EYES WIDE OPEN

How to Make Smart Decisions in a Confusing World

NOREENA HERTZ

HARPER
BUSINESS

An Imprint of HarperCollins*Publishers*

HarperCollins books may be purchased for educational, business, or sales pro-
motional use. For information, please e-mail the Special Markets Department
at SPsales@harpercollins.com.

A hardcover edition of this book was published in 2013 by HarperBusiness, an
imprint of HarperCollins Publishers.

FIRST HARPER BUSINESS PAPERBACK EDITION PUBLISHED 2015.

Library of Congress Cataloging-in-Publication Data has been applied for.

ISBN: 978-0-06-226862-4 (pbk.)

20 21   LSC   10 9 8 7 6 5 4 3 2

To Danny Cohen – the best decision I ever made

Contents

THIS DECISION WILL CHANGE YOUR LIFE

KEEP YOUR EYES WIDE OPEN

BECOME YOUR OWN CUSTODIAN OF TRUTH

GO DIGITAL ... WITH CAUTION

DEVELOP YOUR SURVIVAL SKILLS

SHAKE THINGS UP

THIS DECISION WILL CHANGE YOUR LIFE

STEP ONE
Get to Grips with a World in Hyper-Drive

It's Monday morning.

In Washington, the President of the United States is sitting in the Oval Office assessing whether or not to order a military strike on Iran.

In Idaho, Warren Buffett is deciding whether to sell his Coca-Cola shares or buy more.

In Madrid, Maria Gonzalez, a mother, is trying to work out whether to let her baby continue crying until he falls asleep, or pick him up and soothe him.

I am sitting by my father's bedside in hospital, trying to decide whether I should let the doctor operate, or wait another twenty-four hours.

We face momentous decisions with important consequences throughout our lives. Difficult and challenging problems that we are given the sole responsibility to solve.

On top of this, we have to make up to 10,000 trivial decisions every single day,[1] 227 just about food.[2] Caffeinated or decaf? Small, medium, large or extra large? Colombian,

3

Ecuadorian, Ethiopian? Hazelnut, vanilla or unflavoured? Cream or milk? Brown sugar or sweetener?

If you make the wrong choice when it comes to your coffee, it doesn't matter very much. You make a face and move on.

But make the wrong choice when it comes to your finances, your health or your work, and you could end up sicker or poorer, or lose your job. And if your decisions relate to others – your parents, your children, your country or your staff – the choices you make can irreversibly impact the direction *their* lives will take too. Not only today, but in the months and years ahead.

Errors in decision-making lead young people to under-save for retirement, doctors to miss tumours, CEOs to make catastrophic investments, governments to engage in needless wars, and parents to irreversibly traumatise their children.

This book is about how to make better choices and smarter decisions when the stakes are high and the outcome really matters – whether you are a politician, a businessperson, a professional or a parent.

Think Yourself Smarter

It's actually very surprising how little we think about the quality of our decision-making and how we could improve it. How absent decision-making classes are from educational curricula.

How little we think about how it is we think.

Ask most people why they came to a certain decision, and watch them stumble. How we come to our own assessments, how we arrive at our predictions and choices, are things we seldom scrutinise.

For the sake of our health, our wealth and our future security, we must take it upon ourselves to challenge the way we make our decisions. It's a matter of self-empowerment.

If we do not want to be victims of a future that others dictate to us, we need to get better at making choices with our eyes wide open, our brains switched on.

This means getting better at collecting, filtering and processing information, getting smarter at establishing who to trust and whose recommendations to take on board, getting more adept at analysing different options and weighing up divergent opinions. It also demands that we forge a clearer sense of how it is we come to make decisions – that we understand how our emotions, feelings, moods and memories affect our choices. And that we better know and understand our environment, so that we can master its particular challenges as well.

More specifically, we need to come to terms with three powerful ways in which the environment we now live in can inhibit our ability to think smartly and choose wisely.

Drowning in the Deluge

For this is the age of data deluge.

An age in which advertisers, marketers and media outlets tweet us, text us, and follow us online. An age of Facebook News Feeds and Amazon Recommends. An age in which we are overwhelmed with information, increasingly to the breaking point.

A *New York Times* Weekly Edition contains more information than the average person in the seventeenth century was likely to come across *in their entire lifetime*.[3] In 2008 we were consuming three times as much information as we were in 1960.[4] By 2020 we'll be generating forty-four times more data than we are producing today.[5]

Our stone-age bodies can't cope with this modern-day deluge. Evolution is slow; the deluge has come fast. Confronted with data – some dodgy, some not – our hearts beat faster, our breath becomes more shallow, we sweat: the deluge makes our body shift into crisis mode.[6]

Studies reveal that we can't hold more than seven separate pieces of information in our minds at once.[7] Yet when I enter "Qualities to look for in a surgeon?" into Google, four million hits come up. The sheer abundance overwhelms us. That's why most of us end up looking at just the first few links on the first page of Google's search results.[8] The best answer to our query might not be there, but we can't cope with more.

How can we find the space to think clearly, with all of this data raining down on us? How can we discern intelligence from all this noise?

For there is intelligence amidst the cacophony. In fact, the data deluge has a notable upside: we can now get our information raw, unedited, uncurated. We can now imbibe information direct from source, without the traditional gatekeepers.

This offers a huge opportunity to us as decision-makers. But the question of what, among all the data swirling around the digital landscape, we should give credence to is not straightforward to answer.

In London in August 2011, huge numbers of people rioted, and parts of the city went up in flames. Shops were emptied of expensive trainers and wide-screen TVs. The police looked on powerlessly.

It wasn't that there was no information. Tuned in to social media, police command centres were overwhelmed by the 2.6 million riot-related tweets that circulated during the five days of rioting.[9]

The tales circulating the Twittersphere were plentiful and varied – from the political to something more akin to a child's picture-book: rioters breaking into a branch of McDonald's to cook their own food, the London Eye being set on fire, a tiger being set free from London Zoo.

The problem was, in the face of so much information, how could the police work out which stories to trust and which to reject? Which leads should manpower be assigned to investigate? Which should be ignored?

All of those tweets mentioned above turned out to be false, by the way.

In the age of data deluge, with information so fractured and diffuse, and arising from so many disparate sources, how do we know what to believe and what to reject, so we are able to benefit from the digital dividend? That is a challenge that this book will address.

Drip, Drip, Drip, Ping, Ding, Ring

Add to the barrage of data another twenty-first-century form of Chinese water torture – the drip, drip, drip of "Continuous Disruption" – and you'll be better able to understand the demanding context within which we make our decisions.

In this regard, email is Mental Enemy No. 1. The constant pinging, window signalling or green light blinking, depending which medium it finds you on.

Some saw it coming, saw the inherent problem of a medium which could so easily get out of control.

In 1984, just as email was beginning to enter the mainstream, Jacob Palme, a computer scientist from the QZ Computer Centre at the University of Stockholm with a sideline in writing crime novels, warned that an "electronic mail system, if used by many people, causes severe information overload problems."

The cause of this problem [Palme wrote] is that it is so easy to send a message to a large number of people, and that systems are often designed to give the sender too much control of the communication process, and the receiver too little control ... In the future, when we get larger and larger message systems, and these systems get more and more interconnected, this will be a problem for almost all users of these systems.[10]

And so it was that Palme's prophecy came to be. This is an age of cc and bcc. With the click of a mouse you can send an email to everyone you know. Time and again we find ourselves giving people information they really don't need. In 2012, more than 204 million emails were sent every minute of every day.[11]

How many emails do you receive each day? What are all these messages doing to your ability to concentrate, to think, to plan, to decide?

And that's just emails. Add to this the constant droning background noise of open-plan offices, the rat-a-tat-tat of mobile phones, texts, instant messages, Skype calls, phone calls, the lure of websites demanding your attention, and you'll start to get the picture. These days, we spend three-quarters of our waking lives receiving information.[12] Henry Kissinger built a soundproof office above his garage in which to work, banning his wife or children from entering while he was thinking.[13] But most of us can't physically absent ourselves when we've got decisions to make. Instead we have to operate in a state of nothing less than continuous and relentless interruption.

On average, computer users change windows, and check email or another program, thirty-seven times an hour.[14] Forty-three per cent of college students say they are interrupted by social media three or more times an hour while they are working.[15] And when someone's trying to reach us nowadays, not only will they email us – they'll text us, tweet us, phone and voicemail us too. Often it can feel that there is no escape.[16]

The relentlessness of this bombardment has an effect. A Microsoft Research study which tracked over two thousand hours of employee computer activity found that once distracted by an email alert, computer users take an average of twenty-two minutes to return to the suspended task with the same level of focus.[17] In 27 per cent of cases, it took them more than two hours to return to the task they were doing in the first place.[18] More recent studies have revealed that tasks take a third longer when interrupted by email.[19] Whilst a study of employees at the communications firm Porter-Novelli suggested that the combined effect of incessant phone calls and emails can lead to a temporary drop in our IQ of an extraordinary and disturbing ten points.[20]

As for open-plan offices, the constant background buzz of other colleagues and office equipment makes us 66 per cent less productive.[21] Phones ringing on desks, the background hum of conversations we are not part of, and the chime of emails arriving in our inbox distract and demotivate us at work.[22]

The drip, drip, drip doesn't just make us less able to think, it's also exhausting us. We are spent. Unable to sleep, head-aches ever looming, always tired; our bodies cope with these new demands by keeping us, as we will learn, in a constant state of hormone-induced stress.[23]

Yet we crave these interruptions like catnip. Despite their pernicious impact, we actively seek them out. Forty per cent of people continue to check their work email after hours or while they are on holiday.[24] Eighty-six per cent of us use our mobiles while watching TV (this figure rises to 92 per cent for the 13-to-24 age group[25]). An informal poll of friends reveals a geneticist who checks news sites every five minutes while at work, a TV executive who catches up on his emails on the phone while he's on the stationary bike at the gym, an art dealer who logs on to the *Daily Mail* website sixty times a day.

We are addicted,[26] stressed and overwhelmed, and it's often while we are in this state that big as well as small decisions have to be made.

Whether we can be switched on if we remain switched on is a question I will return to.

The Age of Disorder

Alongside the constant distraction and the drip, drip, drip of the deluge, the third defining characteristic of our times, the triple of the triple whammy, is disorder – a combination of the breakdown of old, established orders and the extremely unpredictable nature of our age.

For this is an age in which accepted wisdoms have been dramatically overturned. An era in which Lehman Brothers – a bank that was "too big to fail" – proved to be expendable. A time when, rather than preventing women from getting sick, it turns out that regular screening for breast cancer may actually make them sicker.[27]

An era when certainties can no longer be presumed certain.

Who would have thought, ten years ago, that serious conversations would be taking place about the Chinese yuan replacing the US dollar as the world's main reserve currency? That a Eurozone country – Cyprus – would impose draconian capital controls? Or that, closer to home, we might no longer be able to trust in the safety of investing in bricks and mortar?

Things we thought we could rely upon now seem ever more vulnerable and chimerical.

Moreover, those who we depended upon to translate and curate the old world order for us have, in just a few years, lost their monopoly of knowledge. Librarians are being usurped by Google, travel agents by TripAdvisor reviewers. Doctors are being challenged by the shared experiences of patients. Grey-haired newspaper proprietors by twenty-something social-media moguls.

Established orders are collapsing all around us.

This isn't necessarily a bad thing. In an age in which our most famous economics sages failed to predict the financial crisis, in which our intelligence services failed to predict the Arab Spring, in which Facebook groups can prove to be better diagnosticians than medical experts (more on this in Step Six), and in which the tabloidisation of the broadsheet press makes us unable to blindly trust even supposedly respectable papers' claims, the increasingly competitive information landscape is in many ways positive.

But that is not to say that this trend is categorically good. What are the agendas of these new curators? How trustworthy are they? Which is more likely to steer me to the right hotel – Joe from Idaho's TripAdvisor testimony, or the advice of my long-trusted travel agent? And while it's true that Wikipedia is in some subjects now as reliable as the *Encyclopaedia Britannica*,[28] will the "crowd" always have my best interests at heart?

In a time of disorder, the past can no longer be assumed to be the lodestar for the future, the future cannot easily be foreseen, and accepted truths and conventional curators of information cannot be unquestioningly relied upon.

Disorder can bring about positive change and innovation, but it can also leave us feeling compass-less and uncertain.

It's really hard to know who to believe. Who to trust. And who to rely on to help us work out what the future will hold.

Get with the Programme – How to Be an Empowered Decision-Maker

OK. You've got the picture now. The context in which we have to make decisions is, to say the least, challenging.

And yet, of course, we still have to make choices. I still have to decide which doctor's advice to follow. The President of the United States still needs to decide whether to strike Iran. The mother hearing her baby cry still needs to decide whether to pick him up or to leave him to cry through the night alone. You still need to decide who to hire for your business, or where to put your retirement funds. We still have to make decisions, important, life-changing decisions, regardless of how distracted we are, how much data swirls around us, how unpredictable and uncertain our world now is. Regardless of how exhausted we feel.

Over time, we've developed ways to do just that, developed short cuts and coping strategies – some conscious, some not – for navigating this difficult terrain. Strategies for gathering information and then processing it in ways that fit with the realities of our distracted, deluged, disordered lives.

We must ask ourselves though how good these strategies really are. Most of us are going through life without interrogating whether our decision-making processes are fit for purpose. And that's something we need to change – especially when the stakes are high and the decisions are of real import.

We need to take more control of our decisions and how we make them. We need to become empowered thinkers.

Without quality information we can trust and effective methods for interrogating it, our decisions are bound to be at best sub-optimal, and at worst very damaging to our needs and interests. So in the coming Steps I'll be expanding on our information-gathering blind spots, and showing how we can do better.

How attuned are you to the most common flaws in experts' thinking? How good are you at spotting statistical cons? How quickly are you able to identify a suspect "fact"? Is the information you are focusing on the right information to be basing your decision upon? What might be worth considering instead? Which unusual suspects might you turn to for advice?

I'll be looking into whether you have dug deep enough to establish the truth of your sources. Do you know how to interrogate new sources of digital information? Or how to evaluate the "answers" churned out by computers? Do you know whom to trust? And why? I'll also look in detail at the way our decision-making is being transformed by new online friends and foes, and point out the pitfalls as well as the quick wins.

In an era of disinformation and misinformation, an era of Photoshop, Fox News, personalised search and ever more spin, I will help you discover how best to interrogate your sources and assess the quality of information you are presented with. And how to widen your net in the first place.

I'll also be investigating the surprising role that we ourselves play in the choices we make, by looking at what's going on, at a conscious and subconscious level, during the decision-making process.

For we are not the robotic, emotionless, experience-less, rational decision-makers of economic theory. A whole host of visceral processes take place within us – neurons fire, memories swirl, emotions feel – at the same time as the analytical part of our brain churns out its computations. As we will see, this dance between subconscious and conscious, intellect and intuition, profoundly affects the risks we take, the futures we contemplate, the forecasts we make. As does the environment in which we operate. Colour, smell, touch – all impact upon the choices we make, as does the language used. What this means is that our immediate response will often need challenging, however natural or intuitive it may feel.

Given how fast-changing our world is, I'll also be exploring whether the models and mental maps we currently use remain appropriate. How is the past affecting your current decisions? Is it locking you into particular patterns or behaviours? Is it leading you to make linear predictions? Or are you able to break free from the past when need be, and envisage a very different sort of future?

And have you assembled the right team around you to help you make the toughest decisions? In an age of dispersed knowledge, are you "crowd-sourcing" your information-gathering? Who is in your inner circle? Yes-men or nay-sayers? Who is acting as your "challenger" or your "translator"? Are you taking sufficient responsibility for your decisions? Or are you attempting to pass the buck to others?

Throughout the book, I'll be combining the latest insights from academia – from psychology, behavioral economics, neuroscience, sociology, anthropology and information science – with first-hand insights from a wide range of people who have to make high-stakes decisions on a regular basis – hedge-fund managers and judges, CEOs and politicians, intelligence officers and fighter pilots, doctors and movie producers. By learning from decision-makers who've sometimes got things right and sometimes got things very wrong, we will get a better sense of those traits and strategies that can help us be good decision-makers, as well as the moves that can serve us ill.

With some traits, this is not obvious.

Take those super-confident forecasters, the ones who are given inordinate airtime. It turns out that the more confident a forecaster is in his predictions, the worse those forecasts prove to be.[29] It's the same with doctors. You know those overly self-assured ones? I've certainly come across some in my time. A number of studies now reveal that the ones who are dead certain in their diagnoses are all too often wrong.[30]

Sometimes the strategies that work are incredibly simple.

We'll learn how a board's decisions can be transformed if the directors are asked to change where they sit.[31] We'll discover how much easier it is to make the right choice when you ask for information to be presented in black and white rather than in colour.[32] We'll learn how we make better decisions if we've had a sandwich.[33]

Winning strategies can be somewhat counter-intuitive. Did you know that you can at times get better advice on how to deal with your illness from a patient than from a doctor? That if you want your team to make smart decisions, you'd do better to make sure they're at odds with each other for a fair proportion of the time, rather than always be of the same mindset? That rather than listening to your boss, you might be better off rebelling? Or that you might want to wait to empty your bladder until you've made your decision?[34]

What it is impossible to do in this book, however, is give you one over-arching, catch-all strategy to follow. This isn't about "Blinking," or "Nudging," or trusting "the Wisdom of Crowds," and leaving it at that.[35] I don't believe there is a one-size-fits-all decision-making template that can work for all of us, at all times. Human life is too complex for that, especially nowadays.

Instead, what I hope to deliver is a "decision-making tool kit." A kit that will enable you to interrogate your own decision-making habits and investigate the information you are given. A kit with the tools that will empower you to make decisions in radically different ways from how you may have been making them until now.

Because ultimately, this book is about empowering you.

Empowering you so that you are able to get past the spin and evaluate the underlying substance. Empowering you so that you can challenge conventional wisdoms and determine what to replace them with. Empowering you so that you are not cowed by authority figures or over-confident experts, and are able to assess their opinions as you would the opinions of any others.

Empowering you so that you're not ashamed to ask for help when you need to, but have the skills to be able to identify who best to get this help from, and how. Empowering you to be able to look into your own psyche, so that you can identify ways in which you may be sabotaging your own decision-making.

The goal of this book is to empower all of us to become more confident, more independent and wiser thinkers and decision-makers. To become people who neither blindly accept the dictates of others nor unquestioningly follow our own initial instincts or analysis – people able to face the world with eyes wide open, and make smart choices and decisions for ourselves.

QUICK TIPS FOR GETTING TO GRIPS
WITH A WORLD IN HYPER-DRIVE

- **Commit to becoming an Empowered Decision-Maker.**

- **See the Ten Steps as the tool kit to help you in this quest.** The Tips that follow will get you thinking – they will get you started on your journey. We will develop them further as the book progresses.

- **Become aware that we have to make over 10,000 decisions a day.** Begin to think about which of these you actually need to make, and whether you are really prioritising the important ones.

- **Start thinking about how it is you make decisions.** Do you consult others and gather a range of opinions, or do you take everything upon yourself? Do you make decisions quickly? Or do you tend to want to mull options over first?

- **Start noting who or what typically influences the choices that you make.**

- **Acknowledge that smart decision-making needs time and space.** Begin to think about how you can reshape your environment to achieve this. How can you limit distractions and disruptions? Can you take technology-free Sabbaths? Can you initiate a new policy at work that limits who is cc'd on emails and under which circumstances?

- **Start considering how you have typically viewed experts and conventional big-hitters until now.** Do you tend to accept their views and ideas without question?

- **Ask yourself more generally who it is you trust and why.**

- **Contemplate your current strategies for dealing with the digital deluge.** Think about the short cuts you take, and how you determine which information to base your decisions on. Begin thinking about how these may be impacting on the quality of your thinking.

KEEP YOUR EYES WIDE OPEN

STEP TWO
See the Tiger and the Snake

The Tiger and the Snake

In 2005, the prominent American cognitive psychologist Professor Richard Nisbett began an extraordinary experiment.

After some careful planning, he showed a group of American students and a group of Chinese students a set of images for just three seconds each. The images were pretty varied: a plane in the sky, a tiger in a forest, a car on the road – you get the idea.

How would the American and Chinese students view these images, the Professor wondered. Would they see them differently? Would they see the same things? If there was a snake on the ground, say, would the Americans or the Chinese notice it?[1]

The Professor's methods were clinical. Upon entering the room, the students were placed in a chair, with their chins in a chin rest at a distance of precisely 52.8cm from the screen. They were then strapped in to 120Hz head-mounted eye-movement trackers. Nisbett could track every squint, glance or flicker of attention.

The differences between the two sets of students were immediately apparent.

The Americans focused on the focal object: the plane, the tiger, the car. They pretty much fixated on these, and barely looked at the background.

The Chinese, on the other hand, took longer to focus on the focal object – 118 milliseconds longer. And once they had done that, their eyes continued to dart around the image. They took in the sand, the sunlight, the mountains, the clouds, the leaves.

So if there was a snake on the ground behind the tiger, it would be the Chinese, not the Americans, who would see it.

All That Glitters ...

In a complex world of hidden dangers and fleeting opportunities we *all* need to be able to see snakes as well as tigers.

We have to understand that the picture we see at first may not give us all the information we need to make the best possible decision. We need to learn to see beyond what is obvious, beyond what we are culturally or conventionally attuned to focus on.

Of course, this doesn't mean that we shouldn't ever act until we've gathered every single piece of information out there that may be relevant to our decision. That would be excessively time-consuming, and our brains wouldn't be able to cope with all that data anyway.[2]

But what the tiger-and-the-snake experiment tells us is that the information we're most prone to focus on may only give us a very partial story, a fragment of the truth, and therefore risks misleading us. Being aware of this, and adjusting accordingly, will make a profound difference to the decisions you make.

Take internet dating. Studies show that men are most attracted to photos of women with large eyes, a big smile and high cheekbones.[3] Glossy hair, full lips and smooth skin are also a big draw.[4] It's also the case that women who describe themselves as "voluptuous" or "portly," or "large but shapely," are contacted far less online than women who are slightly underweight.[5]

That's how it goes with a lot of male browsers. What about women? Well, women seem to focus more on height. Men listed as between six foot three and six foot four receive about 60 per cent more first-contact emails than men in the five foot seven to five foot eight category.

But are superficial features such as the fullness of a woman's lips or a man's height really the best things to focus on if you're looking to choose the right partner?

The answer, unsurprisingly, is a categorical "no." Studies of successful long-term relationships point to less superficial qualities such as sense of humour, shared interests and common values as being much better indicators of whether a couple are well matched.[6] Deep down, most of us know this, yet the majority of online daters only focus on one part of the picture.

Politicians, economists and investors can easily fall in to the same trap.

They tend to focus overwhelmingly on economic growth as the ultimate indicator of how well a country is doing. Yet growth indicators tell us nothing about *how* that growth was achieved.

If you cut all your trees down to sell the wood for kindling, that would be good for growth; but would it really be a measure of how successful you were as a nation? Clearly not. Think of all the problems that the destruction of the rainforests has caused to local habitats as well as its contribution to global warming. Then add to that the very significant associated future economic costs of this kind of short-term thinking.

"Growth" also does not tell us anything about how spoils are shared, about inequality levels, or gender differences, or the rumblings of discontent that can mutate into revolution. It yields, in reality, relatively little information on how a country is actually faring, or will fare in the future. In Russia, the economy has been growing at the same time as life expectancy has been falling.[7] In the United States, during the noughties there was growth, but at the same time median family income declined, and there was no net job creation.[8] So if you are a prime minister or an investor, or just a concerned citizen, the modern economic obsession with digits of growth can end up being the tiger that means you don't see the snake creeping up on you on the forest floor.

Think also of the doctor who no longer carries out a physical examination or takes a detailed case history, but instead focuses overwhelmingly on blood tests or scan results – you've probably come across the type.

While blood tests and scans can of course yield important, often life-saving information, in many cases these static findings cannot on their own determine what is wrong with you. The best doctors are still those who listen to you, touch you and try to establish the individual characteristics of your situation. Such doctors use the static readings of your test results as potential clues to what's wrong, but not as the sole way of defining and diagnosing you.[9] As Dr. Athina Tatisoni, of the prestigious Tufts University School of Medicine, remarks:

> *Usually what happens is that the doctor will ask for a suite of biochemical tests – liver fat, pancreas function, and so on ... The tests could turn up something, but they're probably irrelevant. Just having a good talk with the patient and getting a close history is much more likely to tell me what's wrong.[10]*

Doctors, like investors, like dating-site users, like all of us, need to get better at thinking about the whole picture. We need to look beyond what is immediately obvious or easy to see. For if we are to see a snake as well as a tiger, if we are to see what it is we *need* to see, we must remember that the information that glitters most brightly may not actually be what will serve us best.

24

The Unicycling Clown

Sometimes we are so focused on one thing in particular that we actually stop seeing the other things we need to take into account.

Just ask Dustin Randall.

One might think that, dressed in a vivid purple-and-yellow outfit, with large shoes and a bright-red nose, Dustin the clown would be pretty impossible to miss.

Especially when he was riding a unicycle around a small university campus square.

But researchers at the University of Washington discovered otherwise. When Dustin rode by people who were crossing the square while using their mobile phones, the vast majority completely failed to notice him.[11] It was as if the unicycling clown simply wasn't there.

This is an example of a phenomenon known as "inattentional blindness,"[12] and it's what happens when we're very focused on one thing in particular – in this case a telephone conversation or an important text message. When we are focused like this, we typically don't register new data points, new things that may come in to our sensory orbit. We can even miss highly visible objects we are looking directly at, because our attention is elsewhere.[13] One professor rather brilliantly describes it as being "as if while the eyes 'see' the object, the brain does not."[14]

This is something we are all likely to have experienced. Have you ever bumped into a lamp-post while walking and texting? Or somehow missed seeing an important email in your inbox during a particularly busy week? If so, you can blame inattentional blindness.

There are times, of course, when tunnel vision clearly pays off – think of your hunter-gatherer ancestors, seeking out food and doing everything they could to avoid mortal danger. Once they heard the lion's roar, there would only be two things to think about: working out where that roar was coming from, and running in the other direction. They would not have wanted to be distracted by anything else – the pain in their muscles as they ran, the sound of birds singing above, the sight of their favourite snack hanging from a tree – these would all have been irrelevant to their immediate survival.

But fast-forward a few millennia, and if you don't want to get knocked over by a unicycling clown, miss a critical email or fail to spot a wrong charge on your credit-card statement, you'll need to take your blinkers off and with eyes wide open improve your powers of attention and perception.

Think about what it is that is consuming your focus. At work, this may be your latest sales figures, or your company's current stock price. At home, it may be the football scores. How many times a day do you check these? What might this mean you're not paying attention to? Could you spend a day (or even a few hours) without looking at them? What would you notice that you hadn't previously? And who around you could bring the unexpected to your attention? More on this point to come.

From PowerPoint to Hypnotised Chickens

Sometimes it is not our fault that we've only got partial vision.

Edward Tufte (pronounced tuff-TEE), an American statistician and Professor Emeritus of Political Science, Statistics and Computer Science at Yale University, knows this all too well.

A man of many talents, Tufte was hired by President Obama in 2010 to keep an eye on how his $787 billion stimulus package was being spent.[15] He also has a sideline gig as an exhibiting sculptor. But in his academic career he has undertaken substantial research into how informational graphics impact on decision-making.[16]

One case he has looked at in real depth is the *Columbia* Space Shuttle disaster of February 2003. Seven astronauts lost their lives when their NASA spacecraft disintegrated shortly before the conclusion of a successful sixteen-day mission.

It is now well-known that a briefcase-sized piece of insulation foam from the Shuttle's external fuel tank collided with its left wing during take-off, meaning that the Shuttle was unable to shield itself from the intense heat experienced during re-entry to the earth's atmosphere.

But the official investigation also revealed a story that is both fascinating and curiously everyday in its nature.

A key underlying factor that led to the disaster was the way in which NASA's engineers shared information.

In particular, the *Columbia* Accident Investigation Board singled out the "endemic" use of a computer program. A program we more usually associate with corporate seminars or high-school classrooms: Microsoft PowerPoint.

The investigators believed that by using PowerPoint to present the risks associated with the suspected wing damage, the potential for disaster had been significantly understated.

As the *Columbia* circled the earth, Boeing Corporation engineers scrambled to work out the likely consequences of the foam striking the thermal tiles on the Shuttle's left wing. Tragically, when they presented their findings, their methods of presentation proved to be deeply flawed. Information was "lost," priorities "misrepresented," key explanations and supporting information "filtered out." The "choice of headings, arrangement of information and size of bullets ... served to highlight what management already believed," while "uncertainties and assumptions that signalled danger dropped out of the information chain."[17]

In other words, the very design tools that underpin the clarity of PowerPoint had served to eclipse the real story. They had distracted its readers. They had served to tell a partial, and highly dangerous, story.

Tufte, applying his expertise in information design, investigated these claims further, and found even more to be concerned about.

He analysed all twenty-eight PowerPoint slides that had been used by the engineers to brief NASA officials on the wing damage and its implications during *Columbia*'s two-week orbit of the earth, and discovered that some were highly misleading.

The title of a slide supposedly assessing the destructive potential of loose debris, "Review of Test Data Indicates Conservatism for Tile Penetration," was, in Tufte's words, "an exercise in misdirection." What the title did not make clear was that the pre-flight simulation tests had used a piece of foam 640 times smaller than that which slammed against the Shuttle. This crucial information was buried towards the bottom of the PowerPoint slide. Nobody seemed to take any notice of it – they were too focused on the headline at the top, and did not take in the full picture.[18]

Tufte found that the limited space for text on PowerPoint slides led to the use of compressed phrases, with crucial caveats squeezed into ever smaller font sizes. This created a reliance on "executive summaries" or slide titles that lost the nuance of uncertainties and qualifications.

In cases such as this, in other words, oversimplification leads to the loss of vital detail.

Complexity, a reality of executive decision-making, is something the medium of PowerPoint dangerously disregards.

It's not just NASA or professors who are concerned about the potential of PowerPoint to blinker our vision.

General James N. Mattis, who served as Commander of the United States Central Command after taking over from the subsequently disgraced General David Petraeus in 2010, has always had a way with words. He once advised his marines in Iraq to "Be polite. Be professional. But have a plan to kill everybody you meet."[19] Mattis's assessment of PowerPoint was equally merciless: "PowerPoint makes us stupid," he said in 2010, at a military conference in North Carolina.

This is a feeling corroborated by his military colleagues. Brigadier General H.R. McMaster, who banned PowerPoint when leading the successful assault on the Iraqi city of Tal Afar in 2005, said, "It's dangerous, because it can create the illusion of understanding and the illusion of control." Indeed, so aware is the US Army of the medium's powers of evasion that it intentionally deploys PowerPoint when briefing the media, a tactic known as "hypnotising chickens."[20]

Of course, this is not to say that we don't ever need information to be summarised for us. There are times when we clearly do. But if we're making decisions on the basis of summaries, we need to remind ourselves of the significant risk that in the process key details and subtleties may well be overlooked. Or be written in such small font size that you don't pay attention to them.

We must also take a moment to remind ourselves that what someone else has deemed important may not be what matters most to us, or what will really make a difference to the decision we make.

So next time you're looking at a PowerPoint presentation, or indeed any type of executive summary, look beyond the large font and the bold headline points. The information you actually need may be somewhat more buried. Or it may not even be on the slides at all. Do also put your presenter on the spot. If it matters, ask them to clarify and expand, and provide more information.

If you don't, you risk being shown only tigers, and never snakes.

The Cult of the Measurable

It's not only particular forms of presentation that can blinker our vision.

One *type* of information often dominates our attention – numbers. This in itself can be problematic.

Numbers can give us critical information – if we want to know whether to put a coat on, we'll look at the temperature outside; if we want to know how well our business is doing, we'll need to keep an eye on revenues and expenditures; and if we want to be able to compare the past with the future, we'll need standard measures to do so.

But the problem is that the Cult of the Measurable means that things that can't really be measured are sometimes given numerical values.[21]

Can a wine really be 86 per cent "good"? That doesn't sound right to me, but one multi-billion-dollar industry doesn't agree. Robert Parker, probably the most famous wine critic in the world, ranks wines on a scale between fifty and one hundred. And winemakers prostrate themselves before him, praying for a rating of ninety-two or above, because such a number practically guarantees commercial success, given how influential Parker's ratings have become with wine drinkers.[22]

Yet what really is the difference between a rating of ninety-two and an eighty-six? How can we tell what that six-point difference means?

And are someone else's tastes necessarily going to correlate with yours? I've already raised the question of whether Joe from Idaho on TripAdvisor is really the best person to steer your choice as to where to go on holiday. We also need to ask ourselves whether what I mean by four stars is what you mean by four stars. Whether my Zagat score of twenty means the same as yours. As the *Financial Times*'s wine critic Jancis

Robinson points out on the subject of Parker's influence, "Make no mistake about it, wine judging is every bit as subjective as the judging of any art form."[23]

So, before you make a decision based on a number, think about what the number is capturing, and also what it is not telling you.

Risk is another area where our attempts to assign clear measures are often bound to fail. While it's true that there are some areas where we can meaningfully quantify risk – such as engineering, where we can come up with a number for how likely a building is to withstand an earthquake, say; or medicine, where we can estimate a patient's chance of responding to a particular drug – this approach doesn't work effectively in all spheres. Indeed, in our turbocharged world, in which changes happen quicker and less predictably than ever before, many of our attempts to assign probabilities to future events are likely to be pretty meaningless. As President Obama said, reflecting on the huge range of probabilities that various senior intelligence folk had proffered back in March 2011 as to whether Osama bin Laden was the "high value target" spotted within a high-walled compound in Abbottabad in Pakistan – with confidence levels that ranged between 30 and 95 per cent – "What you started getting was probabilities that disguised uncertainty as opposed to actually providing you with more useful information."[24]

In our desire to reduce everything to some sort of standardised measure, to create universal meanings for things that will always be subjective, and to create the illusion of certainty when uncertainty is in fact what prevails, do we not risk making decisions on the basis of what may seem intelligence-rich information, but is in truth pretty meaningless?

Not everything can be measured, not everything can be compared, especially in a world as complex as ours. Indeed, Obama, realising this, responded to the various probabilities he'd been presented with, "Look guys, this is a flip of the coin. I can't base this decision on the notion that we have any greater certainty than that."[25] A flip of the coin which we now know that President Obama won and Osama bin Laden lost.

All That Counts

Another danger of putting the measurable on a pedestal is that what cannot be measured often ends up being discarded, or dismissed. But just because something can't be quantified, it doesn't mean that we should ignore what it is telling us.

A conversation with a senior director of a multi-billion-dollar international children's charity brought this point home to me in a stark way. Huddled in a Cambridge University ante-chamber, encircled by six of her colleagues, Ms. Broun explained that the key problem children now face in many middle-income countries was domestic violence.[26] She and her colleagues knew this, because they had personally witnessed countless cases of children bearing marks of physical abuse alongside symptoms of mental strain. They'd heard their stories, seen their scars, and noted their teachers' and community leaders' corroborating stories.

Domestic violence, however, is hard to measure. What do you record? The number of bruises? How can you capture in numbers how terrified a child feels? As a result, Ms. Broun had been unable to convince the organisation's head office that domestic violence was something vital for them to target. Instead she was told to focus her efforts on addressing problems for which they could collect numbers, and thereby easily gauge progress on – problems such as under-attendance at school, or children without sufficient vaccinations.

These instructions were given to Ms. Broun despite the fact that in middle-income nations, such measurable and easily trackable problems had to a great extent been resolved, whereas domestic violence was active and growing.

In many ways it's hard to accept this story. It speaks of bureaucratic intransigence and rigidity, and it's also symptomatic of the way in which the Cult of the Measurable can overshadow what really needs to be seen, and what really needs doing. In this case it is incredibly painful, because the happiness and welfare of children is at stake. If the over-importance of numbers can become embedded in this kind of situation, where in your business or personal life could the Cult of Comfortable Measurement be adversely affecting your decisions?[27]

By devaluing that which cannot be measured, we risk not only making poorer decisions, but also distorting our priorities and goals. As was once said, "Not everything that counts can be counted, and not everything that can be counted counts."[28]

Glass Half Full

So we need to be careful about focusing excessively on numbers, or on things in bold typeface, or on the information that others deem most relevant for us, or that glitters most brightly. We also need to start paying more attention to people's stories and testimonies, even if they cannot be quantified.

Beyond this, there's another type of information we should watch out for that is prone to draw us in – information we want to hear, over information we don't.

Neuroscientist Tali Sharot explored this theme by putting volunteers in a brain scanner and asking them what they believed the chances were of various unpleasant events occurring to them in their lifetime. She asked questions like how likely are you to get burgled? How likely are you to contract genital warts? How likely are you to develop Parkinson's disease? That sort of thing.[29]

After each answer, she immediately told her volunteers what the real chances were of such an event happening. So, if someone thought they had a 10 per cent chance of developing cancer, she would reveal that the real probability was 30 per cent – or quite a lot worse.

What Sharot discovered was that when her subjects were given bad news, news that should have led them to be more concerned than they were previously, the part of their brains that should have fixed the mismatch between their prediction and the true chance of disaster showed only low-level activation.

However, when a subject was given information that was *better* than expected – for example, if someone thought they had a 50 per cent of being burgled, but was then told that their real chance of being burgled was only 30 per cent – the part of their brain that processed the information went wild. What's more, when the volunteers were asked to go through the list of unpleasant events again, they actively changed their beliefs when the information they had been given improved their prospects. For example, if they found out that they were actually less likely to suffer from infertility than they had thought, they adjusted to the new risk percentages presented. But if the new information pointed to there being an even higher chance of something bad happening to them, they simply ignored it.

When it comes to things that affect us directly, it seems that many of us dismiss information that suggests that bad things will happen to us, and only pay attention to the good stuff. It doesn't matter what we throw at them, unconscious processes in our brains are determined to show us a rosy glow.

There are obvious dangers to this when it comes to making decisions. If your unconscious belief is that you won't get lung cancer from smoking, then you're unlikely to choose to quit.

For every warning from an anti-smoking campaigner, your brain will be giving a lot more weight to that story of the ninety-nine-year-old lady who smokes fifty cigarettes a day but is still going strong. You're not doing this consciously, but it *is* happening.

Similarly, if you're a trader buying and selling stocks and shares, or an investor looking to buy another property, you'll be paying more attention to evidence of sustained growth and stories of rising prices than to the nay-sayers who predict a crash – a partial explanation for financial and housing bubbles.[30]

The inability to properly process news that suggests something bad may happen to us is clearly a dangerous trait for nearly all decision-makers – not just traders or smokers or property speculators. Dr. Sharot's research reveals that 80 per cent of us are very vulnerable to this mental lapse.[31] Interestingly, however, there is one group of people who it turns out update their beliefs in a more balanced way: people with mild depression appear to be better at balancing the good and the bad when they receive information.

If you're not depressed yourself, however, don't despair. Being aware that you're prone to this thinking error is a start – it means you can challenge your immediate reactions and reflect upon how your decisions would be affected if your optimism *were* overstated. You might also, now that you are cognisant of your ability to trip yourself up, want to take out insurance against the worst happening. As Sharot advises, do carry an umbrella even if you're sure the sun will shine, and do buy health insurance even if you're certain nothing bad could ever happen to you.[32]

How Not to Spot Aspirin Poisoning

It's not just bad news that we have a tendency to unwittingly dismiss.

Take what happened to Dr. Harrison J. Alter, then an emergency-room physician in Tuba City, Arizona, a small town in the Painted Desert just a sixty-mile drive from the Grand Canyon National Park.[33]

Alter isn't your usual medical-school type. Born in Chicago, he attended the prestigious Francis Parker prep school before heading off to Brown to get an undergraduate degree in comparative literature and art history.[34] He still lists reading among his interests, along with his children,[35] but his area of professional expertise is medical, and in particular the hullabaloo of the emergency room.

Alter's emergency room was a focal point of medical care for the Navajo Nation, and during the winter of 2003 he took a routine admission in: Blanche Begaye, a Navajo woman in her sixties. Blanche explained that she was having trouble breathing. At first she just thought she just had "a bad head cold," and did what most of us would do: she drank lots of orange juice and tea, popped a few aspirin, and expected that to be the end of it. But it wasn't. She got worse.

Dr. Alter knew that Blanche worked in a grocery store on the reservation. He also knew that something was amiss within her community. Lately, his emergency room had been full of people with similar symptoms to Blanche's. He'd diagnosed them all with viral pneumonia, a nasty lung infection that can knock you out for weeks. Alter couldn't help noticing that Blanche had quite similar symptoms.

After Blanche was admitted, Alter went through the normal procedures. First came the observations. He noticed that her respiratory rate was almost twice normal. On top of that, she had a low-grade fever – her temperature was up, but it wasn't through the roof. Next came the tests – in particular, the bloods. The first thing he checked was the white-blood-cell count, a typical marker of infection. It wasn't actually raised, but her blood chemistry showed that the acid-base balance of her blood was now weighted towards acid, a red flag for a major infection.

Alter totted up the signs, and plumped for a diagnosis of "subclinical viral pneumonia." Mrs. Begaye's X-ray showed that she didn't have the classic white streaks across her lungs, but he reasoned that this was because her illness was in its early stages. From here on it was routine: admit her, work on getting that fever down, and keep an eye on her heart rate. He had her hooked up to some intravenous fluids and medicine, and put her under observation. Then he moved on to the next bed.

Case closed.

Or so he thought.

A few minutes after Alter had begun evaluating his next patient, the junior doctor to whom he had passed Mrs. Begaye's case attracted his attention. Thankfully for Mrs. Begaye, this wasn't the type of subordinate who was too scared to speak up when he disagreed with his boss. "That's not a case of viral pneumonia," he told Alter. "She has aspirin toxicity."

How could Dr. Alter, who had not only studied medicine at the prestigious University of California at Berkeley, but following his residency had gone to the University of Washington in Seattle to study medical decision-making, have got his diagnosis so wrong? As the always open-to-learning doctor later reflected, "Aspirin poisoning, bread-and-butter toxicology ... She was an absolutely classic case – the rapid breathing, the shift in her blood electrolytes ... and I missed it."

It wasn't that he hadn't been asking the right questions, or conducting the right tests to get to this diagnosis. He had.

Dr. Alter had all the information he needed to make the correct diagnosis right in front of him. The trouble was that even though the information had been plain to see, he hadn't taken it in. And he hadn't taken it in because when he saw Mrs. Begaye, what came to mind were all the recent cases of pneumonia he'd been seeing.

This meant that instead of treating her story as an independent one, and focusing on all the information she gave him, he had zoomed in on the symptoms that fitted the pneumonia diagnosis, and ignored or reasoned away the information that didn't.

This is a common thinking error we are *all* prone to. In fact, it turns out that we actually get a dopamine rush when we find confirming data, similar to the one we get if we eat chocolate, have sex, or fall in love.[36] Having jumped to a particular conclusion, we focus on information that supports it, and ignore everything that contradicts or doesn't conform to our initial analysis. We're especially prone to being overly swayed by what we've most recently seen. It's as if once we've decided that the only danger we can face is tigers, even if we see a snake in the grass we don't process that it could be a danger to us too.

That is what famously happened in 1940 when French intelligence, arguably the best service of its kind in the world at that time, made a catastrophic error. Having undertaken sophisticated analysis of German blitzkrieg tactics earlier that year, the intelligence service came to the conclusion that the brunt of the German attack would come through the plains of Belgium. Growing evidence that the Nazis were planning to invade through the Ardennes Forest instead was ignored, despite information gleaned on the pattern of German reconnaissance flights (which closely mirrored the later invasion route) and aerial photography of German pontoon-bridge construction in the area. Even "hard information," it seems, will be sidelined unless it is received by open eyes *and* open minds.[37]

What should we take from all of this, from these stories and insights?

Well, if we are to make smarter decisions, we need to make sure that we are not overly swayed by what we've seen most recently, or by the information that's most easily available, or by our initial assessment, or by what it is we most want to hear.

We should consciously practise being more observant. Take a raisin. Rub it between your hands. How does it feel? Look at it, examine its contours. Smell it. Lick it – how does it feel against your tongue?[38] Practising mindfulness techniques like this helps us to get better at opening our eyes to what we might otherwise overlook.

We must also force ourselves to actively search for information that challenges our preconceived ideas.

We have to treat each new situation as independent, and each new piece of information as potentially game-changing.

And when making assessments, we must question not only whether things are as we think, but also *what else they could possibly be.*

We can do this on our own, but it's often easier if we have someone who can help. Who could you deploy to help you interrogate your own ways of thinking, help force you to see everything in the jungle, not just what you're most drawn to? So you don't make the same kind of cognitive mistakes as Dr. Alter, or Tali Sharot's volunteers, or the French intelligence services. So you don't get consumed by your confirmation dopamine buzz.

The head of one of Europe's leading hedge funds – a fund that succeeds or fails on the basis of its analysts' assessments of the industries and companies they decide to invest in – tells me that he sees one of his primary roles as that of "Challenger in Chief," as the person who niggles his staff to focus not only on the evidence that confirms their initial assessment or that they want to hear, but also to actively look for data that will contradict or refute it. He believes he must challenge his staff to consider how they could be wrong, and then assess how this might impact on their decision-making.[39]

Who, at work or at home, can serve as Challenger in Chief for you?

Detach from the Past – Lessons from Hollywood and Helsinki

As well as challenging what it is we see before us right now, we also need to consider how the past might be affecting our present-day choices.

For although our past experiences, good or bad, provide us with split-second cues which can often be very useful – I don't put my hand on the gas hob if it's switched on, because I know, having burnt my finger in the past, that it would be the wrong decision – experience, as we will see, can be a double-edged sword.

Richard Zanuck was one of the most successful film producers of recent times. His hits included such classics and box-office juggernauts as *Jaws*, *Cocoon*, *Driving Miss Daisy* and, more recently, Tim Burton's *Alice in Wonderland*, which grossed more than $1 billion.[40] Hollywood royalty who spoke at his funeral and memorial services included Clint Eastwood and Steven Spielberg, who called him a "cornerstone of the film industry."[41]

But when I had lunch with Dick Zanuck at his usual table at George in Mayfair's Mount Street, just days before he died in July 2012, we discussed one of the rare moments when his decision-making had gone very wrong.

In 1965 a movie produced by Zanuck broke all box-office records. A musical about an errant trainee nun in the Austrian Alps, starring Julie Andrews, *The Sound of Music* was a gargantuan commercial success, rescuing Twentieth Century-

Fox from the $40 million wounds inflicted two years earlier by Richard Burton and Elizabeth Taylor's *Cleopatra*. It remains, in inflation-adjusted dollars, the third-biggest-grossing film of all time.[42]

Zanuck was thirty years old, and this was his first big hit. So what did he do next?

Understandably, he tried to repeat what he'd just done.

"I was convinced that the musical was back, and a lot of people, a lot of other studio heads, were convinced that this was the way to go," he told me. He commissioned three more musicals, all in a similar sugary vein.

All three were box-office flops.[43]

Doctor Dolittle, an adaptation of the children's books by Hugh Lofting, contributed to Twentieth Century-Fox posting a staggering $37 million loss in 1967.[44] The next, *Star!*, released in 1968, which starred Julie Andrews and had the same director, producer and choreographer as *The Sound of Music*, also bombed: box-office receipts in the US were just $4 million, and losses were pegged at $15 million.[45] The third, *Hello, Dolly!*, released in 1969 and starring Barbra Streisand, did equally badly, losing $16 million, bringing to a close a disastrous few years for Twentieth Century-Fox, and leading to Zanuck unceremoniously losing his job as production chief.[46]

It's not that the past is never a good predictor of what lies ahead. There are of course many examples we could cite of times when looking backwards, consciously or not, has helped people reach the right decisions. The key, though, is not to be overly wedded to our past successes and failures, or our experience-based instincts, so that shifting tides or new information are ignored.

Nor should we assume a linear trajectory – more so now than ever, as we attempt to navigate today's uncertain and unpredictable digital world, in which things are changing with an ever greater rapidity.

Dick Zanuck explained to me that his movie strategy immediately after *The Sound of Music* fell victim to a fast-changing world, and a shift in cultural mores. When *The Sound of Music* hit movie screens, the appeal of singing nuns and the lush Technicolor greenery of the Austrian hills made sense against the backdrop of the early 1960s. But by the time the back-to-back movie flops were released, things had moved on. The Vietnam War and the Civil Rights movement had politicised the American public, Martin Luther King had been assassinated, pop and rock music were dominant, and saccharine-sweet family productions had lost their appeal.[47]

Success does not necessarily breed success. Just because we haven't seen a snake today or yesterday, it doesn't mean that we won't see one tomorrow. And just because a certain set of ingredients once worked, it doesn't mean they always will.

This was a tough lesson learnt by Finnish communications giant Nokia in 2007. From the 1990s onwards, Nokia dominated the mobile-phone industry. At its peak the company had a market value of $303 billion, and by 2007 around four in ten handsets bought worldwide were manufactured by Nokia.[48] But when Apple introduced its game-changing iPhone in 2007, Nokia was caught sleeping on the job. Hoping to keep its edge on the market, it had piled $40 billion into research, secretly developing an iPhone-style device – complete with a colour touchscreen, maps, online shopping, the lot – some seven years earlier. But the product never hit the shelves. In spite of all the research (which ended up generating about $6 billion-worth of patents), Nokia decided to stick with what it knew: good, solid, reliable mobile phones. As a former employee working in the development team at the time said of that decision, "Management did the usual. They killed it."[49] In fact, when the iPhone was introduced, Nokia engineers sneered at the Apple device's inability to pass their "drop test," where a phone is dropped onto concrete from a five-foot height.[50]

They believed that the past could provide a reliable guide to the future, but as we now know, it didn't. In the five years since the iPhone was introduced, Nokia has lost 90 per cent of its market value.[51] Meanwhile, Apple has sold over a quarter of a billion iPhones.[52] Indeed, in August 2012, at the same time as Nokia's bonds were rated as worse than "junk," Apple's share price peaked at $664.74, making it the most valuable company in history, with the iPhone generating 55 per cent of that value.[53]

What can we learn from these two stories to help us with decision-making? That there is no such thing as a trend? Clearly not that – just ask the erotic fiction writers now bringing home the bacon thanks to E.L. James. Or those who've made their millions off the back of the *Twilight* franchise.

Never to make a musical? Not that either, although with a twinkle in his eye Dick Zanuck joked with me that that was the lesson he'd learnt.

How about that failure is the death knell for future success? Not necessarily. Zanuck went on to make many more blockbusters and critically acclaimed movies. And there are a number of examples of entrepreneurs who've gone on to make fortunes after losing it all.[54]

But what we can take away is this: do not get so attached to past successes or failures that they inhibit your ability to think cogently, and to assess the present challenges with an open and objective mind.

Be acutely aware that the interplay between our environment and its outcomes is ever-changing.

Understand that all trends will come to an end at some point.

Consider the possibility that the same ingredients at another time may not make a tasty cake or a hit movie.

Don't allow success to breed either arrogance or complacency.

And if you get things wrong, remember the imperative to learn from your mistakes.

That's what Dick Zanuck did. He realised that he had based his decisions too firmly on past experiences, assuming that what was right yesterday would be just as successful tomorrow. It is testament to both his creative energy and his willingness to engage in introspection that he came back from these harsh experiences to produce some of the greatest movies of all time.

The Truth about Harry

Being stuck in the past can cause other problems too – a fog of assumptions based on past experiences can obscure the new or the innovative.

This is something that a dozen of the most prestigious British and American publishing houses must now realise.[55]

When a 223-page manuscript of around 90,000 words from an unknown female author landed on their desks back in 1996 they quickly turned it down for a number of understandable but misconceived reasons. The book was too long for kids these days – 50,000 words longer than the average children's novel at the time.[56] Reading by boys was declining, especially of books by women and those light on dialogue. Moreover, this was a straight-on, full-blown fantasy, not a book about the kinds of serious issues such as bullying or broken families that were currently in vogue. It was hard to think of a successful children's fantasy book in recent times.

Penguin, one of Britain's most prestigious publishers, flatly rejected the manuscript. At Transworld it languished in the in-tray of somebody who was off sick.[57] Indeed, twelve of the top British and American publishers turned it down.[58]

It took a publisher new to the game, working in a children's division just a couple of years old, with no past to be stuck in and a belief that a story with emotional resonance would always find an audience, to take the plunge.

Barry Cunningham, a former marketing man and one-time giant puffin (at exhibitions for Penguin's children's books imprint, Puffin, Barry, as Marketing Director, would walk around thus costumed), read all 223 pages. "The skies didn't part and lightning didn't come down or anything," he recounted as we sat in the basement of the nineteenth-century Savile Club, the Mayfair haunt previously frequented by Kipling, Hardy, Yeats and other literary greats, me sipping tea, he his trademark Coca-Cola.

Cunningham simply thought that the manuscript was "really engaging." He negotiated with the author's agent "for about five minutes, because he didn't want very much money and I didn't have very much money," and bought the first two books in the series for the princely sum of £2,000.

As he said to me, "The rest is history." And it sure was.

The author, a first-time writer by the name of Joanna Rowling, who was "so nervous" the first time Barry spoke to her that she "couldn't really talk," was delighted to get the firm offer, especially after so many rejections. And Barry Cunningham, of course, was also delighted. The seven Harry Potter books went on to sell over 450 million copies worldwide, have been translated into more than seventy languages, and spawned a movie franchise worth over $4.5 billion.

Rudyard Kipling was right to caution us to treat both triumph and disaster as "imposters." Yet we're all too prone to letting failure and success become our only guiding beacons. What this means is that not only do we risk ignoring cues that things may be changing around us, but also deny ourselves the possibility of contemplating futures, trajectories and possibilities that are different from what has come before.

How to See with Eyes Wide Open

To make smart decisions we need the right information to guide us. That is a given.

This means being aware of how instinctively tunnel-visioned we can be, of how some information glitters much more brightly than others – some of which may well turn out to be fool's gold.

It means becoming more conscious of the way we are drawn to what's most familiar or most obvious, or closest to what we want to hear. Of how little attention we pay to what we don't want to know. Of just how caught up in our past we can be, and how this can disable our ability to process the present or imagine the future.

Being aware is a start. But there's more that we can do to ensure we see with eyes wide open.

One thing we can do is to give ourselves more time – time both to gather the right information, and to consider it. I know that for many of us time feels like a luxury we just don't have any more. But as Dr. Alter makes explicit, "In order to think well, especially in hectic circumstances [and he's talking about decisions made by doctors in the ER here], you need to slow things down to avoid making cognitive errors."[59]

You need time to ask yourself what you may not have thought about, time to consider alternatives, time for your eyes to dart around the picture.

Time pressures encourage tunnel or distorted vision, while the best ideas often emerge after a reflective pause.

So, can you take a beat before you make your decision?

More generally, is there a way you can give yourself more time so that you can properly take in what it is you need to?

Barack Obama advised David Cameron that "The most important thing you need to do is have big chunks of time during the day when all you're doing is thinking. Without that you lose the big picture."[60] And without the big picture, as we've seen, we risk not seeing those snakes.

So, can you batch your emails and respond to a group of them in one go? Is there anything more you can delegate to others? How else can you carve out your own thinking time? Many of us feel that this just isn't possible in our hyper-hectic lives, but if the President of the United States can find the time, surely you and I can too?

Alternatively, can you just slow down your decision-making process? Who or what can help you take that pause? Doctors and pilots have been found to profit from following a checklist even when doing things they have done many times before. By slowing them down, the list makes them more methodical and less vulnerable to making the kind of cognitive errors we discussed earlier.[61] Might a system like that work for you?

You should also ask yourself who can help you interrogate your own ways of thinking, help force you to see everything in the jungle, not just what you're most drawn to. Who can serve as your Challenger in Chief, as we explored earlier?

Before we move on to the next Step, it's also worth reminding ourselves of the following.

First, that the further into the future the outcome of your decision will play out, the less likely that what worked before will prevail. It's a basic law of probability – so if you can make your decision as late in the day as possible, do.

Second, that decisions are best made with built-in flexibility. So, if possible, don't fix yourself to Plan A. In a world as fast-changing as ours, try whenever you can to have Plans B, C and D in your back pocket.

Third, bear in mind that in order to work from the best intelligence possible, you'll need to make assessments on an ongoing and continuous basis. This means keeping your eye on the present and the future, not only on how things once were. Actively ask yourself, "What is different now?" "What could be different tomorrow?" And then think through the implications of this for the decisions you're currently making and the information you're presently seeking out.

And finally, give yourself permission to break from the past and try something unprecedented, especially if it's an affordable punt. The pay-off can be quite remarkable. Bloomsbury Publishers made a multi-million-pound return on Barry Cunningham's initial £2,000 investment.

As Barry said to me, "Probably the best investment in publishing ever."

Takeaways

In a world of data deluge, distraction and uncertainty, a world in which we increasingly have to determine ourselves which information we should use to make our decisions, it's understandable that we tend to focus on particular forms and types of information over others. Ultimately, it's a kind of coping strategy.

But what we are most naturally or most instinctively drawn to may not actually be the best information to help us make decisions. What's in the foreground, what's most glittery, what's biggest and boldest, stands out the most and grabs our attention, as do numbers over words, information that reinforces what we want to hear over information that jars, and the past, with its promise to be our lodestar. Yet all of these are potentially tigers consuming all our attention, while a snake slithers dangerously towards us on the ground.

We need to be aware of this; to re-calibrate how it is we see the world, re-adjust our focus and deploy others around us to help pull off the blinkers.

But once our blinkers are off, there's more to consider. In keeping with life's complexity, making smart decisions can be thwarted for other reasons too. For we are massively influenced by how *others* shape and form what it is they convey to us – by the words they use, the colours they choose, and even, as we will see, by touch. By factors in the ether that we're not even aware of.

How to strip bare what we are told, so that we can evaluate the information before us, see beyond packaging and wrappers and spin and misleading cues, is what the next chapter is about.

QUICK TIPS FOR SEEING THE TIGER AND THE SNAKE

- **Look beyond the most obvious data.** What you are most drawn to will not necessarily be most relevant. Ask yourself what additional information might be of use. Challenge yourself to think about what you might have missed.

- **Practise becoming more observant.** Introduce a regular mindfulness technique to your day, such as the "raisin practice." This will have a tangible effect on the quality of your decisions.

- **Remember that numbers only tell a partial story.** What are the numbers *not* telling you? What other information do you need to consider?

- **Be aware of the form in which you're receiving your information.** Is it too reductionist? What is the PowerPoint slide not revealing? What is the Executive Summary not telling you? Who can provide you with the requisite nuance or detail? Is there a more in-depth report you need to get your hands on? If so, can you set the requisite time aside to read it and properly absorb the information?

- **Don't confuse a generally happy disposition with unrealistic levels of optimism.** When you're next told that something bad could happen to you, remind yourself of our natural tendency to ignore or underplay this kind of news. Try to contemplate whether your assessment would be different if you took your optimism down a notch or two. Who around you is of the glass-half-empty mindset? They might have a more realistic take on the information. Are you touching base with them frequently enough?

- **Don't just seek out information that confirms what it is you already believe or think.** It's vital to actively seek out information that could prove you wrong. Who in your life can act as your "Challenger in Chief" to remind you to do this?

- **As a general rule, carve out more thinking time for yourself.** If Barack Obama can prioritise this, so can you. Can you batch your emails so as to free up thinking time? Schedule thinking time into your diary as you would any other appointment? What on your to-do list can be postponed or ditched?

- **Slow down, to avoid making thinking errors.** Give yourself time to consider alternative diagnoses and possibilities. We risk accepting the most easy-to-reach answer because we are so rushed for time. Develop a strategy that helps you avoid this. For some it may be a checklist, for others it may be that Challenger in Chief to talk the options through with.

- **Identify those day-to-day distractions which take up too much of your focus.** Can you limit the number of times you check Facebook or the football scores? How about downloading software that stops you from being able to surf the web for specified periods?

- **Don't use the past as too fixed a steer.** There is great danger in assuming that the past will light the way to the future. Think of your favourite Dick Zanuck movie, or that special magician from Hogwarts, as a way of avoiding this thinking error.

- **Have Plans B, C and D in your back pocket, and be willing to change tack.** Accept the fast-moving nature of our world and how quickly things can change. This demands that we monitor our landscape on an ongoing basis.

- **Where possible, don't make big decisions way before you actually need to.** Make your decisions as late in the day as you can, so that you can take into account the hyper-rapid changing nature of our world.

- **Stretch yourself to imagine the unimaginable.** What might future scenarios look like? How might circumstances change? How might they differ from right now? And how does this impact your thinking and the decisions you should make?

- **Accept that not all outcomes can be anticipated.** What can you put in place to mitigate worst-case scenarios? Can you buy insurance? Hedge your decision?

- **Don't allow success to make you complacent, or failure to define you.** Recognise the transient nature of both, and that learning opportunities can arise from either.

STEP THREE
Don't Be Scared of the Nacirema

Body Rituals and Magic

In June 1956, Horace Miner, Professor of Anthropology at the University of Michigan, published an article that electrified the anthropology community.

The journal he wrote in, the *American Anthropologist*, was already accustomed to colourful studies of exotic tribes: the same issue contained articles about kinship networks among the Araucanian Indians of Chile and lineage in the Mundurucú society of Brazil. But Miner's latest study was something else. He was describing a tribe, the Nacirema, for the very first time.[1]

No one, it seemed, had written or even heard about this tribe ever before.

It wasn't just that the Nacirema were new. Their tribal practices seemed particularly bizarre too. Practices that were so unusual, and so shocking, said Miner, that they might even be described as "an example of the extremes to which human behaviour can go."

The Nacirema were gripped by magic. Their days were marked by a parade of rituals based on the human body. This in itself was not exceptional: countless tribes performed body rites, from fasting to tattooing. But what stood out about this tribe was their wacky beliefs about bodies.

To the Nacirema, the human body was fundamentally ugly and prone to decay. Their every ritual was dedicated to reversing this process at all costs. Some of the steps they took to do this verged on the barbaric. The men lacerated their faces with sharp instruments; the women baked their heads in small ovens. They also displayed a curious preoccupation with the mouth, which they would ritually fill with hog hairs and holy powders. It followed that Nacirema society conferred special status on the wise elders – the medicine men, the herbalists – who provided them with the charms and magical potions to stave off decay.

The spectre of physical deterioration was not the only thing that preoccupied the tribespeople: their very peculiar take on aesthetics also seemed to dominate their lives. The Nacirema were consumed by disgust for the body's natural state. When a member of the tribe was too fat, they performed a ritual fast to become thin; when a member of the tribe was too thin, they held a ceremonial feast to become fat. The female breast was singled out for particular concern: the Nacirema used outlandish body-modification techniques to make women's breasts "large if they are small, and smaller if they are large."

Given the burdens they have imposed on themselves, Miner concluded, it is astonishing that the Nacirema have survived for so long.

*

What have you learned about the Nacirema?

That they are barbaric, masochistic? That they have questionable values? Do you see them as primitive, foreign, strange?

If these are the words that spring to mind, you're on the same page as anthropology students today when they are given this study.

The thing is – and forgive me if you've already cottoned on to this – the Nacirema isn't actually some weird, primitive tribe: it is "American" written backwards.

Now that you're in on Miner's joke (or rather, his pedagogical tool), you can see that the behaviour and practices you found so strange are actually rather ordinary. When the men lacerated their faces, they were shaving; when the women put their heads in small ovens, they were under hair-dryers in a salon (this is the 1950s we're talking about). When the Nacirema filled their mouths with hog hairs and magical powders, they were brushing their teeth; when they performed ritual fasts or feasts, they were watching their weight.

So why have so many people from the 1950s to the present day been tricked by Miner's study?

In part this relates to how deferential we are to those who are labelled as "experts." Miner was President of the American Anthropological Association, his article appeared in its house journal, and in it he deployed fellow academics to add weight to his assertions: Professors Linton, Malinowski and Murdock were all cited. We'll be returning to the sway of experts in the next Step.

But it's also down to something else.

The answer lies primarily in the power of language, the ability of carefully chosen words to shape our reactions, change the way we think and influence our decisions.

Think about Professor Miner's choice of language. He introduced his subjects using the word "tribe"; and not any old tribe, but one with "particularly unusual aspects." Throughout the text he used words like "rites," "exorcism," "natives," "body rituals" to further convey a sense of otherness, primitiveness and foreignness, when what he was really describing was the American citizen.

It's a simple technique, but it's very powerful. With just a few words, Miner takes the reader a long way from Manhattan or Kansas City. Unfamiliar language, unfamiliar reference points make the local and known feel distant and alien.

How easily manipulated we are.

The way things are communicated to us – the choice of words, images and metaphors used – has a huge impact on how we process and evaluate information and then go on to make decisions.

Youth-Infused Lies at the Beauty Counter

This is something the marketing industry knows all too well.

Flick through any women's magazine, and choose just a few select turns of phrase from the glossy adverts that dominate its pages.

How about Garnier's "Dark Spot Corrector" – I definitely don't want to be caught out with any "dark spots" – got to add that to my shopping list.

Then there's Lancôme's "Cell Defence": not only does it "fight ageing," it also "fights oxidation" – not sure exactly what that is, but if it needs fighting it must be bad. One of those too, please.

This sounds particularly good – Estée Lauder has just launched a "youth infusing serum" for eyes – huge relief, my eyes could do with some youth infusion; so yes please, I'll take some of that as well.

The language advertisers use to play on women's latent insecurities today may not be as extreme as it was back in the 1960s – a 1969 advert for Guerlain anti-ageing cream was headlined "Are you going to crack up before you're 45?"[2] – nice! But they're still doing a pretty good job of zooming in on women's fears by reminding us in slightly more subtle ways of what we are not and can never really be – all with a few carefully selected words.

I know, of course, at an intellectual level that this is what they are doing. I know that "youth" is not a chemical property that can be "infused," and that Dior's pledge to combine "a scientific breakthrough" and "precious nature" in a bottle of "Capture Totale" is total nonsense. Yet I fall for their combination of fear-mongering and pseudo-scientific babble disturbingly frequently, and add yet another solution-promising beauty cream to my already over-full bathroom cabinet.

This is because our unconscious minds can lead us to make choices that our rational selves would never countenance. It's not just at the beauty counter that this can happen. As we'll see time and time again in this chapter, similar responses to this kind of emotive wordsmithery play out in an extraordinary range of contexts, including those with much more disturbing consequences.

If you're not yet convinced that you need to keep your eyes wide open, this chapter should help to persuade you.

Verbal Avalanches ...

Let's dissect just one paragraph in George W. Bush's 2003 State of the Union address, a speech which took place at a time when war with Iraq was under "discussion" in American political circles.

> *Chemical agents, lethal viruses and shadowy terrorist networks are not easily contained. Imagine those nineteen hijackers with other weapons and other plans, this time armed by Saddam Hussein. It would take one vial, one canister, one crate slipped into this country to bring a day of horror like none we have ever known.*

The rhetorical juggernaut deployed in these few lines is pretty hard to miss. Bush's evocation of 9/11. His linking of that terrible day with Saddam Hussein. His use of the word "imagine" – a word much beloved by advertisers, because it's proven to get consumers to suspend their disbelief. His juxtaposition of "horror," "vial," "chemical," "shadowy," "terrorist" and "viruses," all within a few seconds of each other. Once you've added to the mix "Hitler" and "Communism" and thrown in multiple references to "them and "us," as Bush went on to do, it's no wonder it seemed that Huntington's Clash of Civilisations was playing out in our living rooms.

The first poll published after the speech, conducted by the *Washington Post* and ABC News, showed the impact of Bush's rhetorical choices. The administration received the highest support yet for a war with Iraq: 66 per cent of respondents supported military action, up from 57 per cent just two weeks before.

Bush's speech was short on facts. It was extremely limited in the evidence it provided to justify a nation going to war. Yet many among its audience were swayed by the story-telling and the frightening trigger-words. Many Americans came to a decision on this issue not on the basis of substantive information, but because of the emotive language used. It's an age-old technique, used by leaders for centuries. And it works – for there we go once more, falling for the power of the well-chosen word, whether at the supermarket or in the voting booth.

... and Verbal Snowballs

Having had a few examples to contemplate, you may be feeling more on your guard now against a highly embellished avalanche of words. But be aware that it doesn't necessarily take an avalanche to sway us. A verbal snowball can be just as powerful.

In a study, people asked to give a quality score to two dishes, one labelled "Succulent Italian Seafood Filet," the other plain old "Seafood Filet," rated the "Succulent" dish higher, even when, as was the case here, they were both the same dishes. Similarly, "Tender Grilled Chicken" was evaluated as tastier and more filling than the same dish when it was simply called "Grilled Chicken."[3] It's amazing how a small number of simple but carefully chosen words can transform what your tastebuds actually seem to experience. It's worth remembering this next time you're standing in the queue at a fast-food restaurant.

You might also want to take heed of the findings of a recent study that looked at the way the wording of a CV affects how a job application is perceived. It turns out that an applicant whose CV is presented in the third person, with bullet points like "Communicated with clients globally" or "Managed a large department," tends to be considered more reliable, less boastful, more suitable for teamwork and a stronger candidate overall than an applicant whose CV is formulated in the first person, with bullet points such as "I communicated with clients globally" or "I managed a large department." Even though the content in both cases is the same.[4]

Or look at what happened when, in a recent experiment at Stanford University, two groups were each asked to come up with recommendations for how to combat crime in Addison, a fictitious crime-ridden city in the United States.

Both groups were given exactly the same text:

Five years ago Addison was in good shape with no obvious vulnerabilities. Unfortunately, in the past five years the city's defence systems have weakened, and the city has succumbed to crime. Today there are more than 55,000 criminal incidents a year – up by more than 10,000 per year. There is a worry that if the city does not regain its strength soon, even more serious problems may start to develop.

However, the two groups were given a slightly different opening sentence to the report. The first began, "Crime is a beast ravaging the city of Addison." The second, "Crime is a virus ravaging the city of Addison."

One word different in a passage of seventy-nine words. Yet it turned out to have a huge impact.

Participants who had been told that crime was a "beast" were significantly more likely to propose "catch and cage" strategies – the hiring of additional police officers, the building of more jails; whereas the group who were given the word "virus" leaned disproportionately towards "heal and cure" methods of deterrence, such as crime-prevention strategies, and educational and social reforms.

This was regardless of whether they were Democrat or Republican, conservative or liberal-minded, young or old, male or female.

Moreover, the vast majority of the subjects were totally unaware that it was the metaphorical frames of "virus" and "beast" that had driven their decisions. When asked to identify which parts of the report had been most influential in their decision-making process, only 3 per cent of them correctly identified the metaphor as the driver.[5]

It really is incredible how vulnerable we are to subtleties of language when forming our opinions and making decisions. How unaware we can be of its pervasive powers. But we are. Time and again.

A whole host of other seemingly minor semantic tweaks have been shown to have significant impacts on our decision-making too.

The Trouble with Wayne

When 238 university psychologists were asked to rate the CVs of two fictitious applicants for an academic tenure-track job, from a Dr. "Karen" Miller and a Dr. "Brian" Miller, the results were pretty disappointing for anyone who cares about gender equality.[6]

Although the two CVs were identical apart from the first name, the male Dr. Miller was perceived to have better research, teaching and service experience than the female Dr. Miller. While three-quarters of the psychologists would have recommended hiring Dr. Brian, less than half would have hired Dr. Karen. And it wasn't just male professors who thought this: female professors were just as guilty.

It may be easy simply to put this down to gender bias, but other studies have also found that the way something is named affects how it is perceived. During the dotcom bubble, for example, many firms changed their names to take advantage of the euphoria surrounding "hot dotcom" stocks.[7] These included some that had nothing to do with the internet. For example, North American Natural Inc., which was in the business of producing educational literature, changed its name to Pinkmonkey.com, and saw its share price increase from $1 to $17. In another startling example of the influence a name can have, RLD Enterprises, a potato-crisp manufacturer, changed its name to go-rachels.com and experienced a huge jump in the value of its shares, even though at the time of the name change go-rachels did not even have a website.

Just by changing their names, these companies experienced large increases in their stock prices without any underlying business change. Time-poor investors were heavily influenced by the tremendous optimism about everything associated with the internet at the time, and used companies' names as a short cut on the basis of which to make important financial decisions.[8]

Shakespeare was wrong. A rose by any other name, it seems, does not smell as sweet. In fact, this is literally true: researchers in Montreal found that subjects enjoyed smells more when they had more pleasant names. "A rose by the name of 'rotting flower' would not smell as sweet as if it were introduced as 'fresh rose'," the study concluded.[9]

Remember all this when you're leafing through a pile of CVs, choosing what to buy for dinner in a supermarket, or deciding whom to vote for. Or indeed if you are a doctor diagnosing patients. A British study told two groups of psychiatrists the same story about a young man who had attacked a train conductor. The only difference was the attacker's name. When it was "Matthew," psychiatrists were more likely to diagnose him with schizophrenia; when it was "Wayne," they were more likely to diagnose him with a personality disorder or a drug problem.[10]

This may seem surprising, or shocking, but time and time again studies have shown that anything, from a single pernicious word to a scientific-sounding formula, from a company's name to that of a person, can fundamentally affect the way we process information and choose what to do.

So, whether you're someone who thinks of yourself as a measured decision-maker, or as more of a gut thinker, be aware that such semantic factors may be what is actually driving your decisions.

World-weary and supposedly savvy, we may all think we are well attuned to these linguistic attacks on our ability to think and decide, but the truth is that we remain acutely vulnerable, whether in the supermarket aisle or the polling booth, whether sitting in the classroom, the office or the courtroom.

Beware of Anchors When Buying a House

In Germany, a group of 177 senior trainee lawyers were asked to put themselves in the position of a trial judge having to pass sentence in a rape case.[11]

They were given key aspects of the case to evaluate, including witness statements, expert appraisals and copies of the penal code related to the incident.

However, there was a twist. As they were appraising the case in the courtroom environment, the "trial judges" were interrupted by a heckler. Although this is a common occurrence in emotionally charged legal cases, in this case it was a set-up. The heckler was an actor. And the judges were exposed to one of two types of heckler.

The first pretended to be a boyfriend of the victim, and shouted out to the court, "Give him five years!" The second acted as a friend of the accused, and yelled, "Let him go free!" The judges were then asked to reflect briefly on the interruption and pass sentence.

The results were pretty astonishing.

Even though our judges knew that they should ignore the heckler's interruption – especially as they understood that it was a biased opinion, with the heckler pushing either for leniency or for harsh sentencing depending on his supposed relationship to the accused or the victim – there was a marked variance in response between the judges who were exposed to the "Give him five years" heckler and those interrupted by the "Let him go free" one.

Judges who were confronted with the "Give him five years" remark pronounced on average a sentence of thirty-three months. Those who were confronted with the "Let him go free" remark pronounced on average a sentence of twenty-three months – almost a third less in length.

The judges had "anchored" their sentencing decisions around a biased interjection from a heckler, and had set aside much of the other information provided to them.

If even such highly trained information evaluators can make mistakes like this, it's not surprising to learn that we are all prone to similar "anchoring" errors.[12]

People asked to write down the number formed by the last two digits of their social security number, for example, and then asked what bid they'd be willing to make in an auction, anchored the bid around that number.[13] Even though the number couldn't possibly (except by coincidence) be connected to the value of any object in the auction, they unconsciously based their bids on it. Decisions as varied as the amount people are willing to pay for a house or bid in an auction, and the amount of damages juries award, have also been seen to be affected by similarly spurious numerical considerations.

In each of these cases, the higher the number people unconsciously fixated on, the higher the number they gave as their decision. This is why real-estate agents will usually show you the most expensive house first – so that others will seem cheap by comparison; or, more pertinently, will seem cheap when compared to the "anchor point" they have established in your mind.[14]

So how can we avoid unwittingly basing a decision on an inappropriate number? For we are often asked to make decisions that, whether by manipulation or chance, involve anchors lodged in our minds.

First we need to reflect upon whether a number is actually the right thing to be focusing on at all – to remember one of the lessons in the previous Step: not everything that can be counted, counts.

Assuming that in this case the number *is* relevant, one thing you might want to try is to ask yourself whether there is anything you might be anchoring your decision on. And if there is, whether that anchor might be inappropriate or misleading. Studies show that simply by asking ourselves this question we are able to override the anchor's effects.[15]

The Strange Case of Mr. Jones

There's another strange human quirk relating to numbers that it is useful to be aware of. We process the same number in different ways, depending on the way it has been presented to us.

You may already know that you're more likely to buy meat that is labelled "85 per cent lean" than meat labelled "15 per cent fat" (autistic people, interestingly, do not make this common mistake[16]). But did you know that you are very likely to evaluate fractions differently from percentages?

"Mr. Jones" would wish this were not so.

When two groups of forensic psychologists and psychiatrists were asked to decide whether to recommend the discharge of a "Mr. Jones," a patient at a high-security mental institution, they were given one of two pieces of information on which to make their assessment. The first group was told that "Twenty out of every hundred patients similar to Mr. Jones are estimated to commit an act of violence against others." The second group was informed that "Patients similar to Mr. Jones are estimated as having a 20 per cent chance of committing an act of violence against others."

Although these two ratios are of course equivalent, they triggered very different responses. Forty-one per cent of the mental health experts who were given the findings in relative terms ("twenty out of every hundred") recommended that the patient should not be discharged, while only 21 per cent of the group who'd been given the information framed in percentage terms did so.

Why should this be? It seems that for many of us there is a distinct difference between the way we perceive fractions and percentages. When we are given numerical information in the form of a frequency – i.e. twenty out of a hundred patients – we see clear, and in this case frightening, images before us. A percentage doesn't prompt a similarly clear emotional response.[17]

So, if your doctor tells you that there is a one in ten chance of you having complications from a particular operation, before you freak out, reframe this as a 10 per cent chance. Does that make it sound less bad? And does it therefore impact on your decision whether to have the surgery or not?

See, Hear, Touch, Smell: Why a Waitress Wearing Red Gets a Bigger Tip

Numbers and words are not the only factors that can subconsciously affect our decision-making.

A whole host of environmental cues can affect the decisions that we make, often without us having any idea of them.

Imagine you are at the doctor's surgery for a routine visit. The nurse hands you a pamphlet promoting a new vaccine that could have a major impact on your future health.

What will your decision be guided by? Thoughtful analysis of the information? A considered weighing up of its pros and cons?

To some extent, of course, yes. But you may also be influenced by something you probably wouldn't have expected to play a major role in such an important choice: the colour of the pamphlet.

Countless studies reveal that colour plays a significant role in our evaluation process. Speakers presenting with colour slides are viewed as having higher-quality data than those with black-and-white ones.[18] Men rate women as more physically attractive and sexually desirable when their pictures are superimposed on a red background rather than a white, grey, blue or green one.[19] Football referees are more likely to give penalties to teams wearing black strips than to those in other colours.[20] When researchers sent multiple French waitresses to work wearing different-coloured T-shirts, they found that men tipped them more if they were wearing red rather than black, white, blue, green or yellow.[21]

Even when it comes to our investment decisions, colour has a marked impact.

Doron Kliger is a behavioural economist at the University of Haifa, with an interest in how colour affects judgement in the financial sector. By carrying out experiments on investors, Kliger has discovered that when we are given information about a stock set against a red background, we focus on its potential to fall in value, making us less likely to want to buy it. Whereas if we read the same information on a green background, we focus on the stock's potential for gain, and therefore consider it a more appealing buy.[22]

It may seem extraordinary that decisions as important as the evaluations of people we meet, whether or not to be vaccinated, or what portfolio of shares to invest in, can be affected by the colour associated with the information we are given – but there is a large body of evidence to prove that this is the case.

And it's not just colours that mess with our decision-making.

Studies have shown that wine merchants sell more French wine when they play French music, and more German wine when they play German music.[23] That in restaurants, people spend more when slower-tempo music is being played, or classical rather than pop.[24] That waiters who briefly touch customers receive larger tips than ones who do not.[25] And that individuals asked to sign a petition are also more likely to do so if they've been briefly touched.[26] So, if you're trying to get a favourable response, you might want to touch someone on the forearm when making a request – patients who are touched on the forearm for one to two seconds by their doctors adhere significantly better to their medication regime than those who are not, with the biggest increase being for males.[27]

By triggering emotions, reactions and at times memories, touch and sound have proved capable of powerfully steering our choices in one direction or another.

So too has another of our senses.

What happened when identical pairs of Nike trainers were placed in two identical but separate rooms – one room sprayed with a mixed floral scent, the other not? Eighty-four per cent more consumers preferred the shoes displayed in the fragrant room. They also estimated the "fragrant" pair to cost $10.33 more than the identical pair in the unscented room.[28]

It's not just in supermarkets, restaurants and shopping malls that our senses can be scarily manipulated, without our being aware of it.

Did you know that you're more likely to offer a job to a candidate if you've been handed their CV on a heavy clipboard, rather than on a light one?[29] Or that the way you judge someone's behaviour may depend on something as simple as what you are holding in your hands?

A group of researchers at Yale gave participants either a soft blanket or a hard block of wood to handle. They then read a passage about an ambiguous interaction between a supervisor and employee. Those who'd touched the wooden block judged the employee to be more harsh and set in their ways than those who'd been stroking the blanket.[30]

Did you know that you're more likely to act stingily with your money if the room you're in has a briefcase in it rather than a rucksack?[31] The mere presence of the briefcase unconsciously triggers business-related associations, thereby putting you in the mindset of "grab" and "compete."

Or that you are more likely to make an offer for a house if it smells of freshly baked bread, as that evokes feelings of being cared for and nurtured?[32]

Even the most trivial aspects of our environment can have a profound effect on how we unconsciously assess things. In a recent study, two groups of participants were asked to judge the stability of celebrity relationships – couples like Barack and Michelle Obama, and David and Victoria Beckham. One group were seated at a table and chair that were regular and steady; the other group's table and chair were wobbly. Sure enough, the wobbly group were more likely to see the couples as "likely to dissolve." What's more, when asked which traits they valued most in a relationship, the individuals sitting at wobbly furniture were more likely to value stability. The small change in their environment had given them a greater desire for emotional security, a need to cling on to something to make them feel secure.[33]

If you are a marketer, whether of ideas, policies, ideological positions, or just shampoo, knowing the impact of the right words, frames, metaphors, colours, sounds, smells and sensory experiences is extremely valuable. But if you are continually on the receiving end of these tricks, triggers and anchors, as most of us are, you need to be primed and ready for this continual barrage of deceptions.

If you are not, how can you be confident that the decision you have made is the right one?

So how do we make sure that we're not this easily manipulated? That we're not held hostage to our environments? It's not easy. We can't make real-world decisions in a vacuum. And sometimes the sophistication of the message, or the sheer volume and force of the barrage, can overwhelm us. But there are things we can do.

Reclaim the Truth

The bad news is that it's not enough to give yourself a general note to avoid basing your decisions on anchors, sensory cues and rhetoric.[34] This tends not to make any difference at all.

The good news is that there are ways to regain control of your unconscious, at least to some degree. There are active thinking strategies that do deliver if you suspect you might be being spun or played, or that you might inadvertently be basing your decisions on an anchor.

One such strategy is to get into the habit of imagining an alternate scenario, in which your cue or anchor isn't present. How would you respond then?

So, if you're viewing a house for sale, and it smells of freshly baked bread, force yourself to consider whether you would be thinking less favourably about the property if it didn't smell as good. Or before you turn down a date with Sally from match.com, make sure to ask yourself whether you might have said yes if her photo had been set against a red background rather than a green one. And if you're about to put an offer in for a car in an auction, don't just anchor your offer automatically around the guide price. Instead, ask yourself what offer you would have put in if you were thinking completely independently.

Studies show that simply by posing such "imagine if" questions, which allow us to consider alternative explanations and different perspectives, we can distance ourselves from the frames, cues, anchors and rhetoric that might be affecting us.[35] Liberated from these tricks and triggers, we can consider information through a more neutral, less emotive, more analytical and nuanced lens.

You might also want to do some more active reflecting on the decision you're making – look at prices of similar homes on the market, say, or think about how it is you actually use your car. By asking yourself additional questions – a car for long-distance journeys? A city runabout? A family car, or just for you? – you can dislodge the frames and anchors that others are attempting to influence you with, and substitute them for more accurate data points.[36]

Another tactic that works is to build a case for the opposite option to the one you are leaning towards.[37] So, write down the reasons why not to buy the house, or why to go on a date with Sally, or why to offer just half the guide-price for the car. By articulating possible reasons to do the opposite, you become better placed to look at your initial position in a more objective light.

Removing yourself from your original decision-making environment before you come to your conclusion is another tack to consider. Given that you may have come to your initial response under the sway of temporary influences you weren't even aware of – background music, a smell, the touch of someone's hand, a colour, a word or phrase – by physically removing yourself from the environment of the trigger and taking some time to consider your decision, you will be diluting that influence's impact.[38] Again, if you can, take that beat. That pause that could make the difference between a good decision and a flawed one.

We should also make sure to ask ourselves, as a matter of practice, who is communicating the information to us. What might their agenda be? What is the organisation the "messenger" is speaking for? How does he see the world, and how might that affect how he represents it to you? Does he want you to adopt a particular belief? Act in a particular way? Once you've established the messenger's agenda, ask yourself how the way he's presenting his case might be affecting you.

Alert now to just how sensitive to language we are when making a decision, there's something else to do whether you are evaluating a proposal at work, a politician's policies or an advertiser's claims. Consider what impact the language you are hearing or reading might be having. What metaphors and adjectives are being used? What *kind* of words have been chosen, and why? How is the information being framed? What is the tone? How might all of this be swaying your judgement?

Then ask yourself whether your response would be different if emotional, evocative or politically loaded turns of phrase were not in the frame. Think here of Bush's State of the Union speech, say, and how you might have reacted had fear not been the pervasive tone.

By actively interrogating the language used, and stripping the content of rhetorical flourishes, we can override our immediate responses.

Knowing also now how affected we are by "wrappers" and "form," there are further tactics we can put into regular practice. If you want to make a decision as objectively as possible, ask yourself if there is a way you could strip away the wrapper, or change the very form in which the information has been received. If those colours on the presentation risk leading you down one particular path, maybe ask for a straightforward copy in black and white. What impact would this have on your thinking? Or if you're asking your HR department to send you a selection of CVs for a post you're looking to fill, how about asking them to remove the names of the candidates, so you don't know their gender? The year that University College Cardiff introduced anonymous marking, 47 per cent of female students achieved firsts or 2.1s. In the preceding four years, when graders knew the gender of the person whose final exams they were marking, only 34 per cent of women earned the top grades.[39]

All of the above are possible steps to take, but if you don't have time, there's a simpler strategy that may work. Admit to yourself just how susceptible you probably are to external influences, frames, cues and anchors, and then actively think about the extent to which your assessment may therefore be being distorted. This simple act of self-consciousness can eliminate the effect of the cue, frame or anchor. Reflecting on just how irrational our thinking can be seems to help us to re-establish rational thinking.[40] I tried this technique the last time I was at the beauty counter – and came home with no new purchases!

Takeaways

We'd drive ourselves crazy, of course, if we constantly tried to strip bare every piece of information we're given. And at the end of the day, if you buy the "wrong" moisturiser, it doesn't really matter. But when the stakes are high and the decisions are of import – which house to put a down-payment on? Which business proposal to pick? Whom to employ? Whom to trust? Whom to date? – we need to remind ourselves of the extent to which our decisions are prone to be influenced by situational and environmental factors as well as labels. And we must be aware of how sensitive we are to language, and the way it can distort our responses and our decision-making.

Thus aware, we should think of ourselves as a juror: bombarded by rhetoric and emotional appeals from the prosecution and the defence, by senses and sights and sounds. In the end it's down to us to decide whether or not the evidence holds up. But we can judge most fairly if we apply some basic rules, and distance ourselves from the rhetoric and imagery thrust our way by others, whether they be salesman, politicians, professors or employers. I've suggested a few concrete ways to do this at the end of this chapter.

It's also important, as ever, to retain a sceptical stance. Once we can see where someone's coming from, we're much better able to determine where it is they're trying to take us. Only then can we properly assess whether it is actually somewhere we want to go. We also must remind ourselves of the importance of independent thinking, and where possible take control of our environment. If we don't want others to con us, we need to be alert to their tricks.

Keeping our eyes wide open isn't just about ensuring that those we are listening to are not manipulating us, and that we are not inadvertently conning ourselves. It's also about being sure that we're getting our information from the right people in the first place, and being willing to challenge claims, however supposedly certain and expert the source. Time to ditch deference, and take supposed mavens on ...

QUICK TIPS TO AVOID BEING SCARED OF THE NACIREMA

- **Ask yourself if you could be leaning towards or against a decision because of an irrelevant cue (colour, smell, sound).** If so, imagine if that cue wasn't there. How do you feel now?

- **Strip any evocative or heart-tugging language away.** Write out the key determinants of your decision in as dry a way as possible. Are you still affected in the same way by what you're hearing or reading? If not, revise your initial assessment accordingly.

- **Remember how influenced we are by "wrappers."** How would you feel if the claim wasn't made in scientific language? If you didn't know the gender of the applicant? Would you still be making the same decision?

- **Look out for any anchors in your environment, any numbers or data points that you might be unconsciously basing a decision on.** If you're not sure if or how they've affected you, consider the opposite option to the one you've been leaning towards. Does this make you think differently about your initial decision?

- **Where you have the ability to "dress the environment," create as blank a backdrop as you can.** Blind evaluations so as to remove gender or ethnic bias; limited sensory distractions so as to make your decision as "cleanly" as possible.

- **Play with form.** Turn percentages into ratios, and stories into statistics. Re-frame the information you've been given. Ask for a black-and-white version of a colour document. How do you feel now about the decision at hand?

- **Remove yourself from your decision-making environment for a moment.** Go for a walk before your final decision – or if you can't do that, at the very least leave the room briefly. By removing yourself from cues and environmental influences, their impact becomes diluted.

BECOME YOUR OWN CUSTODIAN OF TRUTH

STEP FOUR
Ditch Deference and Challenge Experts

From Harley Street to the Mayo

I am sick, really sick. I look in the mirror and see hollow cheeks, eyes ringed with tiredness. I am weak. Walking to the end of my street feels like a huge effort. My weight has plummeted by thirty pounds in just three months. In swift succession I have transformed from slim, to thin, to very thin, to looking ill. On doctor's orders I stuff my face with cream cakes, chips and plates of buttered bread. Yet my BMI remains dangerously low; I gain no weight. If anything, I am getting ever thinner.

I've done the round of doctors. From London's Harley Street to New York's Mount Sinai, from Chicago's Mercy to the Mayo Clinic in Minnesota. I've been prodded and pinched, have put on and taken off paper knickers and back-tying hospital gowns more times than I'd care to remember. I've been ultrasounded, X-rayed, MRI'd and CT'd with contrast and without. My blood has been drawn so often we're now looking for veins in my feet. I've swallowed a camera in a capsule, seen my guts in slo-mo and had tubes down my throat. I've been tilted and shocked, my hands have been heated and then plunged into ice. I've been pitched a variety of treatment plans.

Surgeons suggest a range of procedures, from exploratory fact-finding missions to the immediate removal of my (perfectly healthy, and I feel irrelevant to my symptoms) gall bladder this very week. The Professor of Nutrition (so revered he has a three-month waiting list) suggests I eat mainly sugar. The world-renowned gastroenterologist tells me of his personal success with Prozac, and recommends very strongly that I try that. At the impressive Mayo I have two weeks of tests and examinations, yet they suggest I come back and be tested more.

But I don't want to live off sugar, am keen to pass on Prozac – my mental state is fine, while the famous doc seemed pretty loopy – and I would rather not succumb to more investigations. As for surgery – not that appealing, especially as I'm feeling so very weak. And what are they actually looking for? I'm not up for having body parts removed on a whim. And even if surgery is the right decision, which operation? And which surgeon?

What to do? Whom to put my trust in? Which expert to pick? What to decide?

Men in White Coats

In an age of disorder, deluge and disruption, a time when we are ever more conscious of marketers' attempts to mislead, we crave answers and certainty. And experts sell both in spades.

Scientists, professors, doctors, lawyers, investment advisers, management consultants, specialists in a wide range of domains and fields. Men (typically) in white coats or pinstripe suits, usually grey-haired – you know who I'm talking about: the authority figures we see on our television screens or read about in our morning newspapers. The kind of people deemed "trusted sources" on a particular topic, usually but not always their own. We find their utterly self-confident, parent-like aura very reassuring. When they tell us what we can and should do, or what we can't, it's a real relief.

I mean, ever since the Enlightenment we've acknowledged, haven't we, that science and logic are supremely privileged forms of knowledge, to be much revered? And it's experts who know the passwords that provide access to this privileged world. When an expert confidently delivers his opinion, we can almost see centuries of theories, rules, principles, experiments and formulae being channelled through him, in a special secret language that we, the non-experts, are not privy to.

We take these words of supposed wisdom at face value – we can't understand what the experts are on about most of the time, but we nod anyway, and accept what we are hearing. Bludgeoned by their stats and theories, pacified by their institutional affiliations and the letters after their names, reassured by their self-confidence, we surrender our intellect, instincts and power to them.

They know the answers. We do what we are told. It's a tyranny of the experts.

This is no exaggeration.

In a recent experiment, a group of adults were asked to make a financial decision while contemplating an expert's advice. An fMRI scanner gauged their brain activity as they did so.[1]

The results were extraordinary: when confronted with the expert's advice, it was as if *the independent decision-making parts of the participants' brains pretty much switched off.*

An expert speaks, and it's as if we stop thinking for ourselves. It's a really scary idea.

Yet we don't even suspect that there's a problem. Indeed, studies show that the vast majority of college-educated, high-earning, informed adults, CEOs, professionals, executives – people with clout, experience, wisdom of their own, people perhaps like you and me – trust experts more than any other group in society.[2]

But remember how easily misled we were by Professor Miner in the previous Step ...

The Sham in Expert's Clothing

Even fellow experts prove to be overly trusting. In a revealing experiment first conducted in 1972 by a group of professors of medical education from the Universities of Southern Carolina and Southern Illinois, and repeated in many other contexts since, "Dr. Myron L. Fox" supposedly an authority on "the application of mathematics to human behaviour," but in reality an actor named Michael Fox, addressed a lecture hall full of professionals from his supposed field – psychiatrists, psychologists and social workers.

"Dr. Fox" spoke on the subject of "Mathematical Game Theory as Applied to Physician Education" for a whole hour. He then took half an hour of questions. From the feedback forms collected after the lecture, we know that his talk was extremely well received: "Good analysis of subject," "Excellent presentation," "Extremely articulate" were among the comments made. This despite the fact that the material he delivered was actually meaningless – full of "double talk, neologisms, non sequiturs, and contradictory statements ... interspersed with parenthetical humor and meaningless references to unrelated topics."[3] Other studies have similarly found that the more verbose an academic is, the more competent he or she is taken to be.[4]

In this case, not a single audience member saw through the hoax. One even claimed to have read Dr. Fox's publications.

The experts' accessories – the doctor's stethoscope, the fund manager's pinstripe suit, the professor's lectern, the framed certificates and convoluted lingo – all serve as proxies for their reliability and trustworthiness, and protect the frauds, fakes and incompetents as well as your everyday expert.

From Monkeys to Garbage Collectors

But experts do get things wrong. A lot wrong. I'm not talking here about tricksters like Dr. Fox. Or fraudsters such as Hwang Woo Suk, the South Korean stem-cell researcher who claimed to have created the world's first cloned human embryos, but hadn't. Or the 2 per cent of scientists who admit to cheating outright – falsifying or fabricating their results.[5] I'm talking about your run-of-the-mill expert and run-of-the-mill error.

Did you know that studies have shown that doctors misdiagnose one time in six?[6] That of the one in twelve patients who die in hospital because of misdiagnosed ailments, half would have survived had the diagnosis been correct?[7] Or that 50,000 hospital deaths each year in the US and Canada could have been prevented if the real cause of illness had been correctly identified?[8]

Did you know that you are more likely to file your tax returns correctly if you do it yourself than if you hire a tax adviser to do it for you?[9] That 70 per cent of mutual-fund managers underperform the market?[10] Or that in Germany up to 80 per cent of all long-term financial investments are terminated prematurely because of the unsuitable advice consumers have been given by their supposedly expert investment advisers (unsuitable advice which is estimated to cost German consumers twenty to thirty billion euros every year)?[11] And how about the Cranfield Study of companies that had used management consultants? Two-thirds considered the advice they'd been given to be at best useless, at worst actively harmful.[12]

Then there are the forecasts of economic or political experts.

In 1984 *The Economist* set a challenge to four different groups to predict what the world economy would look like in ten years' time. The groups were comprised of four former finance ministers, four chairmen of multinational companies, four Oxford University students, and four London dustmen. Each group was set the same questions relating to inflation, economic growth and the pound–dollar exchange rate. They were also asked to predict when Singapore's GDP per head would overtake Australia's.

Ten years later, the magazine reviewed the predictions to see which group had made the most accurate forecasts. Four points were given for the most accurate answer to each question, three for the second best, two for the third best, and one for the worst.

Who got the highest score?

The dustmen. As for the finance ministers – they came last.[13] No wonder the global economy is in the state it's in.

When it comes to crystal-ball gazing, experts frequently get it wrong.

Some of the biggest moments in the past fifty years – the 1973 oil crisis,[14] the fall of the Soviet Union, 9/11, and most recently the Arab Spring – were missed by traditional intelligence experts, whilst a study of 82,000 predictions by 284 experts over a sixteen-year period, on issues ranging from the future of the then USSR to Saddam Hussein's invasion of Kuwait, revealed that the experts got no more right than a monkey randomly sticking a pin on a board. "It made virtually no difference whether participants had doctorates, whether they were economists, political scientists, journalists or historians, whether they had policy experience or access to classified information, or whether they had logged many or few years of experience," wrote the author of the study.[15]

It's not just metaphorical monkeys who outdo experts, however. The *Observer*'s 2012 Investment Challenge pitted a team of professional investment advisers against Orlando, a flesh-and-blood ginger tomcat. Each began with a notional £5,000 to invest in five companies from the FTSE All-Share Index. Every three months they were allowed to exchange any stocks with others from the index.

While the professionals used their expert knowledge and decades of investment experience to guide their decisions, Orlando selected his stocks by throwing a toy mouse on a grid of numbers, each representing a different company.

At the end of the year, the professionals' portfolio was worth £5,176.60 – a 3.5 per cent return on their investment. And how did Orlando do? He ended up with £5,542.60, a return of almost 11 per cent.

As Justin Urquhart-Stewart, one of the expert wealth managers, good-humouredly said, "It's time to crack open the Whiskas. The cat's got talent."[16]

Still got experts on that pedestal?

From Alan Greenspan to Bernie Madoff

If so ...

What about the financial crisis?

It's really quite absurd, when we reflect on it now, how much trust was put in the hands of those who were considered "experts" in the world of finance. But it was.

From rating agencies to economists, from Alan Greenspan to Bernie Madoff, the proclamations of those deemed experts were taken at face value. On the rare occasions that they were challenged, the very few who dared to do so were ignored or even fired.

So, investments as poor or risky as Icelandic banks and mortgage-backed securities were A-rated by Moody's and Standard & Poor's, and therefore deemed safe to buy and sell, without anything like the appropriate caveats or enquiry, simply because these supposedly "expert" agencies had given them the stamp of approval.

Equally shockingly, sophisticated investors like Banco Santander and Bank Medici invested in a fund that promised a steady return of over 10 per cent, despite the near-impossibility that anyone could deliver such steady performance, simply because of the faith they put in one man – Bernie Madoff.

Meanwhile, economic mavens such as Alan Greenspan and Larry Summers sang the praise of derivatives – Greenspan actually claimed that they made the global system less risky – despite a whole host of warnings on their dangers.[17] And fellow economists claimed that a bankruptcy like that of Lehmann Brothers could be expected only once every billion years, even though similarly "impossible" events, such as the collapse of the LTCM hedge fund and the 1987 stock-market crash, had occurred twice in the previous fifteen years.[18]

Experts were taken at face value simply because they were *perceived* as being expert.

If only those oh-so-smart economists, with their oh-so-slick theories about the efficiency of markets and the rationality of those who inhabit them, had been properly interrogated. If only those financial gurus – whether Alan Greenspan, former Chairman of the US Federal Reserve, with his endless proclamations about the safety of the financial system, or Bernie Madoff, fund manager extraordinaire, with his promises of steady returns of over 10 per cent – had been viewed as fallible humans, rather than haloed mavens. If only the rating agencies, Standard & Poor's, Fitch and Moody's, had been seen for what they were – conflicted organisations, ill suited to objectively assess hyper-complicated situations – and then been treated with appropriate scepticism.

If only all the supposed experts had been challenged, and the dissenting views at least been considered. There were even some hedge funds before the crisis, big names such as Paulson & Co. and Lansdowne Partners, who were "short the market," thereby signalling that they thought we were heading for a fall. Yet, as one of the principals pointed out to me, no one ever asked them why they were thinking differently from most others in the market, and had taken such a position.

And if only experts in the worlds of finance and economics weren't so prone to move in packs, and dissenters weren't so often sidelined, then a vast edifice of flawed models, regulatory prescriptions and computer simulations would never have been established; Park Avenue dowagers, Holocaust survivors and ordinary taxpayers would not have faced financial ruin; and the world would not have been plunged in to a far-reaching financial maelstrom.

Let me get something clear here. It's not as if experts have not powerfully contributed to our world and our knowledge. Of course they have, and they continue to do so. Nor am I suggesting that years of training, technical skill and deep immersion in a particular area count for nought – of course these things matter. What I am saying is that the conflation of expert with unchallengeable guru, experience with accolades, scientists with exemplary scientific method, and claims of certainty with actual veracity, puts us in peril.

I'm saying this not only as someone who has had to deal with experts a lot in my private life, but also – and I'm aware of the irony here – as an "expert" myself. A professor, someone who advises prime ministers, heads of big companies and international organisations like the World Bank.

But I am an expert who thinks not only that others must be more challenging of *us*, but also that as a group we need to change. We need to be more open to people challenging our points of view, more accepting of uncertainty and the limits of what we can know. And we need to be more willing to admit to our own limitations.

For while there are of course many exceptions – wonderful, civilisation-enhancing exceptions – experts can be both flawed and biased.

I mean, they're human, after all.

Follow the Money

Expert error is not only down to unconscious thinking errors like those I described in the previous chapter, however.

Up to a third of scientists admit "changing the design, methodology or results of a study in response to the pressures from a funding source."[19] Eighty-one per cent of biomedical research trainees said that they would be willing to select, omit or fabricate data to, among other things, "win a grant."[20] A recent study looking into the accuracy of scientific papers in leading medical journals – highly prestigious publications such as the *Journal of Clinical Oncology*, the *American Journal of Cardiology* and the *New England Journal of Medicine* – revealed that over 40 per cent of the best-designed, peer-reviewed scientific papers that have been published there have misrepresented the actual findings of research, largely due to funding pressures.[21] And "Numerous studies have shown that industry-sponsored clinical trials are often biased in favour of the sponsor, sometimes in ways that can only be detected with access to the original data and study protocol."[22]

Bear this in mind as you happily eat your dark chocolate bar, in the "knowledge" that dark chocolate is good for you. It turns out that the research that underpins this claim was predominantly funded by the confectionery company Mars.[23] And that in fact flavanols – the chemicals in dark chocolate thought to be good for the heart – are often removed during manufacturing, due to their bitter taste. (And that's presuming that there's much chocolate in the bar in the first place: many of them have a thin coating of chocolate, and are mostly sugar and fat.)

Also, think twice when you take a swig of your sports drink during exercise. It turns out that the scientific "facts" that prompted you – you've got to keep drinking to stay hydrated; your brain doesn't know when you're thirsty; it reduces the risk of water intoxication – may be less impartial than you had reckoned with. A study in the *British Medical Journal*, conducted to coincide with the London Olympics, found that all of these claims are based on highly selective research funded by, wait for it – the makers of drinks like Gatorade, Powerade and Lucozade.[24]

So, if you're planning to turn to an expert for important "objective" advice, find out in advance whose payroll they are on, and what conflicts of interest this may present.

That was something the US Federal Drugs Administration did not do when it convened a panel of experts to determine whether a group of painkillers – COX-2 inhibitors, commonly known as "coxibs" – should be removed from the market. These drugs were among the most heavily marketed in pharmaceutical history: their manufacturers spent billions of dollars on advertising, touting them as miracle drugs, "super-aspirins" that relieved pain without the risk of stomach ulcers. Soon they ranked among the most prescribed drugs in the US. However, mounting evidence linked them with cardiovascular problems: the most controversial of them, Vioxx, had been aggressively promoted in ad campaigns featuring Olympic gold medallists Bruce Jenner and Dorothy Hamill, only for an FDA whistleblower to later estimate that it may have caused up to 140,000 heart attacks.[25]

At first glance, the FDA's decision to convene a panel of experts to help it decide what to do made sense. The experts comprised professors, scientists, statisticians and patient representatives. They sounded like a very sensible group of people to take advice from. Following three days of public hearings, the panel reported back. Although they recognised that these painkillers did increase the risk of heart attacks, the panellists felt that the benefits outweighed the risks. Voting on each drug in turn, they recommended that all three drugs in that class – Celebrex, Vioxx and Bextra – be permitted to stay on the market. (Vioxx had actually been withdrawn by then, so in its case "returned to the market" would be more accurate.)

A week later, it was revealed that of the thirty-two panel members, ten had financial ties to the manufacturers.[26] These individuals had voted 9–1 in favour of keeping Vioxx and Bextra on the market. If their votes had been excluded, only Celebrex would have passed muster.

When experts are on the payroll of the very companies that they are asked to evaluate (a pretty common practice – a survey of two hundred such expert panels revealed that a third of those on them had a financial interest in the drugs they evaluated), there's a good chance that they will not be impartial.

We see these potential conflicts of interest in the world of finance, too.

Take those credit rating agencies, agencies like Standard & Poor's, Moody's and Fitch. We saw during the financial crisis the huge impact their ratings have on how companies are perceived by investors and lenders. But did you know that they are often paid by the very institutions that they review?[27] And there is evidence that this affects their judgement. A recent report for the European Central Bank, based on 39,000 quarterly bank credit ratings from 1990 to 2011, revealed that those banks that gave significant business to a rating agency – you guessed it – got better ratings from the agency in question.[28]

How about closer to home? When your financial adviser suggests a particular product for you to buy, is this because it is in your best interest? Or is it more a reflection of the commission he will make by selling that product to you? An investigation by the UK's Financial Standards Authority found that commission payments by insurers, banks and other financial institutions often distorts the advice supposedly "independent" financial advisers provide.[29]

So, whether at your GP surgery or your bank, if your financial adviser or doctor seems to be pushing a particular product especially hard, ask them outright whether they have any potential conflict of interest, if there is any associated commission or perk they are likely to receive. This may feel uncomfortable, but you might just be shocked by their answer.

Who is incentivising your expert to say what?

We need to be asking this question.

We need to make sure our eyes are wide open and our brains are switched on, and that we are thinking for ourselves.

Follow the Practice

Experts' testimonies need to be viewed with caution for other reasons too, some much more humdrum, and some even more shocking than those we have already seen.

Take the much-touted "fact" that the average British citizen can expect to be captured three hundred times a day by CCTV. You may well have come across this claim in your newspaper. It's a figure that has appeared in the *Evening Standard*, the *Daily Mail* and the *Sunday Times*.[30]

But where did it come from? Those papers took it from a landmark report on Britain's Surveillance Society. Commissioned by the government and edited by David Murakami Wood, a sociologist of significant standing, it soon became highly influential received wisdom in the surveillance debate.

But where did Wood get it from?

The figure derived from a study by Clive Norris and Gary Armstrong, two British criminology lecturers who analysed a day in the life of Mr. Thomas Kearns, a middle-aged salesman who lived on a housing estate with his wife and two children.[31] According to the study, Mr. Kearns left home at 8:15 in the morning, took the lift downstairs, and dropped his children off at their respective schools. Click. Then he stopped off to buy petrol at a service station, bought a newspaper and took the train to work. Snap. During his lunch break he went to the maternity ward to visit his sister, who had just given birth. Click. From there he headed to Heathrow Airport to meet some potential clients. Snap. From there he escorted his guests to a car park, where a rental car awaited them. Click. That took them to a Chelsea match at Stamford Bridge. Snap. After the game they headed to a restaurant in Streatham, South London, but took a wrong turn – Click – and ended up in a red-light district by mistake. Snap. Eventually they found the restaurant, ate, and went their separate ways. Click.

Poor, exhausted Thomas Kearns only got home just before midnight. Over the course of the day the study revealed that he had been snapped, clicked and captured by more than three hundred security cameras. Our surveillance society, it seemed, was out of control.

The information, however, had one major flaw: Thomas Kearns did not exist.

Thomas Kearns was a "fictional construction," the invention of Norris and Armstrong. The authors stated clearly in their study that the account of his day was a hypothetical scenario to illustrate how the average person might come into contact with security cameras.[32]

The trouble was that Professor Wood, who used the oft-quoted "three hundred cameras each day" figure in his report, had failed to disclose that it was based on imagined events. When journalist David Aaronovitch questioned him about this oversight, Wood responded that the actual numbers were unimportant; the purpose of the report was to start a policy debate. "There are probably all sorts of questionable things in it," he added. "In fact, I hope there are many."[33]

While academics are of course capable of inadvertent error, that isn't what happened here. This was a case of an academic keen to make a noise. As a rule of thumb, the better the sound-bite, the less the expert's claim should be unquestioningly accepted.[34]

When the Facts Change …

Furthermore, despite John Maynard Keynes's possibly apocryphal maxim, "When the facts change, I change my mind," it should be noted that in practice, experts tend to remain wedded to *their* truths, even if these are way beyond their sell-by date.

If you live in the United States and had impacted wisdom teeth as a young adult, you've probably had them removed. Right?

The consensus among American dentists has long been to remove impacted wisdom teeth. Around ten million healthy, asymptomatic wisdom teeth are extracted from young patients in the United States every single year, despite such procedures involving considerable risk. Between 1997 and 2007, up to 175,000 patients suffered permanent paraesthesia – numbness of the jaw or tongue, with symptoms that include drooling, disfigurement of the lip, and impaired speech and taste – as a result of wisdom-teeth surgery.[35]

The conventional wisdom among US dentists is that delaying wisdom-teeth removal is simply "postponing the inevitable." "Who knows when they could flare up?" they ask. "In the middle of the semester? The middle of exams? The first day at your first job?"[36] They toss around ominous warnings about the risks of retaining wisdom teeth. A 2010 press release from the American Association of Oral and Maxillofacial Surgeons said that 80 per cent of young people who retained formerly healthy wisdom teeth "developed problems within seven years."[37] "It is critical that both patients and healthcare providers fully understand how harmful retaining these wisdom teeth can be," says Dr. Louis Rafetto, who led the AAOMS task force on third molars. "Inaction," he adds, "can have serious long-term health consequences, including increased systemic inflammation which can lead to cardiovascular disease and pre-term birth."[38]

The problem is that these figures that the experts have been bandying around, the fear-filled stories about "cysts" and "bacteria" that will harm you unless you have surgery, are not backed up by convincing research.

A landmark investigation conducted by the University of York in 2000 reviewed the forty most rigorous international studies, reviews and trials of the previous twenty-five years on the effect of surgery on patients whose impacted but non-infected wisdom teeth were removed. It concluded that there was "no reliable research evidence to support the prophylactic removal of disease-free impacted third molars," and that evidence had been found of significant risks to such surgery.

These findings corresponded with earlier investigations. A previous study had found that of a large group of middle-aged people who had declined to have their impacted wisdom teeth removed, only 12 per cent had suffered any kind of complication.[39] A thorough review of the literature in the periodical *General Dentistry* in 1996 found that "In more than 98 per cent of cases, there is no apparent benefit to prophylactic third-molar extraction in adolescents."[40]

It wasn't that American dentists were unaware of such studies. Some of them were American studies. Moreover, US researchers had recently come up with evidence that further corroborated such findings. An article in the prestigious *American Journal of Public Health* in 2007 revealed that as many as two-thirds of all such extractions were unnecessary.[41] And in 2008 the American Public Health Organization issued a statement arguing that wisdom-teeth extraction was insufficiently justified by evidence, and "subjects individuals and society to unnecessary costs, avoidable morbidity and the risks of permanent injury."[42] Yet to this day, teachings on the "evils of wisdom teeth" are prevalent in American dental schools, and the removal of impacted wisdom teeth remains the norm in the US.

Just think of how many other supposed expert truths and standard practices have similarly endured way past their sell-by dates. The risks of Hormone Replacement Therapy and PIP breast implants had been written about for years before the bulk of doctors admitted the dangers. As we've seen, Alan Greenspan was repeatedly warned of the risks that irresponsible lending practices could bring, yet despite this he continued to stick to his guns. Economists continued to preach non-interventionist policies even after the financial crisis, when the limits of the free market had been made all too explicit.

Paradigms are notoriously hard to shift. Experts are notoriously wedded to their way of doing things, especially when they've been doing it their way for some time, and it has proved lucrative – approximately 75 per cent of oral surgeons' incomes come from "defensive" treatments such as the removal of impacted wisdom teeth – and when those at the top of the profession continue to beat the old drum.[43]

When the facts change, in all fields of expertise, all too many experts decide to stay put.

So, when you're considering whether to trust a particular expert, one thing to do is to ask them whether they're up to date with latest research and findings, and if so, how they've modified their thinking. If they balk at this sort of question, beware. I quickly ran from one of the UK's leading gastroenterologists after he proudly admitted that he didn't have the time, or see the need, to stay on top of the latest research.

Experts in Conflict – Why You Need More Rather Than Less

If at all possible, you should also do your best to gather different expert opinions. Because experts won't always agree.[44]

Each of the ten surgeons I saw during my period of illness had a radically different approach. Five touted open surgery, two a laparoscopy. Three were intent on sparing me anything too radical; the others were gung-ho, keen for me to face full-on battle. Six wanted to strike pre-emptively; one suggested we wait and see. Two argued for robotic, five wanted manual. Most advised the insertion of drainage post-operatively, although one dissented. Two suggested Arnica pre- and post-surgery, five said don't bother. And each surgeon's approach had a substantially different level of associated risk, each had a different prognosis, each had a different expected recovery time. The Mount Sinai maven told me I would have to take six months off work. In Harley Street the surgeon was hopeful that he'd get me back at my desk within six days.

Decisions as diverse and important as whether to have surgery or a vaccination, whether to take on more staff or increase your advertising budget, will have experts of different hues trumpeting diametrically opposed positions.

So when the stakes are high, the first step is to remember that you may need to listen to a number of different expert views before you decide anything.

How to Pick the Right Expert

But then you have to work out how to pick between experts.

How to know which to trust over another?

Who to trust, and why, are questions I'll be coming back to time and time again in this book.

One generally applicable strategy to adopt is this: do everything you can to become an expert yourself. If it's a decision that really matters, you need to build your own knowledge-base, think for yourself, be ready to know what the right questions are, and what kind of answers you might receive. You've got to make sure you understand what it is your experts are telling you, what they're recommending or advising, so that you can properly consider their steer.

This is what some of the early AIDS sufferers in the US, although not medically trained or scientists, realised. If they could talk the talk, they'd be taken more seriously by doctors and researchers, and would therefore be better able to manage their condition. Mark Harrington, a coffee-house waiter-cum-freelance screenwriter who'd studied German art and film at Harvard, recalled staying up all night "making a list of all the words he needed to understand." Brenda Lein, a multiply pierced AIDS activist and punk rocker, reminisced about reading "a stack about a foot high about granulocyte macrophage colony stimulating factor about ten times so as to understand the lingo." By immersing themselves in the academic literature, attending scientific conferences, scrutinising research protocols and learning from sympathetic professionals, a group of AIDS patients emerged in the late eighties who were impressively versed in virology, immunology, molecular biology and biostatics.

These self-taught experts soon reaped the benefits, not only in terms of better management of their own conditions, but also of getting a seat at the table. Fluent in the language of medical science, they were invited to publish in scientific journals and to present at formal scientific conferences. Before too long they were being asked to sit on national institutes of health and FDA advisory committees, on institutional review boards at local hospitals and research centres, and on advisory boards established by pharmaceutical companies.

To quote Brenda Lein, "I mean, I walk in with, you know, seven earrings in one ear and a mohawk and my ratty old jacket on, and people are like, oh great, one of these street activists who don't know anything." But once she demonstrated that she knew her stuff, she found that she was able to have meaningful conversations about treatment options.[45]

If you want to be able to evaluate experts' recommendations, but the experts you're dealing with are incapable of translating, or unwilling to translate, their impenetrable jargon, either get up to speed in expert-speak yourself, or find a good translator whom you can trust. We're not all going to be able to understand these specialised worlds, nor will we always have the time to become fluent in expert lingo, but who might help us make sense of what we're hearing? Might there be someone in your life who can lend a hand?

When a friend's husband was injured in a skiing accident, and left in a coma as a result, she convened a board of smart individuals – not doctors, but people good at processing medical speak – to help her understand the various opinions she received.

Who do you have in your network who can act as translator to decipher the opinions of experts? Or is there a group of like-minded individuals somewhere in the world, with the same issues or problems, that you can join forces with? More on this in the next Step.

Second – and again this is a lesson more broadly applicable than just for choosing between experts – don't be a lemming. That is, don't simply go with the majority opinion. History is littered with examples of minority expert opinion eventually prevailing. Darwin, Galileo, Copernicus and Pasteur all had their scientific ideas either rejected, ignored or attacked by their peers.[46]

More recently, contrarians such as economist Nouriel Roubini, law professor Frank Partnoy, risk manager Rick

Bookstaber and myself were just a few of the voices who warned about the fissures in the global economic system before the financial crisis. All of us were ignored by the mainstream in our fields.[47]

This isn't to say that maverick opinions are always right. If they're prompted by financial or ideological interests, or by the desire for fame, or are shoddily researched, you must tread carefully. In Step Eight I'll be sharing some tips on how to spot bad research. And bear in mind that mavericks are just as capable of mistakes as anyone else.

What I'm saying is, don't discard minority views just because they are unpopular. All expert advice needs to be considered on its own merits. Indeed, the more we keep our brains switched on and think for ourselves as well as learn from others, the more successful we will be in our endeavours.

Third, check out your expert's track record. How good have their assessments and predictions been in the past? How experienced are they in the area in which you need their help? A recent study in the United States found that patients who had surgery to open up clogged arteries in their necks in order to reduce the risk of a stroke were more likely to die within a month of the operation if their surgeon was inexperienced in that particular procedure.[48]

This isn't to say that the past is a perfect steer for the future – we've seen cases when it definitely wasn't. Nor is it to say that mistakes are never acceptable: no one will get every single decision they make right. But if your expert has made some howlers, at the very least you'll want to know about them, so you can interrogate their current assessment especially carefully. So do ask the surgeon you're considering how many times he has carried out this particular operation, and how many times anything has gone wrong. And do check a pollster or forecaster's previous batting average.[49] If it's poor, you probably want to look elsewhere.

Fourth, if the expert before you appears cocksure and dead certain, run away from him or her, quickly. Time and again I've found that the smartest, most considered people are those who are still hungry to learn from others. Of course they have their own opinions and views, but their minds have remained open.

Absolute intellectual certainty is very often the sign of a mind eclipsed by its own ego.[50]

I do understand that the more uncertain the times are, the more we want our experts to claim certainty. That we equate certainty with apparent ability. And that the harder the situation before us, the more we want to absolve ourselves of responsibility and hand over the power to decide to someone who seems godlike in their assuredness.

But the reality is that, for most of the issues one's likely to seek expert advice on, certainty is a luxury that simply doesn't exist, especially in a world as unpredictable and fast-changing as ours. Better an expert who acknowledges this than one who attempts to deny it.

Studies show that the best political forecasters are those who are self-deprecating. That the more confident a forecaster is in their predictions, the worse their forecasts prove to be.[51] That radiologists who perform poorly also tend to be very confident that they are right – at the very times they are wrong.[52] And that intensive-care doctors who are "completely certain" in their diagnoses can be wrong as much as 40 per cent of the time.[53] Certainty, whether about why something is or what will be, is something that should set alarm bells ringing.

Conversely, the courage to admit when we've got things wrong, and to learn from it, is a trait we should actively seek out in our expert.

The Austrian economist Friedrich August van Hayek said in November 1974, at a time of terrible economic crisis not dissimilar to that of recent years: "Economists are at this moment called upon to say how to extricate the free world from the serious threat of accelerating inflation which has been brought about by the very policies which the majority of economists recommended and even urged governments to pursue ... We have indeed at the moment little cause for pride: as a profession we have made a mess of things."[54]

Hayek didn't say this as an off-the-record aside, by the way. It was the introduction to his acceptance speech when he was awarded the Nobel Prize for Economics.

If your expert is stubbornly rigid in their opinions, unaware of alternative positions or unwilling to accept their own human limitations, they're unlikely to be the right person to trust.[55]

Finally, don't pick an expert simply because their analysis corresponds to what you already believe, or because their advice is precisely what you want to hear. We saw in Step Two just how prone we are to this sort of behaviour.

Just because an expert's views correspond to yours, it doesn't mean that they are right. If we are to make smart decisions, we have to be willing to contemplate views wildly different from our own. More on the value of dissent in Step Ten.

Takeaways

To sum up, experts are not a homogeneous group. Their ranks are made up of a diversity of opinion, ideology and competence. Not all are equal. Some are clearly better than others, and many get much wrong.

Remember this when you are seeking out an expert, and don't automatically give them a free pass. It's imperative both to recognise the limitations of experts, and to keep the independent decision-making part of our brains switched on.

We can't afford not to, especially when the stakes are high.

So, treat each expert's advice with appropriate caution. Remember that they are human, and therefore subject to a whole host of potential failings. At best, look upon your expert as an investigator bringing you different assertions, rather than as the custodian of definitive facts.

Always be willing to challenge them, but also be ready to challenge your own response to what it is they say.

And widen your net when it comes to who you get your steer from – experts are not the only source from which to seek counsel. That is what the next Step is about.

QUICK TIPS FOR DITCHING DEFERENCE AND CHALLENGING EXPERTS

- **Take on the challenge of becoming an expert yourself.** Do your own research. This gives you the best chance of asking the right questions and reaching the right outcomes. If you can't understand something, who can act as an interpreter for you on your journey?

- **Shop around – not all experts are equal.** Their ability, expertise and intellectual open-mindedness will vary a great deal.

- **Get second and third opinions, at least.** Seeking out just one "expert opinion" may well leave you with flawed information. A range of perspectives will give you the knowledge you need to ask the right questions and understand all your options.

- **Don't confuse arrogance with competence.** They are not the same thing. You don't want an arrogant expert. Intellectual curiosity and a lack of ego are often the signs of the most impressive experts.

- **Look for the expert who admits to not knowing everything, rather than the one who claims certainty.** He's more likely to get things right.

- **Make sure you've looked at your expert's track record.** If it's a surgeon, you want to know how many times they've performed the procedure; if a management consultant, who they have worked for and what did they achieve there. Work out a way in which you can find out how good this person really is at their job.

- **Discover how up-to-date your expert is with the latest research and techniques.** If they dismiss this question, they are dismissing your right to play an active part in your own decision-making, and they may just have something to hide. At this point you might want to find someone else.

- **Check your expert's reasoning, and ask to see their evidence** (future Steps will help you brush up on how to evaluate this). It's OK to ask: experts do get a lot wrong.

- **Remember, experts are human, which means they are prone to a whole host of thinking errors and biases.** You are too. (We've already touched upon this but more still to come.)

- **If your expert won't engage with you, or patronises you, they're not the right person to be seeking advice from.** You need a dialogue with your expert, not an expert who expects you to receive their decrees from on high.

- **Never forget that you have a mind of your own.** And never unthinkingly hand over responsibility for the decisions you make to another person, even if they are wearing a white coat.

STEP FIVE
Learn from Shepherds and Shop Assistants

Radioactive Sunday Roasts

Imagine the scene. We are in Cumbria, in the north-west of England. A beautiful part of the British countryside, immortalised by Coleridge, Wordsworth, Ruskin and Beatrix Potter.

The year is 1986.

Some 1,800 miles away, a terrible nuclear accident has taken place in the Soviet city of Chernobyl.

A week after the disaster, the scale of the calamity is becoming clear. The fallout is four hundred times that of Hiroshima.[1]

The British government becomes concerned that heavy rain has meant that the radioactive fallout from Chernobyl did not disperse in the air above the UK, but fell to earth. In particular they are worried about what this will mean for Cumbrian lamb – a major export of the region.

So they send a group of eminent and highly qualified nuclear scientists to Cumbria to give their assessment.

The experts determine that the Cumbrian sheep will not be contaminated as they graze. They estimate that within three weeks any remaining traces of radioactivity in the air will have dissipated, and the sheep will be completely safe. Farmers are told to "hold on" until then, and in the meantime to feed their sheep on "imported straw."

The scientists have based their assessment on how the alkaline clay soil found in the valleys of the lowlands responds to nuclear fallout: it tends not to seep through this type of soil. The trouble is, that's not the only place Cumbrian sheep graze.

As every shepherd in Cumbria knows, sheep also graze in the highland hills, where the land is not alkaline clay but acid peaty soil. And unlike clay, acid peaty soil does not lock up nuclear fallout. It remains mobile, and moves easily from the soil back into the vegetation which the sheep graze. Indeed, the shepherds had direct experience of this some years previously, when a leak at the local Windscale/Sellafield nuclear plant exposed their sheep to radioactive waste.

The shepherds attempted to share their knowledge with both the scientists and the authorities. They tried to explain the full story of where their sheep grazed, and the differing soils this encompassed. They passed on the information about what had happened following the Sellafield incident. But the powers that be refused to listen to them.

I mean, they were shepherds, after all. Why on earth should their "opinions" be taken more seriously than the confident claims of scientists? We saw in the previous Step just how drawn to men in white coats we are, and how susceptible to meekly accepting their advice.

It was only after a period of weeks, when the measured levels of radioactivity showed no signs of abating, that the government conceded that the experts had been mistaken, and the shepherds correct.

A long-term ban restricting sheep movements in the area was imposed, which was only fully lifted on 1 June 2012, twenty-six years after Chernobyl.[2]

If it wasn't for the shepherds, you might have eaten radioactive lamb in your Sunday roast.[3]

From Migraine Mavens to Schoolboy Raconteurs – Expand Your Notion of Experts

It's not just shepherds who can trump scientists.

Imagine you are the CEO of a pharmaceutical company looking to come up with a new product, or a government minister looking to improve the health of your citizens, or a migraine sufferer looking to work out how best to manage your condition. Or a day trader deciding what to invest in. Or a banker trying to understand a particular sector.

Who should you turn to for an effective steer? Traditional experts – researchers, academics, doctors, analysts? Despite their limitations, quite possibly. But not to the exclusion of a whole other constituency – people I call "lay experts," who may not have the formal status or training of traditional experts, but instead have relevant and deep first-hand experience.

A whole host of Western medical "breakthroughs," including the development of drugs like morphine, the anti-malarial quinine and aspirin, have been built not on the laboratory discoveries of PhDs, but the direct experience of indigenous people's local knowledge of plant and animal remedies, repackaged in pill format.[4]

Levels of child malnutrition in Vietnam fell dramatically once mothers of the healthiest babies in villages, rather than trained paediatricians, were tapped to share their experience of child-rearing. It turned out that they spread their infants' feeds over more meals a day than their peers (four or five versus two), which meant that their children were able to consume twice as many calories at each feed. They also supplemented the staple rice diet that the other mothers fed their babies with snails, crabs, shrimps and the greens of sweet-potato tops, meaning that their children digested many more nutrients – a feeding plan that certainly didn't figure in any traditional paediatric-care manuals.[5]

If you're coping with a chronic condition, rather than turning to your overworked GP, your fellow patients might well be a better bet. When 191 active members of online support communities, people managing such conditions as breast cancer, ovarian cancer, prostate cancer and hepatitis C, were asked who supplied them with valuable information most effectively – specialists, primary-care practitioners or online support groups – their answer was unambiguous. Online support groups came out on top by a country mile in a whopping nine out of ten categories, including not only emotional support, compassion and empathy, but also medical referrals, practical coping tips and the provision of in-depth information. They also emerged as slightly preferred in the category of "best source of medical and technical knowledge."[6]

The value of "lay experts" can also extend to the boardroom. Morgan Stanley learnt the value of tapping into direct experience when they asked an intern in their London office to write a report describing the media habits of teenagers. The resulting paper had clear insights on newspapers ("Teenagers cannot be bothered to read pages and pages of text while they could watch the news summarised on the internet or on TV"), pop-up ads ("extremely annoying and pointless"), music ("very reluctant to pay for it") and everything in between.[7] Edward Hill-Wood, the baby-faced executive director of the European media team at Morgan Stanley, said of the report that it was "one of the clearest and most thought-provoking insights we have seen."[8] Flooded with six times the normal level of calls and emails from clients and CEOs, he commented, "It is far and away the most significant reaction to a note we've ever been involved in, and is certainly going to go down as one of the most widely-read notes ever published by Morgan Stanley."[9] The paper was even discussed at the Allen & Co. conference, attended by media moguls and techie billionaires like Rupert Murdoch and Bill Gates.

So who was this young person who had become "the world's most famous intern since Monica Lewinsky"?[10] A Harvard MBA in between his first and second year? A law graduate from Oxford hoping to make the transition to investment banking? No – he was Matthew Robson, a fifteen-year-old at Kidbrooke comprehensive school in Greenwich, whose mother had secured him a summer placement after the family dog Rudy made friends with the wife of a Morgan Stanley media analyst in a local park. A teenager who researched his paper by asking his friends – fellow teenagers. There were no textbooks, no footnotes, no references. Just conversations and observations. He simply reported on the mood of a generation that he was part of.

Cast Your Net Wider

Don't think of this as simply a matter of traditional experts versus lay experts, however. Think of it like this: traditional experts come to the table with particular skills and knowhow. These are valuable. Yet all too often they make their pronouncements from on high, without sufficient mindfulness of context or local conditions.[11] Lay experts, on the other hand, necessarily have their feet on the ground. This means that they are capable of delivering insights that those looking down from up top, however qualified, may never discover or volunteer.

For although neither the Vietnamese village mothers nor your fellow migraine sufferer nor the Cumbrian shepherds nor the Morgan Stanley intern Matthew Robson were in any traditional sense experts – they had no formal education in the subject at hand, they weren't versed in science, they were unlikely to have been able to explain why things worked as they did, or why they saw as they saw – in each of these cases the insights and knowledge they had by merit of their first-hand experience and immersion in the matter proved uniquely valuable.

Experience is not the poor relation of expertise.

PhDs and fancy titles are all very well, but they do not necessarily deliver better insights than those gleaned by the people at the coalface.

So if we want to make smart decisions it is not enough that we challenge and better scrutinise traditional experts, we also need to *expand our notion of who it is we should turn to for advice and guidance.*

We need to value what our Nobel Prize-winning economist Friedrich Hayek described as "local" knowledge – the dispersed wisdom of those on the ground.[12] This means casting our nets much wider than we are traditionally prone to do, and seeking out the most experienced and best-placed lay experts, wherever they happen to be.

It's not rocket science. If it is caring for children that you want to get insights into, parents will probably have something valuable to share. If it is the management of rivers you're trying to get a handle on, you probably want to consider the input of anglers and canoeists. If it is new product innovations you are considering, tap into the insights of the product's existing fans.

More generally, if it is issues at work you are trying to get a perspective on, there's a significant constituency you might well not be deploying effectively – *your workers*, or the teams you personally manage. They might just have the answers that expensive management consultants, swooping in for a few weeks with no direct experience, are less likely to discover.

That being so, let's take some time to look at ways in which we can actively and effectively seek out lay expertise in our workplace. Doing so may profoundly affect the decisions we make.

From First-Class Luggage to Toyota's Poka-Yoke

The airline industry gives us some great examples of how tapping in to the on-the-ground experience of workers can pay off.

British Airways revolutionised how it delivered first-class baggage on its carousels because of the insights of ... a baggage handler.[13]

Ian Hart worked at Heathrow Terminal 4. In 1993, standing by the carousel all day, he spotted a pattern: the bags that came out first always had black-and-yellow tags. Hart did some investigating: it turned out that these tags were given to standby passengers, who were the last onto a flight if all the seats had not been sold. As their luggage was the last to be put into the hold, it came out first.

As standby passengers were those who paid least for their flights, it was pretty ironic that they were getting their luggage first. Moreover, first-class passengers had clearly clocked this: many of them had asked Hart, "How do we get a tag too?" So he had a thought: shouldn't first-class passengers get this treatment for forking out the extra cash for their tickets? He suggested a way to give them what they want: loose-loading first-class luggage into the front hold, so it could be removed first and fastest.

The suggestion was trialled on selected routes in the summer of 1993. It proved a huge success, slashing the average waiting time for luggage for first-class passengers from twenty minutes to twelve. British Airways had improved their customer service and found themselves a USP not from a graduate consultant, but from street-smart, close-to-the-customer Ian Hart on the floor.

The idea that employees throughout your organisation could have valuable insights is not a revolutionary one. Indeed, the first recorded formal suggestion programme in a workplace is from 1770, when the British navy, realising the need for a process for soliciting every sailor's ideas (at that time, the mere mention of an idea that contradicted a captain's opinion was likely to be punished by flogging), put in place a suggestion-box scheme.[14]

A hundred-odd years later, NCR became the first American company to implement a company-wide suggestion programme.[15] Its owner, John Patterson, realised early in his career that while employees often had valuable ideas, management structures often prevented these ideas from surfacing. To counter this, he introduced "convenient receptacles placed throughout the factory where anybody can deposit signed suggestions."[16] Patterson described this scheme as his "hundred headed brain," and it really took off. Soon he had 7,000 suggestions a year flowing in from his 3,700 employees, with a third of them being implemented. The results were powerful. By the time of Patterson's death in 1922, the company controlled 90 per cent of the American cash-register market.[17] When it went public three years later, it was the largest-ever public offering on the US stock market.[18] By valuing the people on the ground, Patterson had built an industry powerhouse.

By World War II, suggestion boxes had entered the mainstream of business globally, and their impact grew in the decades that followed. British Airways didn't just benefit from Ian Hart's lay expertise, it capitalised on its cabin crews' simple suggestion of descaling on-board toilet pipes, saving the company £600,000 in the process.[19] American Airlines made an annual saving of $567,000 thanks to first-class flight attendant Kathy Kridel's suggestion that they replace the 200-gram tins in which they were serving caviar with 100-gram tins. Smaller tins would mean less waste, and less cost.[20] Tesco nowadays puts barcodes on the bottom of baguettes, so cashiers don't have to perform the juggling act of scanning the bag and hoping the baguette doesn't fall out, thanks to the insights of checkout staff.[21] Kellogg's now uses the same thickness of card for all manufacturing plants in Europe – bringing an annual saving of £250,000 – thanks to a suggestion that came in through their employee suggestion scheme, "Snap, Crackle and Save."[22] Toyota has received over ten million ideas from employees over the past few decades, on issues ranging from cutting costs, to speeding up the production process, to "poka-yoke" – techno speak for strategies which enable the errors workers repetitively make on the factory floor to be avoided.[23]

Insights from the shop floor can clearly deliver. Yet despite all these examples of successful employee suggestion schemes, most organisations do not actively seek out input from those in their lower echelons. Indeed, lay expertise remains significantly underappreciated in the workplace, a poor cousin to customer feedback, and an even poorer cousin to the ruminations of management or the musings of experts. In most cases it is these groups who continue to be the sole providers of opinions on what are deemed important matters. As a result, most companies continue to massively undervalue their internal lay knowledge.

How much lay expertise is hidden within your business that you are missing out on?

Even if a company does have some sort of suggestion scheme in place, thereby tacitly acknowledging the importance of views from its "lower-down" echelons, it does not mean that all employees will rush to provide their input. Certain types are more likely to contribute – those looking to be noticed or to curry favour. Moreover, enthusiasm can quickly wane after an initial flow of ideas. The suggestion boxes can then lie dormant, becoming at worst nothing more than receptacles for the anonymous poison-pen letters of disgruntled staff. At other times they can end up as mere receptacles for the mundane musings of the unfocused.[24]

In order to be truly effective, these kinds of schemes need consistent attention and careful management thought. So rather than soliciting open-ended suggestions, how about posing specific questions that your company needs input on? In doing so you will not only provide a clear steer as to what you are *not* looking for, but will also have a degree of control over what kind of suggestions come back.

Betting on the Shop Floor

If you want to ensure that dispersed and differing perspectives from throughout your organisation, including contrarian and heretical ones, are gathered, there's something else to try – a mechanism that both encourages a frank exchange of ideas and enables you to effectively and efficiently tap into your staff's experience in a wholesale form. One can only imagine how many employees it took to read through Toyota workers' millions of ideas, and at what cost.

The mechanism I have in mind, which has delivered on all these fronts, is known as a prediction market. It is a way of collecting and aggregating information from disparate parties on what they think the likelihood of future events occurring is – via what is essentially a betting market.[25]

Such markets have been used to aggregate views from diverse sources on future outcomes in spheres as varied as movies (box-office returns and Oscar-winning performances) and election results, with considerable success. The Iowa Electronic Market, which predicts presidential election outcomes, outperformed the polls 74 per cent of the time between 1988 and 2004.[26] On the eve of the 2012 election it predicted a 50.9 per cent share of the vote for Obama – pretty much spot on: Obama got 50.93 per cent.[27]

When the crowd is diverse and decentralised, and opinions within it are independent of each other, these kinds of betting markets can deliver.[28]

Where such prediction markets have been set up within businesses, the results have been even more transformative. A number of companies, including Google, Microsoft, Eli Lilly, Intel and Siemens successfully use such markets to tap into their internal lay expertise on an ongoing basis, thereby improving forecasts on sales, revenues and new product launches, as well as a whole host of other key strategic matters.

Why they work so well is because within an organisation much is going on that managers, focused on day-to-day business and their individual briefs, simply don't know about, but those on the shop floor and in lower echelons might well do. This means that critical information, that can have a significant impact on decision-making, may often be hidden within the organisation in places that management doesn't even think about looking. So if a market for information is set up, which all employees are encouraged to participate in, and in which they can make trades on the basis of their specific knowledge and their direct experience, the organisation, through monitoring prices and movements in "shares," will be able to access this hidden lay knowledge.

The market works in a straightforward way. Employees are given things to bet on – will this product launch in September 2014 as planned? Where should we open a new office – China, Russia or Brazil? What will sales be next year? They are incentivised to participate either via cash prizes for correct predictions or top-trader recognition – at Google what's at stake is a coveted T-shirt.[29] Then, by aggregating the opinions of all those who bet, a market price for the different outcomes is reached. A price which essentially reflects what employees think the answer to the question is, a price that goes up or down, depending on whether those participants betting think that the estimate is accurate or not.

Take the "Will this product launch on time?" question. If the product launches on time, participants are told they will get a dollar. They need to decide at what price they would be willing to buy shares at that particular moment. A price which will reflect what they think will happen. So, if someone thinks there is only a 70 per cent chance that it will happen, they will be willing to pay seventy cents for this contract. By aggregating what all the different participants would pay, a market price will be reached which will signal the best information possible as to whether or not the company will hit its deadline.

This is a really clever way for an organisation to discover the hidden knowledge within, because those placing bets are likely to be the people who truly have privileged insights and knowledge, and can improve upon the current market forecast.[30] Workers who have dynamic, real-time information, but whose voices might otherwise not be heard. Moreover, because of both the anonymity the market accords and the personal incentive to call it right, prediction markets tacitly encourage participants to challenge group opinions, provide their honest thoughts unfiltered by what they think will be most likely to curry favour with their bosses or least likely to be contentious, and also to seek out superior information.[31] This combination leads to better prediction-making.

In a fast-changing, uncertain world, in which traditional forecasting methods are increasingly unsuitable because they rely on historical data and a self-limiting assumption of stable conditions, prediction markets provide something especially useful. They enable companies to constantly revise their forecasts and predictions by revealing unexpected changes and new developments as they happen in real time – as the facts change, so will the market price. This can be crucial for decision-making, especially in situations where new information accords the possibility of new strategic directions.

The technology to tap into lay expertise in this way is not new. It has been knocking around the business world since the 1990s. Former CEO of Hewlett Packard, Lewis Platt, remarked during his tenure, "If only HP knew what HP knows, we would be three times more productive."[32] And he put this insight into action, implementing twelve "internal prediction markets" over three years. They delivered. By using them to predict sales, for example, HP gleaned more accurate forecasts than its internal processes had been generating.[33] In fact, prediction markets outperformed official forecasts 75 per cent of the time.[34]

Other companies deploying internal prediction markets saw similar results. An internal market at Siemens in the nineties correctly predicted that the company would definitely fail to deliver on a software project, even though its traditional planning tools put it right on schedule.[35] A few years back the American electronics chain Best Buy realised that its flagship China store wouldn't open on time when, a few months before the scheduled date, shares for "on time" delivery in its internal market dropped in price from $80 to $44.[36] Google has used internal prediction markets (staff place bets with play money called "Gobbles") to predict whether projects will launch to deadline ("When will the first Android phone hit the market?"), when a new office will open ("When will Google open a Russia office?"), consumer demand for new products ("How many Gmail users will there be on 1 January 2009?"), and whether profits will be up in the coming quarter.[37] Those who do well are rewarded not only with Gobbles and those coveted T-shirts, but also with a presence on the prediction market leaderboard.

By allowing hidden knowledge within an organisation to emerge and be properly absorbed, by encouraging those who, because of their position in the hierarchy or their personality, would not otherwise have the opportunity or the confidence to reveal their proprietary information or share their views, by smashing the silos that partition off managers as thinkers and workers as doers, prediction markets encourage "a conversation among employees."[38] Former Google executive Bo Cowgill describes this as "a conversation that is happening without politics and no one has any incentive to kiss up, fudge the numbers or sandbag."[39] Participants could be betting against their team leader, a fellow worker in the company cafeteria, or even CEO Larry Page – but they'd never know it. Frank assessments of situations, without thought about how they might play with one's boss, without fear of redress, or skewed by a desire to be rewarded or by social pressure to conform, can thereby be solicited. The result can be golden information that your company might otherwise never have discovered.

Prediction markets are of course just one way to access your organisation's internal lay expertise.[40] In Step Ten we will be considering lower-tech ways of getting diverse, different and often unheard views to the table to help improve your decision-making. We've already considered the value of old-fashioned suggestion-box schemes. More frequent dialogue between management and staff can also be a very good low-tech start.

But research into prediction markets reinforces a key point that this chapter has been stressing: *those lower down in an organisation can have insights far superior to those higher up.*

Indeed, research carried out at Google into the effectiveness of its prediction markets revealed that the more senior the employee, the less accurately they were able to predict outcomes within the business.[41]

This makes sense. Management, tied up in boardrooms and meetings, will often not have the detailed on-the-ground insights that lower-level employees, whose opinions are rarely sought out, will be privy to. Another example of experience trumping status and traditional expertise. Yet somehow companies all around the world are still failing to tap into this extraordinary value, and to make dynamic use of the ideas and feelings of the people right on their doorstep.

How much expertise may be going to waste at your workplace because the dialogue between management and staff is infrequent, untrusted or even non-existent?

What Not to Ask Your Shepherd – the Limits of Lay Expertise

Traditionally, knowledge has been viewed as the preserve of accepted experts and those with high status. But by acknowledging the saleswoman, the production-line assistant, the cleaner, the mother and the fellow illness-sufferer as potential custodians of valuable information – as potential experts themselves – by recognising the value of local experience, and where possible deploying technology to maximise our efforts, we can access salient information and important insights that we would not have done otherwise. Provided, of course, that our lay experts feel able to speak their true minds, and that we give proper consideration to their views, however unexpected.

Of course, don't ask your Cumbrian shepherd for a steer on soil types in Kathmandu, or your Vietnamese mother for insights into honeymoon destinations. Lay expertise will typically be local.

If the lay experts you're seeking advice from have no direct experience of what you're asking them, their input is likely to be useless.[42] Or even actively harmful. The Finnish football club Pallokerho-35 misunderstood the nature of lay expertise when it asked fans to text in suggestions on its training programme, match-day tactics and player recruitment policy.[43] The results were pretty catastrophic – the team had a very poor season, the manager was fired, and the fan text-suggestions system was scrapped.[44] Fans may watch a lot of football, but that doesn't necessarily mean that they know how to spot raw talent or manage players.

Also bear in mind that if your fellow migraine-sufferer in a health forum reveals that she had terrible side-effects from the very medicine your doctor has just suggested you take, this doesn't mean that her experience will necessarily be applicable to you. Indeed, from her direct experience, from this single testimony, all you can know for sure is that bad side-effects are possible – it could be that the odds of them happening are very slim, and that she was the unlucky one. It could even be that her side-effects stemmed from an unrelated cause. It's not that hearing her story has no value. You may not have been made aware of potential side-effects by your doctor, or they may not have been stressed sufficiently. So, based on her story, you might want to do some research into this drug yourself, both to assess the odds of side-effects occurring (how to assess such probabilities is something I will return to in Step Eight) and also to be able to discuss with your doctor the possibility of an alternative treatment.

It is important to also note that as lay expertise is essentially anecdotal, it will not necessarily lead to generalisable claims. So, in the case of the Cumbrian farmers, before taking their words as evidence that *all* Cumbrian sheep are in danger, you would be well served by testing the soil in various places, to check that it wasn't just one particular shepherd's flock that was affected by the radioactive clouds. In the case of Matthew Robson, you might want to commission additional research to see how representative his and his pals' insights really are of teenagers at large before you take this particular group's views as gospel. In the case of the Vietnamese mothers, you might want to run a pilot programme that fed infants in this way, and evaluate their progress, to determine whether there were any other factors making these babies healthier before rolling the diet out to others. The extent to which the lay expertise you have come across is both generalisable and applicable to you is something you always need to consider.

If it's a crowd of lay experts at work whose wisdom you are hoping to tap into, whether via a suggestion scheme or a prediction market, you also want to make sure that you have provided the right incentives to encourage the non-usual suspects – the introverts, the shy, and those of lower organisational status – to participate.

These incentives can be financial. John Patterson, the owner of NCR, provided a $1 reward for the instigator of every idea that was adopted, rising to $30 for the best (this was the 1890s, remember, so in those days that was a significant prize).[45] American Airlines' caviar queen Kathy Kridel got a cheque for $50,000 for hers. But money doesn't have to be at stake. Patterson also hosted a biannual "Prize Distribution," to which employees and their families were invited for music, food and drink, and the best ideas were singled out and celebrated. Heads of departments and their assistants were not eligible for prizes. This was explicitly about valuing workers and mobilising them.[46]

In general, if you want people to volunteer their lay expertise, at work or elsewhere, it's important to make sure that their experience and insights including those insights that may challenge your own thinking – are valued. We'll come back to the import of soliciting dissenting views in Step Ten.

Takeaways

The claims of lay experts need to be challenged as effectively as the claims of any other purported expert, and it is important to acknowledge the specific limitations of this sort of intelligence. But by casting our net wider, while at the same time retaining our scepticism, by making experts a more meritocratic club that allows in people who may not have formal qualifications or fancy titles, but whose experience has much to teach us, we are likely to gain access to insights, knowledge and inspiration that we'd otherwise never even have contemplated. In this way we can significantly enhance our ability to make informed, smarter decisions.

I'm not advocating that you junk traditional experts in a knee-jerk way, and simply replace them with the voices of those on the ground. It's not that straightforward. Not only are there limits to lay expertise, but there are of course skills and technical knowledge that traditional experts have that no lay expert ever will. So I'm not advocating that you seek out a shop assistant to remove your appendix rather than a surgeon, or that you ask a shepherd to teach you physics. Let me be clear on that.

Nor is it necessarily a case of making a choice between a lay expert *or* a traditional expert. Often you'll be well served by thinking about how to maximise the contributions and insights of both. Often, it's the interaction of the two that proves most potent – pharmaceutical companies were able to transform the experience of lay expert village herbalists into billion-dollar businesses by getting their scientists to study the indigenous medicines the villagers used, and then translate them into mass-producable chemical compounds.

But assuming your eyes are wide open and your brain is kept switched on, and that you apply as questioning a mind to what you learn from the bottom as to what you're told from the top, the point of this chapter is this: the experience and testimonies of lay experts can be invaluable when it comes to information-gathering or decision-making. The shop floor is well worth walking, and the coalface mining, even if you're senior management. Technology can massively scale up our ability to tap into not just "a hundred heads" simultaneously, but thousands of brains all at once, brains that may be many miles away yet have valuable insights to share.

Also be aware that if there's a problem you are grappling with, there are almost certain to be others out there who've dealt with a similar situation, and whose experience can prove more helpful to you than the recommendations of professional problem-solvers. People who, although limited by their own direct experience, may well be less interested in touting a particular line than traditional experts, who as we have seen can at times be too attached to their own recommendation, people who may have carried out more research on their situation than the traditional expert you'd expect to consult.

It's not just those with deep first-hand experience whose insights can be invaluable, though. So too can people with much less deep and significantly shorter-lived experiences. Welcome to the world of citizen journalists ...

QUICK TIPS FOR LEARNING FROM SHEPHERDS AND SHOP ASSISTANTS

- **Actively seek out stories and testimonies from people with direct experience of the issue you're trying to address** – remember, experience can trump expertise and status.

- **Think about schemes you can champion at work to tap into the wisdom within.** Can you set up a prediction market? Or improve your current suggestion-box scheme (or if you don't have one in place, set one up from scratch)? Can you commit to walking the shop floor more regularly?

- **Is there a regular time-slot you can establish for managers to receive and respond by email to ideas, suggestions and concerns from people throughout your organisation?** How about holding physical or virtual "office hours" in which anyone from any part of the organisation can get in touch?

- **Think too about what you can do to clearly signal that you are keen to listen to and learn from not only those you directly manage, but also from the wider organisation.**

- **With challenges in your personal life, work hard to gain insights from a wider range of people.** Identify online forums in which people who are confronting the same challenge or problem as you are sharing their experiences. What can you learn from these insights? Think about what you could post on Facebook or Twitter that will prompt relevant lay expertise from your own social network.

- **Push yourself to tap into the lay experts in your immediate environment who you are not sufficiently valuing.** What suggestions might your cleaner have about potential home improvements? What might your nephew be able to teach you about technology? Ask them directly to share their experience and ideas with you.

- **Of course, use lay expertise correctly.** Don't ask shepherds for leisure-industry stock picks, or fellow migraine-sufferers for hotel recommendations. Acknowledge too that someone else's experience may not be directly applicable to you. And that explanations provided for why something has happened may not always be well-reasoned.

- **As ever, keep your brain switched on, and apply your own judgement to the insights your lay expert is providing.** Ask yourself how their version of events differs from that of a traditional expert or source. If they do differ, it doesn't necessarily mean that they're wrong, but you should at least know how they compare, so you can work out what may need further research or interrogation.

GO DIGITAL ...
WITH CAUTION

Co-Create and Listen In

Geiger-Counting in Tokyo

Another nuclear explosion. Not in the USSR this time, but nearly 5,000 miles east.

It's Friday, 11 March 2011.

Workers all over Japan have left their homes as usual and are heading to work. For thousands of men living in the Fukushima prefecture, this means the local nuclear power plant. They turn up and knuckle down to a typical shift – another day of administering repairs, cleaning equipment and performing checks. Or so they think.

At 2.46 p.m. an 8.9 magnitude earthquake strikes 130 kilometres off the north-east coast of Japan, about twenty-four kilometres below the earth's surface.[1] There is a darkening on the horizon.[2] Then the tsunami hits. Within the hour, the Fukushima power plant is slammed by seven tsunami waves, some reaching as high as fifteen metres.[3]

Horror follows horror. In a short time, the usually clear skies of Japanese springtime are clouded by the billowing smoke and steam of a nuclear meltdown. Who is at risk? How bad is the safety breach? Which local areas will soon have unacceptably high levels of radiation?

These questions were quickly being asked by local residents and the media, and many would have expected that the government would be the best source of this kind of emergency information. Surely in these circumstances the Japanese authorities would operate differently from those of the former Soviet Union, whose government notoriously issued no images or information when news of the Chernobyl explosion first broke.

Unfortunately, if as a local resident you had attempted to rely on government sources, you would have been in serious trouble. On this occasion, unlike in our Cumbrian shepherds story, this was not because the scientists had taken centre stage. The problem lay with the Japanese government itself. For while it had access to excellent scientific data detailing the spread of radiation – their System for Prediction of Environmental Emergency Dose Information (SPEEDI) provided them with real-time information on this within hours of the accident – they did not share this with the population. Nor did they share the information the US authorities had provided them with on the direction of airborne particles.

Even worse than this, the Japanese government provided erroneous information to its people. Yukio Edano, the minister fronting the government response, told reporters on 16 March, five days after the disaster, that there was "no immediate health risk." It later emerged that the government had been all too aware of the dangers by then.

Thankfully for Japan's population, not everyone meekly accepted the official line. Instead, a group of sceptical local people stepped in to determine the truth for themselves. Armed with personal Geiger counters picked up for around 60,000 yen, or £500, from local electronics stores, they started recording radiation levels.[4] In fact, by May 2011, just two months after the disaster, Fuji Electric, one of Japan's Geiger-counter manufacturers, was producing four to five times the normal quantity of the devices to meet the growing demand of concerned ordinary citizens who felt that they needed to gather accurate information themselves if the government was not going to provide it for them.[5]

Soon people set up webcams to film their Geiger counters as they took twenty-four-hour, non-stop readings of radiation levels, and streamed the readings online in real time. Concerned citizens could therefore log on and check out radiation levels in multiple locations at any hour of the day. This was minute-by-minute information direct from source – something the Japanese public could not get from any official outlet.

Then things got even more professional. The thousands of individual pieces of data on radiation levels from these local fact-finders were collated by online communities like Safecast and Pachube, which was set up by British artist-cum-architect-cum-techie Usman Haque in 2008.[6] This information was then combined with the very limited official data available to produce as accurate a picture as possible of what was really going on in Japan. Some contributors to the community even started measuring water radiation.[7] One enterprising individual, Seigo Ishino, took things a step further, connecting all Pachube's dots to create a bilingual Android app called "Wind from Fukushima." This organised all the crowd-sourced knowledge onto a map, complete with information on which way the radiation was heading and details of evacuation points.[8]

These information-gatherers were in no sense traditional experts. They weren't employed by Japan's Nuclear and Industrial Safety Agency. They didn't have access to the Japanese government's SPEEDI system. They didn't have training. They may not have even understood without help what the readings on their portable Geiger counters actually meant. Nor were they lay experts – people with deep experience of an issue: shepherds, mothers, shop-floor workers – the kind of people we explicitly valued in the previous chapter.

Instead, we can think of them as more akin to citizen journalists. A new generation of investigators-cum-reporters-cum-broadcasters – not trained in a formal way in any of these roles, nor with any particularly deep or long experience of the situation at hand, but each with a personal story to tell and a motivation to share it. Citizen journalists who came together and combined their individual stories and observations via their computers or mobile phones, and were thus able not only to expose the Japanese government's misinformation, but to actively fill the gaps where the government failed to provide data by co-creating a body of knowledge that was far more credible than that emanating from official sources. Citizen journalists whose ability to collaborate and produce powerful results had been utterly transformed by the joined-up, real-time possibilities of our digital age.

From the Iranian Elections to School Meals in Scotland

We are in the midst of an information revolution. A time when the old notion of knowledge as something handed down to us from on high, with you and me as passive and unquestioning supplicants, is being radically challenged by the democratisation of the information-gathering and broadcasting process. A time when the authoritative voices of the past are being challenged by the direct testimonies of eyewitnesses on the ground – thanks to a whole host of technological advancements that enable information to be "crowdsourced" with great ease and at negligible cost.

Of course, citizen journalism is not only about co-created crowd-generated testimonies. The anonymous bystander who emailed the video of the death of Neda Aghan Soltan at the hands of Iranian security forces to the *Guardian* and Voice of America single-handedly exposed the depth of repression taking place during the Iranian elections of 2009. He or she was also a lay journalist.[9] As were those Chinese factory employees who uploaded pictures and videos of confrontations between workers and security forces at the Foxconn Technology Plant (makers of the iPhone) to YouKu and Sina Weibo, the Chinese versions of YouTube and Twitter.[10] As was Martha Payne, the nine-year-old schoolgirl from Lochgilphead in Scotland who uploaded photos of her £2 school lunches to her blog, NeverSeconds, exposing the nutritionally inadequate meals and meagre portions offered by her local education authority to a worldwide audience.[11]

This is a time when, thanks to social media and mobile telephony, people across the world can broadcast their own scoops singly – and make a splash. A time when those who report on situations no longer need to have press credentials and affiliations to be heard. With over six billion mobile-phone subscriptions worldwide, five billion of them in developing countries,[12] phones which increasingly have video cameras and 3G connections as standard features, there is almost nowhere on earth that one can't communicate from, almost nowhere on earth that cannot be snapped or filmed and then transmitted instantaneously. A time when the distinctions between "producers," "consumers" and "audience" are being blurred.[13]

For us as decision-makers, navigating this new landscape poses significant new challenges. All these citizen journalists' testimonies amount to a massively higher volume of information than we've ever had to manage before. In the absence of traditional gatekeepers and trusted fact-checkers, we need to take on the role not only of information collator but also of information-quality-checker ourselves, because what we are getting is raw, and unverified. The real-time nature of much of today's citizen journalism means we can be confronted with supposed scoops that demand immediate responses before we've had a chance to check whether they are authentic or credible. These are challenges that we will come back to in the next Step.

Yet the information revolution also offers us a huge opportunity. For we now have the ability to make decisions on the basis of unfiltered, unspun, unedited, real-time information, straight from the ground, direct from source to us. Imagine you are in the midst of the Colorado Springs forest fires in late June 2012, for example. Want to know where the fire's moving, and whether you need to pack up and evacuate? You could try the local government website, but that may not give you the most up-to-date, on-the-ground information. Instead, your best bet would be to head to Esri, a website that was mashing up trusted government data with real-time, first-hand accounts to create constantly updating, accurate mapping of the fires and their path. Or to Google Maps, which thanks to people posting their direct testimonies in the form of pictures and live webcam streams was able to provide real-time information on how well contained the fires were, and pictures from the last hour.[14]

Across the Pacific, consider if you were the Thai Prime Minister trying to work out where to deploy resources during the widespread flooding of late 2011. In this case you would have been well served by looking at the Thailand Flood Crisis Information Map. Powered by Ushahidi, the tech company that pioneered the software for mapping crowd-sourced data, this took over a thousand reports from lay journalists when the floods headed inland, and logged and mapped them, providing real-time, up-to-date advice. It collated reports of roadblocks, offers of accommodation and alerts of where people had requested help from volunteers or asked for items like torches, pumps and sandbags. All this before official sources had a handle on it.[15]

The opportunity to make decisions on the basis of unfiltered, unspun, unedited, real-time information, straight from the ground, direct from source to us, can be invaluable not only in emergencies, but in *all* situations where either official information is suspect or partial, or traditional journalists are untrustworthy, biased or hard to find.

Imagine you're thinking of setting up a factory in Maharashtra, India. How do you determine the true lay of the land? In the past you would have had to rely on a combination of official government information, the opinions of potential overseas partners, and perhaps, if you could afford them, "intelligence reports" from a company such as Kroll. Today, you may well get better-quality information were you to visit www.ipaid abribe.com, where Indian citizens register when they've paid a bribe, how much it was, and to whom. The site aggregates these testimonies to find out where local governments are most corrupt. Your ability to choose the right place to invest in a new factory may be radically transformed by this information.

By tapping in to citizen journalists' testimonies, testimonies which, ostensibly at least, are independent and driven by the highest motives – a desire to help others, and to tell the truth – we all now have the potential to gather information that is unblemished by spin, bias and agendas, in super-fast time.

Note, though, that co-created information is not just something we have to hope others are generating. If something matters to us, we can take the lead in co-creating it ourselves.

This is something police forces in some countries are increasingly doing. Seven hundred and seventy people were arrested in Britain, for example, after the police uploaded photos to a Flickr gallery of individuals thought to be involved in looting during the August 2011 riots, and asked for the public's help in identifying them.[16] If you run a business you might want to consider asking the help of your customers to provide you with on-the-ground intelligence on your competitors, for instance, or on local trends and fads.

It's a process we can easily set in motion ourselves too, via our social networks, with the potential to have an extraordinary impact on our personal lives.

Facebook Flu at the Playboy Mansion

Nico Zeifang knows this all too well. Two days after partying at the Playboy Mansion in Los Angeles at the closing event of the DomainFest Global Conference 2011, this twenty-eight-year-old internet entrepreneur from Germany woke up feeling rough. He had chills, a fever and chest pain.

Now, in the pre-co-created information era, what would have happened next? Most likely, Nico would have curled up in bed with an aspirin, and possibly called a doctor, an expert, for advice.

But being a techie, and having discovered that he was not the only one to have been taken ill – four of his colleagues had similar symptoms – instead he deployed Facebook to find out how many more of his fellow partygoers had been struck down.

"Domainerflu count, who else caught the disease at D.F.G.?" he posted.

The response was rapid. The initial five sufferers quickly grew to twenty-four. By the end of the week there were ninety-three attendees from all over the world who had been stricken with the mysterious "domainerflu." And this wasn't idle chit-chat. A "friend request" here and there led to conversations about the symptoms and the sharing of thoughts on what the cause of the illness might be.

By pooling their insights, Zeifang's fellow citizen journalist flu-sufferers were able to collate enough information to identify common threads and themes, and thereby to self-diagnose their condition as an airborne water-based flu. This was later confirmed to be Legionnaires disease.

Zeifang and his online network were able to make this diagnosis far faster than would have been possible had they relied on traditional experts. As fellow patients in a digital world, they were able to connect the dots with speed and skill. By the time the US government Centers for Disease Control and Prevention had even confirmed that there was an outbreak, they'd already created their own Wikipedia page.

To have worked out what was wrong with the Playboy Mansion partygoers in the traditional way, doctors and nurses or public health officials would have seen the victims one at a time. Each would have been tested individually. The data would then have been collated. The process would probably have taken months, not the week or so it took Zeifang and his fellow sufferers to make the correct diagnosis.

The era of citizen journalism allows us to co-create and crowd-source information ourselves at speed. By issuing calls on Facebook, Twitter, LinkedIn or Google Plus, and aggregating and mapping individual testimonies, we can not only detect particular events quickly, but also identify patterns and trends much faster than ever before. We can then go on to make decisions with a speed and effectiveness that simply was not possible in the pre-digital age.

Listen In and Stay Ahead

In the stories above, people contributing their testimonies knew that these would be used by others to advance knowledge. Today, however, we can "listen in" surreptitiously on those with potentially useful information for us, whether lay experts or citizen journalists, via their outpourings on blogs, social media or online forums. We can collate their testimonies, fears, passions, condemnations and applause, and draw out relevant threads, themes and shapes, without them even being aware that this is what we are doing.

For some time now, companies and government authorities have been able to track people's behaviour via their credit card expenditure, their club card shopping patterns, the websites they click on. Many of the world's biggest companies have now placed this customer data at the heart of their strategy and decision-making. Walmart – a company that every single hour captures 167 times the amount of information contained in all the books in the American Library of Congress, the biggest library in the world – has been able to improve its inventory management systems through intense analysis of past sales data. It was able to discover, for example, that just before a hurricane strikes, its stores don't just see a run on batteries and torches, but also on ... Pop Tarts.[17] By analysing huge tracts of historical customer purchasing information, Target, the major US store chain, can now identify that a customer is pregnant as early as her second trimester, and target her with specific offers – an innovation that has on occasion proved problematic. One customer in Minneapolis complained to a store manager when his teenage daughter, still in high school, began receiving mail-outs advertising cots and baby clothes. Was the store encouraging her to get pregnant? Target apologised, only to be met with a sheepish response. It turned out that following a talk with his daughter, the customer found out that he was indeed going to be a grandfather.[18]

The analysis of our data trail – what we spend, where we go, what we do – is increasingly valuable to those who can access it. But our ability to listen in on people's conversations, hear their concerns, passions, desires, beliefs, what they think and say rather than what they do, may well prove even more revolutionary. For accessing data on what people spend, how they shop, what they click on remains a possibility only for those with whom these people intersect directly – their credit card retailer, their search engine, the store whose card they use – unless such bodies sell data to third parties.

Listening-in data, on the other hand, in a world in which thoughts, cares and concerns are published primarily in publicly accessible online forums, is information we can *all* potentially access and make use of, provided we have the ability to properly process it.

It is revolutionary for another reason too.

In the past, if we wanted to know what people thought, believed or wanted, we had to ask them – in the knowledge that by so doing their responses were likely to be affected by how they wanted to appear to us, whether they would make them appear to be a "good," "honest" or "smart" person. Now, by listening in, we can monitor people's thoughts *directly*, without the intervention of survey-takers, pollsters, focus-group leaders or social peer pressure.

Where the volume of testimonies is relatively low, we can manually process what we listen in on with relative ease. By following what women were sharing online with each other about banks and building societies on the UK's leading forum for mothers, mumsnet.com, I uncovered evidence in 2011 of British banks and mortgage lenders discriminating against pregnant women and new mothers.[19] This discovery prompted an extensive government enquiry into gender discrimination by financial institutions, which in turn led to the admission by UK lenders that there was indeed a serious problem, and the subsequent implementation of major reforms. A simple act of digital listening-in will now lead to a fairer deal for women who, as individuals, did not realise that their experience was part of a wider problem.

In some cases there is, however, too much information to manage manually. When there are thousands, or hundreds of thousands, of tweets and posts and comments to navigate – in the four and a half hours of 2012 US presidential election debating twenty-four million tweets were sent on the #debates hashtag; at the start of the Arab Spring there were 2,200 tweets generated every second, adding up to 190 million tweets each day[20] – you'll need to automate your listening-in process.

The technology you need to do this is still in its early stages. So to learn about both how one could automate listening-in to this new world of digital information, and also how this might inform our decision-making, I put together a team of leading social scientists and computer scientists to run a real-time experiment. We looked for a subject that would provide mass data on a weekly basis which would allow us to learn and refine our methodology. In the end, the subject was right there for us on prime-time television – could we predict winners and losers on the UK's talent contest *The X Factor* by listening in on the hundreds of thousands of tweets and Facebook and YouTube posts that were issued by viewers around the show's "voting window"? We developed a computer program to do this, and a proprietary algorithm. And we did better than good: our predictions played out ten out of twelve times – indeed, had we bet on them, we'd have more than doubled our money.[21]

Other studies have also shown that digital listening-in can deliver an entirely new dimension of predictive power. A recent piece of work suggests that if we track the mood of the public on Twitter we may have an advantage when it comes to predicting stock-market movements – early research in this area points to a potential correlation between how calm the Twittersphere is and stock-market rises.[22] There is also research that points to success in using Twitter data for making movie box-office predictions.[23] The United Nations' Global Pulse Project's two-year study of half a million blogs, forums and news sites revealed that conversations online foreshadowed the unemployment rate and yielded advance data up to three months ahead of the official stats.

No wonder a number of police forces are trying to harness Twitter's crystal-ball potential by automating the collection and analysis of social media so as to determine the "temperature" of local communities and take preventative action where trouble might be brewing.[24] In the US, several other government departments are investing in technology that allows them to monitor online activity. The Department of Homeland Security has already been at it for a few years, creeping through social networks and analysing traffic. Reports have suggested that the CIA is doing it too, having invested in a program, "Visible Technologies," which monitors blogs and forums as well as social networks. On 19 January 2012 the FBI laid down the gauntlet for contractors, asking them to create an app with a "search and scrape capability" across social media so they can better predict what "bad actors" will do next.[25]

Automated listening-in systems are of course not something I'm expecting you to program yourself from your living room. But given that these technologies are likely to be used more and more in the workplace, if you want to be at the forefront of smart decision-making, it's important to have a sense of how they work and how they might add value to your business.

Golden Sources Amid the Digital Noise

It is not just patterns that listening-in allows you to discover. Amidst all the noise there may be signals that can yield critical information on their own.

In the aftermath of the April 2010 Deepwater Horizon BP oil-rig explosion, for example, Justin Grindal, a sub-contractor from Houston who was based on one of the rescue vessels, took to his Twitter account to air plenty of dirty laundry.[26] On the same day that BP Chief Executive Tony Hayward remarked that "The operation is proceeding as we planned it,"[27] Grindal tweeted, "Flowrate is the major variable right now. This is what is giving engr's headaches."[28]

Looking back, it seems that Grindal was more on the money than the soon-to-be-resigning Tony Hayward – just over a month after the spill, on 26 May, he tweeted, "This is a true worst-case, and the industry will be paying for it for years." The challenge we all face is how to make sure we hear individual voices like Grindal's when we really need to.

One answer might be provided by a new British company, Curation, which has created a content-management system to track all tweets that mention particular oil and gas companies, and single out those which refer to crises. In doing so, they hope to gain valuable information in these critical moments both unfiltered by corporate spin and significantly faster than via traditional channels.

For the speed at which information is uploaded on social media in general can be quite remarkable – Osama bin Laden's death was reported on Twitter before any major news network was running the story. The death of Whitney Houston was reported just twenty minutes after paramedics stopped trying to revive her, and hours before news outlets ran the story, when the singer's hairdresser's niece tweeted: "My Aunt Tiffany, who works for Whitney Houston, just found Whitney Houston dead in the tub."[29] During the 5.8 magnitude Virginia earthquake in August 2011, people in New York and Toronto reported receiving tweets from friends on their newsfeed that an earthquake had hit them seconds before they felt the tremors themselves.[30]

This is an era in which people tweet even faster than seismic waves move through rock,[31] which means that by listening in to people via social media we can potentially discover truths long before an analyst has crunched them, a broadcaster has transmitted them, or the market has factored them in.

This can be extremely valuable. Imagine you are a CEO: how useful would it be to have an early-warning system via social media of a looming PR crisis before it blew up, so that you could plan your response strategy in advance? For those who invest in the markets, there's another obvious benefit – timely information. Just think of the trading advantage you'd enjoy if you were able to glean critical insights before the market had absorbed them.[32]

The danger, of course, is that not only truths, but lies and slander can also spread within seconds. On 14 December 2012 "Ryan Lanza" was a trending topic on Twitter, where he was named as the killer at Sandy Hook Elementary School in Newtown, Connecticut. Several news organisations even published images from a Facebook profile of a man with that name.[33] It was later discovered that his brother Adam had in fact been the murderer, and that Ryan had been at work at Ernst & Young in Times Square when the massacre took place. In the immediate aftermath of a crisis, confusion, Chinese whispers and misinformation are commonplace. So before you react to information, take a pause and evaluate its credibility – I'll return to how to do this in the next Step.

Google Trends and the Value of Your Home

Listening in to social media outpourings and pooling citizen journalists' testimonies are just two of the ways we can gain an information advantage in our digital age.

Google provides us with another way of making a difference to our private lives and our future prosperity in the form of Google Trends, which collates data on how often people type in particular keywords on their search engine. For our yearnings, hopes, fears and desires are not only expressed by what we say, but by what it is we search for.

And again, when pitted against traditional information-gathering services, Google Trends seems to deliver.

Forecasting models which attempt to predict current economic data (such as unemployment figures or consumer confidence) *before* the government publishes such statistics have been shown to be 5–20 per cent more accurate if they include information from Google Trends keyword searches.[34]

By using Google Trends data on searches for "flu" and related words, regional outbreaks of flu in the United States have been predicted seven to ten days before the Centers for Disease Control and Prevention – which receive approximately $1.3 billion from Congress precisely so that they can make such calls in a timely fashion – did so.[35]

It's not just governments or investors or businesses that can benefit from such trend-spotting powers.

We all can.

A recent study carried out by the Bank of England revealed that if you're thinking of investing in property, say, and want to gauge the true state of the real-estate market, you'd be better off looking at Google Trends than relying on official statistics.[36] The researchers found that by monitoring search trends for "estate agent" on Google, and looking to see if the volume of searches for this term was rising or falling, they were able to predict the direction of the housing market with more accuracy than if they had used data from traditional expert sources – the Home Builders Federation or the Royal Institution of Chartered Surveyors. A similar study in the US suggested that a spike in the search term "foreclosure" indicated troubles in the housing market before official sources realised there was a growing problem.[37]

It makes sense that what we search for can foreshadow what then happens.[38] But what makes Google Trends particularly useful is just how quickly it identifies how people's concerns or interests are evolving. With most official data subject to a significant time-lag – in the UK, for example, house-price indicators are only released monthly by the Land Registry – the real-time insights we can get from looking at how search volumes today differ from the past provide us with much more timely and relevant information. And these real-time insights can be damn specific: one study the Bank of England drew on in its report showed that for every percentage point increase in Google searches for the term "estate agent" in the US, there was an additional sale of 67,700 houses the following quarter.[39]

No wonder Prime Minister David Cameron (I'm told by the person who set this up for him) now monitors unemployment figures on his iPad via Google Trends rather than waiting for official data to come out from the Office for National Statistics. British unemployment figures are issued only once a month; Google Trends offers up what's happening right now, in a form that's easy for all of us to access.[40]

But! A Tiger-Shaped Warning ...

Co-created and crowd-sourced information have opened up a world of possibilities to us as decision-makers. Listening in to social media is proving to be a new frontier for businesses seeking a competitive edge, and we've also seen the way in which simply clicking on to Google Trends may help us navigate the property market to our advantage.

But this doesn't mean that there are no associated challenges or ways in which we can make a mess of this digital dividend.

We can't just assume, for example, that every single person within the crowd will be a reliable witness. Remember the hoax tweets about the tiger being released from London Zoo during the August 2011 riots? Supposed eyewitness pictures posted to social media networks during 2012's Hurricane

Sandy in the United States included a Photoshopped *The Day After Tomorrow* movie poster, and "rainy" pictures, purporting to be real-time photographs, that were taken well before the storm.[41] Even in times of crisis, not everyone can be counted upon to be driven by altruistic motives.[42] How to assess the credibility of online data is something I will return to in the next Step.

When it comes to listening in to people's conversations on social media, there are a number of particular issues to bear in mind.

First, there are ethical considerations. Listening in may at times not be the good and fair thing to do. Indeed, there are serious issues relating to privacy, intrusion and consent.[43] So if you're considering using such techniques in your information-gathering, consider the situation on a case-by-case basis, and think about how appropriate and justified unsolicited listening-in actually is.

Then there are questions as to what exactly you can read into what you are hearing. Questions of representativeness.

For who exactly are the Twitterati? Or those who post on Facebook? Or in forums?

People who tweet tend to be aged between eighteen and twenty-nine,[44] although the persistence of One Direction and Justin Bieber among trending topics (along with the fact that most studies of user demographics fail to consider the under-eighteen age group) makes me wonder if they are not in fact somewhat younger. The majority are under fifty. Eighty-three per cent have at least some college education.[45] 72.6 per cent of people using Twitter are from outside the United States.[46] On Facebook, 81 per cent of users are from outside North America,[47] and they are typically slightly younger than users of Twitter.[48] By contrast, users of eHealth, a healthcare forum with ten million visits a month, are typically aged eighteen to forty-five, and 60 per cent are female.[49]

What this means is that if you're listening in via social media, you're probably only hearing a very particular group, representative at best only of those with similar demographic characteristics. Until you know and understand those demographics, it's important not to assume too much from the data.

You also want to be careful about what you extrapolate from monitoring tweets using real-time searches on your desktop or phone. As there are over 340 million tweets circulating each day,[50] the chances that you will be able to read all the tweets on a "hot" topic in real time are pretty small. Think back to the 2012 US presidential debates, when over 80,000 tweets were issued using the #debates hashtag each minute. Given that you might have been physically able to read perhaps twenty a minute, at a stretch, any back-of-the-envelope assessment was bound to be highly inconclusive. In such cases it's a bit like dipping a cup in the ocean a thousand times and only retrieving water, never fish. You can't conclude from that that there are definitely no fish in the ocean.

So if you're searching for negative news on your company during a time of high-profile crisis, or trying to get a read on the sentiment of a trending topic, beware – just because you didn't come across anything bad, it doesn't mean it's not out there in the Twittersphere. You can't just do a word search for your company and think that's the end of it. You could of course deploy a social-media analysis company to track your brand – such companies automate the listening-in process, and so can process many more tweets than we can ourselves. But be warned that the accuracy and reliability of such service providers varies massively.

Also important to bear in mind is that we're still figuring out the relationship between what people say online and the actions they subsequently take. If someone "likes" Hershey on Facebook, presumably that means that they have tried the company's chocolate. But how many Hershey bars does this mean they will buy, and how often? If someone tweets favourably when the boy band comes on during *The X Factor*, does that mean that they will definitely vote for them? Possibly. But only once? Or multiple times? Data scientists and social scientists are currently working on answering such questions. But for now, when you are interpreting social media – whether you are buying a house or working on a business plan – it's important to be aware of what this digital stream can't yet definitively tell us, as well as embracing all the new and useful information it can provide.

Do Computers Know What Love Means?

There's another problem with making sense of social media that relates specifically to attempts to automate the process. For although we're moving towards a future in which computers are likely to be able to make sense of large numbers of posts and tweets, we're not there yet.

This is in large part because, despite the considerable progress being made on computational semantics, even if programs are built which can read vast amounts of online data, computers are still pretty poor at determining what it is that people actually mean, or feel. They hoover up text, but that text is decontextualised, stripped bare of human meaning, motive and intention.

Take how the very particular vernacular people use on social media and in forums can create misunderstandings. If someone posts that "Little Italy's on fire right now," for example, should you call the fire brigade, or assume it's a really fun place and that you should head on over? The answer may be very straightforward to you, but less so to the current generation of computers.

More generally, listening-in is hampered by the difficulty computers have in discerning humour, irony or sarcasm – although computer scientists are working hard to overcome this challenge, and the technology underpinning the iPhone's inbuilt personal helper Siri suggests that they are moving in the right direction.

This doesn't mean that current computer programs and algorithms are useless. Far from it. We could never deal on our own with the volume of social media data, or identify patterns and trends and spikes within it, as they so easily can. But it is likely that there will remain a significant role for humans to play in analysing what these spikes and trends actually mean, in assessing how representative those we are listening in on really are, and in putting what it is we hear into context.

Contextualisation is the golden rule to apply whenever you're provided with new information, but especially in cases where those providing the information are not known to you, and whose trustworthiness you cannot yet determine. We will come back to this in the next Step.

As for Google Trends, while the opportunities it presents when it comes to pattern-spotting and predictions are signifi-cant, remember that although it does a great job at identifying big meta-trends, it doesn't tell you *why* people are searching. So if you see a spike in searches for a new film, for example, before you book your cinema tickets, be aware that you don't know if people are searching for it because they want to see it, or because it's had really bad reviews. To determine that defini-tively you'd need to do a bit more digging.[51]

Google Trends can also steer you off course for a much more prosaic reason. Look at what happened at No. 10 Downing Street on 6 October 2011. That morning the Prime Minister's inner circle was shocked to discover that there'd been a huge spike in searches for "jobs" overnight. It was only later that day that they realised this was actually down to the death the previous afternoon of Apple co-founder Steve Jobs.

If we're to maximise the opportunities such a tool now affords us as decision-makers, we will need, as ever, to keep our brains firmly switched on, and to properly interrogate any new information it delivers.

Takeaways

The democratisation of both the production and the dissemination of information that we are currently witnessing, and the technological advancements that allow us to process many views and testimonies at once, provide us with significant opportunities to ramp up the quality of the information we base our decisions on. For today we are able to access information that in the past we might never have come across, with an ease and at a low level of cost that are unprecedented.

Much of this information is also discernibly different from what we could access before. Today we can hear what it is people *really* think, and get insights into what matters to them, without their views being tempered by how they come across to the questioner (a common problem of traditional surveys and polls), or because of how a question is phrased. When we listen in online we therefore have the potential to discover something quite unique – not that it will always be palatable, nor that people's views will always be independent.

This is truly revolutionary.

But without in any way diminishing the exciting opportunities this dis-intermediated information landscape provides us with as decision-makers, there are a few questions we must be sure to ask before acting on any of this new pool of raw intelligence. How representative is it? How well have we analysed it? How much can we rely on our computerised screening tools? So, do ask your market-research team how they are tackling these issues when they present you with their Twitter analysis. And don't bet your house on the privileged information you just came across on Twitter – it may not tell the story it initially seems to tell.

More generally, we need to ask who exactly are those sharing their experiences with us on Twitter or Facebook, via an online crowd or indeed on the internet as a whole. Are they even who they claim to be? Can they be trusted? Can we believe what they say?

The credibility of online sources is a major issue, with serious ramifications for how we interpret and act on the information they offer up. One that is increasingly ours to address. For of course, making smart decisions isn't only about being smart about who to turn to for advice, or where to get your information from. It's also about screening the information before you, and assessing whether or not to believe it.

Getting smarter about how to do this is what the next Step is about.

QUICK TIPS FOR CO-CREATING AND LISTENING-IN

- **Seek out crowd-sourced and co-created information websites on topics of interest to you.** From information on traffic jams and speed cameras, to the real-time status of floods or fires, to on-the-ground cultural insights, to people's sharing of illness symptoms, there might well be a crowd-sourced form of information out there that trumps the data provided by traditional sources.

- **If co-created information doesn't already exist on the issue that matters to you, take the lead and issue a call for it yourself.** You don't need to do this in a high-tech way – you can use your Facebook or Google Plus network or Twitter feed to ask for specific testimonies. Remember how Nico Zeifang discovered he had Legionnaires disease by calling for and piecing together fellow "flu" sufferers' testimonies.

- **Be aware that not all on-the-ground testimonies will be credible.** How to screen your sources will be covered in the next Step.

- **At work, start thinking about how you might use listening-in techniques** to get new insights into your customers, obtain advance warning of looming crises, get intelligence on your competitors before it hits the news wires, or improve upon your current forecasting or prediction models. Think about whether you should buy an off-the-shelf "social media surveillance" product, or commission something bespoke instead. But make sure you understand the limitations of current surveillance technology, as well as the current biases of social-media data.

- **Be careful about what you extrapolate from tweets you're following on your mobile device.** If the topic is trending or hot, you'll probably only manage to read a very small proportion of what's out there. It's unlikely to be representative of the whole, or to give you the full picture.

- **At home or at work, use Google Trends to get a heads-up on looming trends, shifting fashions or even pandemics before official data comes out.** If you're worried about the Novovirus, say, and don't trust the official information, look at whether searches for flu symptoms have been going up in your area. If you're thinking of buying an investment property, track search terms like "estate agents" or "foreclosures" to get a more up-to-date sense of the housing market than you can from official figures. But be careful: digital searches can give misleading results at times – remember how searches for "jobs" spiked after the death of Steve Jobs.

Scrutinise Sock Puppets and Screen Your Sources

A Gay Girl in Damascus

In early 2011, if you'd wanted to get the "truth" about what was unfolding in Syria, you probably would have listened to what Amina Abdallah Arraf al Omari had to say. This Syrian-American lesbian, living in Damascus, shared her on-the-ground insights in compelling detail on her blog "A Gay Girl in Damascus," and soon became a go-to source for journalists worldwide.[1] She gave interviews, corresponded with a member of the Associated Press, and was the subject of a profile in the *Guardian*, in which she was described as the "unlikely hero of a revolt in a conservative country."[2]

So when on 6 June 2011 Amina's cousin Rania Ismail took to the blog to report that Amina had been kidnapped by members of President Assad's Ba'ath party, ripples spread quickly through Twitter and the blogosphere. Activists launched a campaign to try to get her released. The BBC reported the news,[3] as did the *Guardian*, which uploaded a story at 1 a.m. on Tuesday, 7 June about her disappearance. The story featured the image of Amina she had supplied for their profile the previous month.

At 4 p.m. that same day, the *Guardian* received a phone call from a very distressed-sounding woman, a Croatian administrator from the Royal College of Physicians in London, who claimed that the photograph was actually of her. The *Guardian* ignored the call, thinking it was an attempt to undermine Amina by some kind of pro-Assad agency. The woman, Jelena Lecic, notified the Press Complaints Commission, and the photo was taken down by 6:45 p.m. The *Guardian* uploaded another image to the website, one that Amina had supplied some weeks earlier, and printed it in the next day's paper. But Jelena Lecic was distraught to find that that too was an image of her. After a wrangle with the paper, all images of Amina were removed from its website by 6 p.m.

Everyone was confused. Had Amina stolen Jelena's photographs in order to protect herself, to hide her identity? Or was there something more complicated or mysterious taking place?

Soon, it emerged that no human being had actually communicated with Amina in person. The US Embassy later reported that it had no record of anybody with dual citizenship who matched her details.

Who, or what, was Amina Abdallah Arraf al Omari?

The truth emerged on 12 June, when it was revealed that Amina was neither Syrian nor a lesbian, nor even a woman, but a bearded, forty-year-old American PhD student in Edinburgh named Tom MacMaster. MacMaster had taken photos of Jelena Lecic from her Facebook account, and had built up and sustained his fabrication for over *five years*, creating a persona complete with friends, readers and even a girlfriend.

Major media organisations around the world, along with many individual web browsers, had been tricked with apparent ease.

As we shift from receiving our information from traditional sources to finding it ourselves in the virtual infosphere, from being supplicants to whom wisdom is handed down from on high, to individuals gathering testimonies ourselves,[4] as we shift from a world in which information is in limited supply to a digital world of plenty,[5] where citizen journalists and lay experts jostle against their traditional peers and where anyone and everyone can self-publish, the problem of verifying sources becomes one that we all need to think hard about if we are to be effective decision-makers.

Today we have the opportunity to make decisions on the basis of better information than we've ever had access to. Provided, of course, that the information can be trusted.

Tom MacMaster had been spinning a fictional history, and accumulating trusting followers, long before the Arab Spring. By the time "Amina" became an international figure, he had created a large online community vouching for her existence. The ruse had fooled smart people in many countries. No one probed beyond the surface until it was far too late.

In a final twist to the "Gay Girl in Damascus" story, one of the very people responsible for Tom MacMaster's exposure also turned out to be a fraud. "Paula Brooks," a respected lesbian blogger and the website editor responsible for eventually tracking MacMaster down to Edinburgh, was revealed by the *Washington Post* as actually being Bill Graber, a fifty-eight-year-old construction worker and former US Air Force pilot.[6] He and MacMaster had interacted as lesbian writers and activists for years, without either knowing that the other had a fraudulent identity. An improbable coincidence, surely?

Sock Puppets

But what really are your chances of encountering an online "sock puppet" – a completely false identity?

Greater than you might expect.

The case of Amina Abdallah Arraf al Omari–Tom MacMaster is no isolated anomaly. Increasingly, we face questions of online authenticity in a range of spheres.

Here are just a few examples.

On the medical website WebMD, a fake gynaecologist offered to answer questions. Thankfully, he was reported by a member of the online community before he could do too much damage.[7]

The supposedly deaf and quadriplegic blogger David Rose, who wrote powerful posts for his blog "David on Wheels," supposedly using a Tobii infrared eye-tracker, turned out to be a hoax.[8]

John Dirr set up a Facebook page to document his five-year-old son Eli's battle with cancer, and garnered 6,000 followers. He went on to share the tragic tale of his wife Dana's car crash at thirty-five weeks pregnant – Dana had "miraculously" held on in the hospital just long enough to give birth to a daughter, the couple's eleventh child. But Mr. Dirr turned out to be a childless twenty-two-year-old woman living in her father's home.[9]

President Assad's 19 March 2012 tweet claiming that "Documents published yesterday by a UK newspaper are hoaxes created against Syria and my family" – a denial briefly picked up by the *Guardian* – turned out to be issued by Tommaso De Benedetti, a Rome schoolteacher with a fake Assad Twitter account.[10]

Through the journalist–source matching service "Help a Reporter Out," Ryan Holiday manipulated numerous trusted media organisations into printing lies and exaggerations in his quest to see how easily the media could be duped. The online marketing specialist, while working for American Apparel, posed online as a valid source or credible commentator for a whole slew of articles on topics about which he knew nothing. Many of the stories he told were pure fabrications: extolling the joys of vinyl records despite never having owned a turntable, or discussing the insomnia from which he doesn't actually suffer.[11] Yet they were reported by a circus of reputable outlets, including ABC News, MSNBC and the *New York Times*.

These are extreme cases. But more generally, when you click on a link on a Google search page, how much thought do you give to who or what lies behind the site? Delving beneath the surface, it's clear that numerous websites that look authoritative and impartial are actually fronts for very specific ethical agendas or corporate strategies.

Imagine, for example, that you are a woman facing a very difficult decision – whether or not to have an abortion. You search online for "abortion risks," and the second link on Google's results page points you to www.afterabortion.org.

After abortion – well that's what you're interested in understanding more about. Dot org – must be credible, surely. So you click on the site. The logo "Elliot Institute" in the left-hand corner looks pretty professional too. And "Institute" – that implies scientific and disinterested, doesn't it?

So you read what's on the home page – studies that claim women who have had an abortion are four times more likely to die in the following year than women who carried their pregnancies to full term; that you're more at risk of getting liver cancer if you've had an abortion; that you're more likely to bear a handicapped child in future pregnancies if you have had an abortion in the past.[12]

Frightening stuff. Likely to influence your decision.

But who exactly is behind the "Elliot Institute"? Dig just a little, and you'll see that rather than a scientific research institute, it's actually a front for the work of its founder and director, David C. Reardon, a "biomedical ethicist." Dig a bit more, and you'll find that David Reardon obtained his biomedical ethics PhD from Pacific Western University – an uncredited correspondence school. Dig a bit more, and you'll see that "pro-life and pro-family leaders applaud [the Elliot Institute's] research." Dig into where Reardon propagates his views, and you'll find that he is a frequent guest on Christian radio and television talk shows, and often speaks to pro-life organisations.

Now that you know all this, would you attribute the same weight to the Elliot Institute's claims?

Presumably not.

This "digging" took me less than a minute – much of the information came from the Elliot Institute's own website. Yet how often when looking at information online do we carry out even the most cursory screening process? Many of us tend to let our guard down, and end up being tricked by what are often actually superficial and easily detectable ruses.[13] It's as if because something is published, we believe it to be true.

Of course, most of those who tweet or post or blog or set up their own websites are not dissembling or using the internet as a figleaf for their own political, ideological or corporate agendas. We saw in the previous two Steps how the internet is a haven for those with powerful stories to tell and deep experiences to share, who in the pre-internet era might well never have been heard. And there are countless examples of highly credible websites set up by individuals or communities to share experiences and knowledge.

But the cases referred to above should serve as a reminder to exercise some caution. For although the opportunity we now have to be our own custodians of truth is to be embraced wholeheartedly, we must remain alert to the fact that the web, while largely enlightening, is also a breeding ground for ideologues and extremists, liars and imposters, hoaxers and pranksters.

Astroturfing and Fakery Factories

People masquerading as others to trick us is of course not a new phenomenon.

Remember your Shakespeare?

In Act II Scene I of *Julius Caesar*, Brutus paces back and forth. He's unable to sleep, he's got too much on his mind. Should he join the plot of his friend Cassius to assassinate Caesar, who, it is feared, is on the verge of turning Rome into a tyranny?

As he struggles with his indecision, he reads one of many letters he has received from anonymous citizens urging him to act against Caesar. Believing that public opinion is on his side, Brutus makes a decision: he will join the conspiracy. "O Rome! I make thee promise," he says after reading the letter.

In fact, the letter did not actually represent the views of the citizens of Rome. It was written by Cassius to try to persuade Brutus to join the plot. Cassius had written many letters "in several hands … as if they came from several citizens."[14] But his effort, while successful, was a crude one-man gambit.

Today, there are entire businesses whose purpose is to write letters in "several hands" for the online age – by posting fake reviews and comments on forums, social networking sites and social media.

Dissembling online is big business.

Its modern-day manifestation is known as "astroturfing." The term was coined back in 1985 by long-standing Texas Senator Lloyd Bentsen, best known today as the Democratic vice-presidential candidate who told Dan Quayle in 1988 that he was "no Jack Kennedy." In his in-tray was a heap of cards and letters opposing recent insurance legislation – cards and letters that had clearly been written by the insurers themselves. "A fellow from Texas can tell the difference between grassroots and AstroTurf [fake grass]," said Bentsen of these letters. "This is generated mail."[15]

In the internet age, astroturfing is becoming more and more insidious, and more and more difficult to spot. How do you know if the reviews on Amazon or the comments on TripAdvisor that you're reading are faked or not? Is Joe from Idaho actually who he says he is? Has he actually ever stayed in that hotel in Tokyo? And if you are suffering from migraine, how do you know that the kind fellow-sufferer giving you advice on a web forum even gets headaches? It's actually quite strange that, when it comes to some pretty big personal decisions, we invest so much faith in people we've never met, and can't be sure we should trust.

For while 70 per cent of us trust online customer reviews, the fakers out there are not limited to the odd case of an embarrassed author caught posting positive reviews of his own work or negative reviews of the work of his rivals.[16] There are now systematic, highly organised operations churning out biased information for financial gain.

Online "factories" pay individuals considerable sums to write positive reviews. One American entrepreneur, Todd Jason Rutherford, briefly earned $28,000 a month from a website, GettingBookReviews.com, in which self-published authors paid him to write four- and five-star reviews of their work on an industrial scale.[17] Ads on Craigslist promise payment for positive reviews,[18] while an investigation by *The Times* in June 2011 revealed that hotel owners were paying up to £10,000 to companies that employ teams of writers to post hundreds of fake reviews.[19] There was even a website, now closed down – postingonlygoodreviews.com – which openly offered to write up to 1,000 positive reviews for just over £900 a month.[20]

Nowadays, such "businesses" tend to be less conspicuous in their marketing, yet astroturfing remains a lucrative trade.

Professor Bing Liu, a specialist in data mining at the University of Illinois, estimates that today about a third of all online consumer reviews are fake.[21] Others put the figure at a lower but still worrying 5–10 per cent.[22]

Indeed, pretty much all the big user-recommender sites – Amazon, TripAdvisor, Yelp (a site where readers can find over thirty million consumer reviews of everything from restaurants to doctors) – have been accused of publishing fake reviews.[23]

It's a trend that's likely to persist, despite the US Federal Trade Commission recently suggesting that each fake review could be subject to a $16,000 fine.[24] In fact, the more that people are seen to trust lay experts over traditional "expert" reviewers, and citizen journalists over traditional specialist reviewers, the bigger the market for false online testimonies is likely to become.

While buying the wrong book on the basis of a fake review is annoying but not devastating, ending up honeymooning in a dump described as a castle on TripAdvisor would be pretty upsetting. If you ended up in the care of a dodgy doctor because of fake positive reviews (and nowadays there are review sites for almost everything, including a number for doctors), the consequences could be disastrous.

So before you choose your surgeon on the basis of testimonies on healthgrades.com, or your honeymoon resort on the basis of some of the choice reviews it garnered on TripAdvisor, don't just reflect upon whether the reviewers' tastes are similar to yours, or on the other points raised in previous Steps. Also consider the possibility that the reviewer either doesn't exist, or made his or her testimony up in return for money.

When it comes to astroturfing, it is not just information on products and services that is being distorted by fake reviews and reviewers. It's not simply that you may choose to buy the wrong product or seek out the wrong expert on the basis of such false information – this kind of dissemination of online falsehood is seeping into more and more areas. Even politicians across the world are getting in on the game.

An Army of Bots

The Chinese government is believed to employ 280,000 people to write pro-government posts in chatrooms, newspaper comment sections and social networking sites, steering discussion away from sensitive topics. These people are known as the "fifty mao party," as they are paid fifty mao – half a yuan – for each post, the equivalent of about ten pence.[25]

When HBGary Federal, a security technology company working with the US government, was hacked by the Anonymous group in 2011, it was discovered that the US government was also planning to invest in astroturfing, potentially on an even bigger scale. Washington, it seems, had been inviting bids for the development of "persona management" software, which would help astroturfers create an "army" of social-media bots who could then post pro-government comments.[26]

These particular fake reviewers were highly sophisticated and duplicitous. HBGary Federal's astroturf software "pre-aged" new accounts by not only automatically creating a built-in back story, but also generating an online life, complete with an entire fake network of friends and contacts – thereby making it difficult to tell the difference between a real person and a robot or sock puppet. Indeed, the program was capable of creating *all* the online furniture that a real person would have: name, email addresses, Facebook and Twitter accounts, you name it. If you went into the account it would appear as if a real person had been living a normal online life for years.[27]

Although HBGary Federal was never awarded the US government contract, probably because of the hacking incident, can we be sure that no similar army of lifelike bots from a different contractor has ever been deployed by US federal agencies?

As these robots take on ever more "realistic" habits, their ability to fool us will grow dramatically. Some now have the capacity to "react" to real-time events, and to follow a normal sleep/wake cycle, so they tweet at realistic times and about the things you'd expect them to. You don't have to think very hard to imagine how companies, organisations or even individuals could use this technology to create "chatter" online. "Woooo! I'm on safari!! This Nikon camera is awesome!" along with a snap of the African savanna.[28] "Amazing performance by David Cameron at the election debates" posted just after the debate airs on television.

It's a problem that's likely to get worse. Facebook recently revealed that 7 per cent of its overall users are fakes and dupes – that's 83.09 million potential robots, just on that medium.[29] Although many of these will simply be real people, wary of how data is gathered and sold, choosing to have anonymous or alias Facebook accounts, rather than deliberately misleading fakers, whose interests might the bots among them, or those posting for payment, be serving?

Where might they be hoping to point you? Towards a particular product, political party, or ideology?

Which of your decisions might they be hoping to sway?

Are You Who You Say You Are?

In an era in which we will increasingly have the opportunity to navigate the information landscape ourselves, we need to take all the concerns mentioned above very seriously.

For if we are to maximise the value of our new online world of blogs and posts and searches in order to make smarter decisions, we need to feel confident that what they say can be trusted.

In the absence of traditional gatekeepers, the responsibility will increasingly fall on us to establish the veracity and credibility of our sources – if we don't pay attention to this, no one else will.

I don't underestimate the challenge this poses.

Tom MacMaster convinced some of the most hard-nosed and sceptical people going – journalists from the *Guardian*, the BBC and CNN – that he was a lesbian Syrian blogger.[30] In his commitment to the deception he even developed a romantic relationship with Sandra Bagaria, a woman from Montreal, Canada.[31] Websites that were actually fronts for corporate or ideological propaganda or spin have caught out numerous journalists and commentators over the years.[32]

In an age in which much of what we come across is anonymous, with even those sources that are credited likely to be unknown to us or unproven, outing the outright liars – particularly those who have invested huge amounts of time or money in their duplicity – will always be extremely tricky, especially given the volume of information we now have to sift through.

But there are some simple hoax-detecting steps you can take.

If it's a personal testimony you're thinking of relying upon to make a decision – a blogger's, or someone you've come across in a chatroom or an online forum – is there a way you can contact them directly via another medium? By telephone? Email? In person?

If this person claims to be in a position of authority – like the WebMD gynaecologist – are they to be found in the directory of the hospital they claim to be based at? If they give a contact number or contact details, do these actually work? These methods aren't foolproof: any forms of communication can be tampered with, and identities can be stolen. Some journalists did indeed attempt to meet Amina/MacMaster, and were left waiting in Damascus cafés as she/he feigned the very real concerns of being followed by the secret police.[33] But if your source fails any of these tests, it should set serious alarm bells ringing.

If it's a review or blog you're relying on, there are a growing number of giveaway clues and online solutions which may help you separate the "real" from the "fake" in years to come.

Researchers at Cornell University have developed a sophisticated algorithm that can tell fake reviews from real ones. It turns out that fake hotel reviews, for instance, are much more likely to focus on who the person was with (using phrases like "my husband and I"); more likely to use the pronouns "I" and "me"; and less likely to mention the name of the hotel.[34] At the University of Illinois at Chicago a computer program is being developed to track a reviewer's internet protocol address so as to determine what else he or she has been reviewing, how often they generate reviews, and whether they follow a particular pattern of praise.[35] Software developed by scientists at the Stevens Institute of Technology in Hoboken, New Jersey, now allows you to check the gender of anyone you read online. In the case of Tom MacMaster, the software predicted with 63.2 per cent confidence that Amina's posts were actually written by a man.[36]

As the power of online fakery grows, a counter-market in this kind of detection software will surely develop. But until such technologies are mainstream, there are some low-tech questions you can ask yourself. Are there numerous reviews written in a similar voice, using similar words and phrases? Does the language being used in a review or blog sound like a real person, or more like an ad? And what is the purported reviewer's or blogger's or tweeter's name? Is it a real name, or a random jumble of letters?

All of these are potential red flags signalling that you are in what may well be a treacherous landscape. They tell us that we need to do more work, spend a bit of time being an online detective, before acting on what we've read.

Short Cuts That We Might Just Regret

Of course, the problem is not just one of veracity or authenticity. It's not just a problem of unmasking fake reviewers, Walter Mitty-esque lay experts, dissembling lay journalists and agenda-heavy website creators.

Even if someone is who they say they are, even if you have been able to verify that your source is who they claim to be – is what they say to be trusted? Or what they show you?

How in these Photoshopped times to distinguish truths from lies? Hoaxes from credible witness testimony? Spin from substance? Evidence from speculation? How can we, even if we've determined that our source is real, know whether to trust what it is they say, show us or claim?

Some of the typical ways we do this are fundamentally flawed, and this can lead us to make some pretty bad decisions if we are not careful.

We tend to use the gender of a blogger as one indication of how credible they are, with males perceived as more credible than females[37] – not that there is any reason why this should be. We are also very influenced by design – graphics, readability, layout, typography and colour scheme. 54.6 per cent of people use visual appeal as the primary determinant of credibility for finance sites, 41.8 per cent for health sites.[38] Yet although a very cheap-looking site with typos and spelling mistakes should raise an alarm, anyone can nowadays hire top-drawer graphic designers from less developed countries at an affordable cost – good design doesn't equate with truth of content.

On Twitter we judge those who tweet by their number of followers, even though one can actually buy followers for a song – the going rate for a thousand is currently somewhere between $5 and $10.[39] We're also swayed by such measures as the tweeter's Klout score, which purports to measure social influence. But what is Klout really measuring? Influence, or noise? And what does it reward? The echoing of what's already out there, or original thought on new and important, though perhaps unpopular, matters?

On Google, the short cuts we use are also problematic. We consider most trustworthy those links that appear highest up on Google's search page – the top three results on page 1 of a Google search receive almost 60 per cent of clicks.[40] Yet Google sorts its results on the basis of a website's popularity: in broad terms, the more people who link to the website, the higher up in the results it will be. And popular does not necessarily mean trustworthy. Ideologically charged websites with a high hit rate can easily edge out sound scholarship or truthful testimony – if you search for "truth about the holocaust" on Google, eight of the top ten results are, disturbingly, holocaust-denier websites. One of the first results on Google if you search for Martin Luther King, the respectable-sounding www.martinlutherking .org, is in fact a grotesque combination of lies, slanders and outright racism hosted by the white-supremacist group Stormfront.[41]

Nor should you take a high volume of corroborating tweets or posts or reviews as evidence that what you're reading must be credible. We've all done it, decided to trust a review because everyone seems to be singing the same song. But herding behaviour online is a significant problem – if people see a five-star review they're more likely to give five stars themselves, if a poor review they're more likely to follow suit, even if this doesn't correspond to their real feelings.[42]

Given the data deluge we now face, and the time pressure we're frequently under to make our decisions, it is under-standable that we use short cuts to distinguish between good-quality information and bad. But it is important to be aware that some of these short cuts could lead us to make very poor decisions.

What to Do about It – How to Seriously Scrutinise

So, what might be better ways to deal with the fundamental question of how to identify good, trustworthy information online?

Below is a comprehensive list of steps to take. I'm not suggesting that you go through each of these every time you consider online information from a source you can't immediately vouch for. Life's too short, and time too precious. But for those moments when it really matters if the information before you is true or false, at those times when the high-stakes decision you're facing will be substantially affected by whether or not you can trust the information at hand, here are some thoughts on what to do.

Who?

The first step, as already described above, is to determine if your source is who they purport to be. This means asking yourself, *who* is purportedly speaking? Is there an obvious reason why they might not be who they claim to be? An extreme viewpoint can sometimes be a clue.

Can you reach them via another medium – ideally by phone or Skype – to verify that they are who they say they are, or even that they actually exist? Is what they say consistent with what else you might know about them already? If you have any information on them, do they have a track record for telling the truth?

If they are unknown to you, can someone else vouch for them? Is anyone you trust referencing them too? Can you see who's funding them?

If you've come across them via a review site or an online forum, or their testimony has been mapped by a crowd-sources aggregator, how good are these filters' own screening processes?

What gives you confidence that your sources are even human – is the language they use exhibiting any obvious traits of a bot?

How?

Next, you want to think about *how* they got their information. Are their claims based on first-hand direct experience? Eyewitness testimony? Or second-hand info only? Are they reporting what they have seen or experienced directly, or echoing what others have already said? Is what they are reporting something they claim to have witnessed recently? If so, is there a time-stamp on the information to establish this? Every tweet, for example, has a time-stamped URL that shows the exact time and date it was posted. Or might it in fact be old news?

If it's supposedly academic research they are touting, how credible is this? (More on how to assess such research in the next Step.)

Where?

Then, can you tell *where* your source is? If so, this may give you a steer as to whether their claims are to be trusted. If their knowledge is supposedly local, is there a way to prove this? Are they communicating in the right language for their location? Have they a geo-location tag? The BBC's User Generated

Content Hub, which is responsible for verifying claims from social media, uses Google Earth maps to check whether the location at which a photograph was supposedly taken corresponds to the actual terrain. It also checks that the weather on the day and at the time the picture was claimed to be taken corresponds to historic weather data.[43]

What?

Critically, you need to look into *what* your source is saying. Is it opinion? If so, be mindful that they might have a particular world view, certain tastes, beliefs and affiliations, and potential agendas or biases. How might these be shaping what they are saying? How might this impact their relevance to you? How might their interpretation of events muddy or distort matters? If it's a conclusion or analysis they are offering, how did they reach it? Is their reasoning sound? Are the inferences they have made sensible? (More on how to determine this in the next Step.)

There's a vast difference between on-the-ground reporting and the proffering of an opinion or explanation, so it's important to establish which of the two is before you.

If what the source says purports to be fact, what is the evidence for it? If it's a supposed eyewitness photograph, can you run it through a database and see if it matches any photos already published? The BBC used a technology that can do this, TinEye, to evaluate a gory image of Osama bin Laden's head that circulated online soon after his death – it turned out that this was another corpse onto which bin Laden's features had been Photoshopped.[44]

More generally, how does the source's testimony fit with what you already know about the topic? If you were trying to make sense of posts from Tahrir Square during the Arab Spring uprising, for example, how did these fit with what else you knew about Egypt, and how the situation was evolving? Are there any factual inaccuracies that sound an alarm? If women who have had an abortion really are four times more likely to die in the next twelve months, surely you'd have heard that at least once in the past?

If you don't know anything about the situation or topic yourself, who might be able to help you get up to speed? Is there someone with relevant experience or expertise you can deploy? If what you're learning doesn't seem to fit with the established narrative, who can help you to work out if this alternative narrative is credible or not? Who can you cross-check it with?

Who Else?

It is important, too, to ask yourself *who else* is making a similar claim. What supporting evidence is there for it? Are there at least another couple of sources that corroborate it? Sources that you have reason to trust? Or is there other information out there that contradicts it?

Both triangulation – the identification of at least two other independent sources to corroborate a testimony – and falsification – the identification of credible information that contradicts a claim – are important tools to use when assessing the credibility of an online source. Indeed, these are the techniques most commonly used by journalists, academic researchers and intelligence officers for this very purpose in the offline world, the stock-in-trade of the inquisitive and the sceptical through time.

Although it is more complex to corroborate or falsify in a digital environment, because it's harder to be sure your sources are independent and not echoes of each other, that doesn't

mean you shouldn't use these techniques as part of your verification and authentication process. It's a matter of being
aware that sheer numbers don't cut it by themselves – a million
tweets echoing each other are less credible than three reliable
sources that are truly independent, reinforcing and supporting
what each says. It's also about looking for offline forms of
corroboration and falsification as well, if at all possible.

When we can't find these, we can, somewhat counter-
intuitively, be well served if we ask the crowd itself for help.

This is what Andy Carvin, the Senior Strategist at NPR
(National Public Radio) in Washington, DC, did. While he was
covering the Arab Spring he noticed how hard it was to verify
some of the Twitter reports he was getting. So what did he do?
He simply re-tweeted them with tags like "Anyone else reporting on this yet?" or "How unusual is this?" or just "Source?"

On 12 March 2011, Carvin got a tweet from a friend saying
there was a rumour that Colonel Gaddafi was attacking rebels
in Libya using mortars made in Israel. The rumour looked as
if it might check out, given that there was a picture circulating
of a man in a camouflage jacket and a black-and-white-checked
scarf holding an 81mm mortar decorated with a Star of David
and an odd crescent shape.[45] Carvin took to Twitter to try to
find out what kind of mortar was pictured, and if it was indeed
Israeli. "They ID it as Israeli. Maybe, maybe not. Need help to
ID it. Anyone?" he tweeted. Within minutes he was receiving
useful responses. Contrary to the earlier reports, these tweets
revealed that the mortar was actually an 81mm illumination
round, which is basically a mortar with a flare and a parachute, designed to illuminate enemy territory as it descends.
The star (a flare) and the odd crescent shape (a parachute)
were infographics used to show what kind of mortar it was.
One response Carvin received showed a sketch using the same
symbols for a weapon from World War I.[46] Carvin had figured
the whole thing out by seeking help from the crowd, while

news outlets including Al Jazeera were continuing to report an Israeli connection.[47]

Seeking help from the crowd to verify your source and what it claims is a technique we can all deploy. So if you're trying to work out whether the tweets you're seeing about an escaped tiger in your area merit you staying in tonight, or if the Facebook photos of labour abuses in one of your subcontractor's manufacturing plants are for real, or if you're trying to establish whether that website you've come across which claims that global warming is nothing but hysteria is correctly representing the current state of science, how about issuing a call for help via your social networks. Might someone within it be privy to information that helps you establish what's what? Or, at the least, might you thereby be able to apportion some of the hard and time-consuming verification work to others?

In a world in which co-created information is gaining in currency, so too will co-created methods of verification.

Takeaways

I don't underestimate how hard a task it is to determine whether the content we are receiving is to be trusted or not, especially given the volume of information the data deluge spews out, its 24/7 nature, and the pressure we are often under to respond in real time too.

And yet, because not every tweet, post, blog, review or website that we come across will be trustworthy, and because online rumours are all too easy to stoke and disseminate, at those times when we need to be confident in the credibility of our information in order to make a decision, it's important that we give ourselves sufficient time to identify red flags, and go through basic verification and credibility assessment processes, before we act upon it. Even then, such a process can never be completely foolproof. We've seen how sophisticated fakers nowadays can be.

When we don't have the luxury of time, we have to at the very least acknowledge that the data before us may be wrong or misleading, or may be occluding what it is we actually need to know. Not that I'm suggesting that we can only act on the basis of certain information – frequently we have to act without this. But by acknowledging the potential limitations of what it is we know, and by being clear too about what it is we may not know at all, we can better decide whether to act or to hold back, whether to pause or to react immediately, and also better prepare for different scenarios to play out.

But identifying good information that we can rely upon is not just about making sure we've cast our net wide enough, and screened our sources properly to determine their credibility. It's also about ensuring that we have the requisite skills to be able to properly interrogate any claims and assertions we may face. When did you last brush up your logical reasoning and your math survival skills?

QUICK TIPS FOR SCRUTINISING SOCK PUPPETS AND SCREENING SOURCES

- **If you're not sure that what you've found online is to be trusted, do some digging.** Even a quick investigation can be illuminating. Two minutes' detective work may make you feel very differently about a source.

- **Try to establish who your source actually is.** Are they who they purport to be? What is their likely motive and agenda? Can someone you trust, or a website with long-standing bona fide credentials, vouch for them? Are there any obvious giveaways that they are bots or sock puppets?

- **Determine whether your source is sharing opinion or fact.** If opinion, what values are informing their slant? If fact, how did they get their information? Do they have any verifiable documentary evidence for what they claim? If so, does it stack up? Any obvious photo-doctoring? Does the time-stamp fit with what you're being told? If their claim is based on research, are there any glaring methodological flaws? (I'll be looking in more depth at how to establish these in the next Step.)

- **If a claim sounds extreme, look into it especially carefully.** This doesn't mean that the claim is necessarily wrong, but it does demand extra analysis.

- **Ask yourself whether what your source says fits with what you already know.** Does it seem to make sense? Again, if it doesn't, that doesn't mean you should automatically rule it out, but you do need to ask yourself what additional information or context you need in order to evaluate it properly.

- **If the subject is new to you, is there anyone who can help you evaluate these claims?** Seek out this guiding hand, whether in person or through making digital connections. Is there a way you can use the crowd to help you verify or corroborate online information? Who in your social network could potentially help in this regard?

- **Scan the landscape, and determine whether others are making the same claims.** If so, ask yourself whether they are independent of each other. If they are, consider whether this amounts to robust corroboratory evidence, or merely to echoes of the original voice? Remember that herding behaviour online is common.

DEVELOP YOUR SURVIVAL SKILLS

STEP EIGHT
Overcome Your Math Anxiety

Inside the Brains of the Math Anxious

With his floppy hair and neat specs, Ian M. Lyons has an air about him of Hugh Grant in the movie *Notting Hill*. But whereas Grant's character was an aspiring intellectual, Lyons is the real deal. A freshly minted Doctor of Psychology, he earned those three letters after his name by studying what's going on in our brains when we number-crunch. Not how we do it, but how we *feel* about doing it. As it goes, some of us feel pretty darn bad.

Working a few blocks from Lake Michigan, amidst the manicured hedgerows and terracotta rooftops of the University of Chicago, Lyons developed an experiment with fellow psychologist Sian Beilock to study how people felt when they anticipated doing a math problem.[1]

Lyons didn't use any old crowd to participate. First, he screened potential participants to check that they weren't generally anxious people – asking questions about how often they felt cool, calm and collected, or able to make decisions easily. He was particularly interested, though, in how they *felt* about doing math, selecting fourteen people who felt relaxed about it and fourteen who didn't. The latter group self-reported feeling anxious at the prospect of things like receiving a math textbook, walking into a math class or being given a set of addition problems to solve. Digits got them feeling all hot and bothered.

Lyons gave all twenty-eight subjects some simple and some hard problems to solve – half were word problems, and the other half were math problems. In the case of the math, hard meant needing to employ a "carry over" operation when subtracting (you know, if you're subtracting 17 from 41, in order to take 7 away from 1 you would "carry" or "borrow" 1 from the 4 …).

How they dealt with the tasks wasn't that important, although Lyons did find that the higher the anxiety, the worse the performance. What he was more interested in was the anticipation. Before each task the participants would be flashed a yellow circle or a blue square. One meant a word problem was on its way, the other meant a math problem was coming. Lyons wanted to pick over the seconds between his subjects getting the cue and getting the problem: what happened to their brains when they knew a math challenge was coming, but it hadn't yet hit?

All the participants were hooked up to an fMRI scanner. They wore what's called a "Head Coil," which looks like a cross between an astronaut's helmet and an upturned laundry basket. While they were anticipating doing their math task, Lyons took thirty-two "axial slices" of their brains. Taken from above, these 3.5mm slices dice the brain like layers of rock, so you can see what's going on from all angles. This gave Lyons the inside track on the brain's inside track – and for those who felt anxious about solving a math problem, the track was pretty thorny.

When math-anxious people knew there was a math problem coming their way, the areas of the brain showing activity were the same as those that are activated when we experience real physical pain. And not only that: the activity registered in the part of the brain, the dorso-posterior insula, that is activated when we feel the pain and rejection of the break-up of a romantic relationship![2]

For those who consider themselves to be "math anxious," math really does hurt.

So what kind of people consider themselves to have some form of math anxiety? Are they a very particular bunch? A tiny percentage of the population that you seldom come across?

Not at all. Up to two million children in Britain are thought to suffer from math anxiety.[3] US studies point to higher-achieving children being more likely to suffer from it than their peers.[4] In Canada, at the University of Waterloo, over a quarter of students in psychology classes were found to be math anxious. Many of them were also science and engineering students, all subjects that require pretty solid math skills.[5] Over 70 per cent of Indian secondary-school students have at least moderate levels of math anxiety. One in five are highly anxious around numbers. And this is regardless of gender or socio-economic advantage.[6]

Indeed, so many people have such an aversion to mathematics in general that even Professor Stephen Hawking, then Lucasian Professor of Mathematics at the University of Cambridge, was persuaded to avoid it almost altogether when writing his first book on cosmological physics. He was warned that book sales would halve for each equation he included – so *A Brief History of Time* contains only one: $E=mc^2$. It sold over ten million copies.[7]

Even NASA Makes Math Errors

Given that math is a key feature of many decisions, the fact that there is such a high preponderance of math-anxious people is in itself a concern.

But it's not simply that so many of us are frightened of math: many of us are rather bad at it too.

In the UK, just 65 per cent of people know that 20 per cent is the same as $^1/_5$;[8] in the US, 36 per cent of final-year high-school students fail basic mathematical calculations such as 0.3 x 360.[9] Many of us don't correctly understand what a weather forecast predicting a 30 per cent chance of rain the next day actually means. A majority of Dutch, Italian, Greek and German people think it means that it will rain for 30 per cent of that day.[10] In fact it means that on 3 out of 10 days like tomorrow there will be at least a trace of rain.

It's not just the general public who struggle with these basics. Many professors of journalism describe their students' grasp of numbers as "notably insufficient."[11] A study of Danish doctors revealed that most were unable to understand the most basic statistical terms needed to make sense of medical research papers.[12] A recent probe into the math skills of ninety-seven British MPs revealed that more than half couldn't correctly answer one of the most basic probability questions there is: "If you spin a coin twice, what is the probability of getting two heads?" The correct answer is of course 25 per cent (½ x ½), yet only 40 per cent of the MPs got the answer correct.[13]

Given that all of these professions involve making important decisions and assessments on the basis of numerical data, these findings are especially worrying.

Even the crème de la crème fall foul of the basics from time to time. In 1999, NASA sent a $125-million Climate Orbiter into space to make the 140-million-mile flight to Mars. On its first orbit around Mars on 23 September it was destroyed. It later transpired the Orbiter had been thrown far off course during its nine-month journey, and had flown too deep into the Martian atmosphere. The cause? A discrepancy that would be embarrassing even for the average high-school student.

The navigation team at the Jet Propulsion Laboratory had been working in the metric system – millimetres, metres and newtons – while the people who designed and built the Orbiter, Lockheed Martin Astronautics in Denver, had been working in feet, inches and pounds. So when the navigation team planned the course, and worked out when the spaceship's thrusters needed to be fired up, their calculations turned out to be disastrously wrong, because they were assuming that Lockheed's data would be in newtons, not force-pounds. One pound of force is equivalent to just under 4.5 newtons. This meant that over its nine-month journey, every time NASA used these numbers to measure the thruster impulse as they corrected the Orbiter's trajectory, the manoeuvres were 4.5 times too strong.

This simple error in the number format meant that by the time the Orbiter reached Mars it was over a hundred miles off-course. It smashed straight into the planet's atmosphere and incinerated itself.[14] "That is so dumb," remarked John Logsdon, the burly Director of George Washington University's Space Policy Institute at the time.[15]

Simple math can floor all kinds of experts, not just those with a mind for interplanetary travel.

In 1999, the British solicitor Sally Clark was wrongly convicted of the double murder of her two infant sons on the basis of bad math from someone who should have known much better. The prosecution's expert witness, paediatrician Professor Sir Roy Meadow, claimed that for a family like hers, the likelihood of two infants suffering cot deaths, or Sudden Infant Death Syndrome (SIDS), as the defence argued, was well-nigh impossible – citing the probability to be as low as one in seventy-three million.

But Meadow had calculated wrongly. He came up with these odds by multiplying the chance of one death from SIDS in a family like Sally Clark's ($1/8543$) by itself, which is what one would do if the two deaths were independent. (Think how you'd calculate the chance of tossing a coin twice and getting two heads – you'd multiply ½ by ½). In fact, one child's death from SIDS makes it far more likely that a sibling will also die in the same way, for a number of genetic and environmental reasons – two deaths are therefore unlikely to be independent of each other.[16] It's what common sense would suggest. The probability of two children in the same family dying from SIDS actually turns out to be somewhere between one in 138,000 and one in 169,000, rather than one in seventy-three million.[17]

These dramatically different odds may well have been the difference between Sally Clark being found guilty or innocent. Indeed, the Foundation for the Study of Infant Deaths had data on approximately two such double tragedies having occurred every year between 1988 and 1999.

Perhaps if the jury in the Sally Clark trial had been given this information they would not have convicted her. Unfortunately, all they had before them was Sir Roy Meadow's deeply flawed one in seventy-three million calculation.

In the era of the Cult of the Measurable, an age in which experts are lionised, what is striking is that the math skills of so many of them are so weak, sometimes with tragic consequences. Not that we necessarily recognise number illiteracy in ourselves. Around three-quarters of those British MPs who were polled about coin tosses said that they generally felt confident when dealing with numbers.[18]

The Importance of Being ... Math Literate

Being number literate is *essential* for understanding the modern world and making the right choices. It's essential for smart decision-making.

We cannot avoid graphs and charts, numbers and statistics, polls and surveys – whether we're a chief executive, a junior manager, a doctor, a journalist, a marketer, a lawyer, a finance director, a juror or a stay-at-home mother.

Decisions ranging from whether to wear a helmet when riding a bike, which financial adviser to hire to help ensure a comfortable retirement, who to vote for, or how to interpret medical test results are all predicated on an understanding of probabilities, polls, stats and studies.

This means that whether confronted with numbers in the boardroom or the courtroom, whether weighing a "scientific" claim at the doctor's or the beauty counter, whether assessing risk at the casino or in the emergency room, or looking at research produced by your marketing department or the government, we need to get much better at deciphering what numbers are telling us if we want to avoid being manipulated by the information we receive, or making decisions from a position of only partial understanding.

We have to become much more number savvy, much more au fait with all kinds of mathematical challenges, if we are to be empowered decision-makers.

Now, I appreciate that many of my readers will not be even slightly scared of numbers, and a fair few will undoubtedly be highly number literate. So for those of you for whom terms like probabilistic reasoning, methodological bias and time slicing of data are familiar, I suggest skipping this chapter, or merely skimming it.

For the rest of us, what I am going to do in this chapter is single out a few potential mathematical, methodological and statistical stumbling blocks, a few things you may not have thought about since high school or university, or that no one may ever have explained to you, that if we're to make smart decisions we need to be much more conscious of.

Risk, and What It Might Mean for Your Breakfast

Let's start with the hard stuff – assessing risk. We have seen in earlier chapters how problematic this can be at times. Remember Mr. Jones, and the story of how almost double the number of mental-health experts wanted to have him incarcerated if the odds of people like him committing acts of violence was expressed in the form of a ratio rather than in percentage terms? Or Professor Sharot's research into how people process probabilities differently depending on whether they are signalling good or bad news?

Assessments of risk can flummox some of us because of the emotional connotations and visceral feelings that different representations of risky events or different qualities of risk can provoke. But even if we get past that hurdle, understanding risk throws up more profound challenges for most of us.

In November 2007, newspapers all over the world published some of the results of a huge study, sponsored by the World Cancer Research Fund. The study looked into the links between lifestyle factors and various kinds of cancer.[19]

In Britain, the press seized in particular on the risk the study highlighted from eating processed meat, and focused on the apparent threat from a much-loved national snack – the bacon butty. The *Daily Mail* let out a battle cry, calling it "The Great War on Bacon." The *Daily Mirror* moaned, "Have a long, healthy and miserable life. Avoid cancer, cut out everything you enjoy." The *Sun* rose to the occasion in style: "Careless Pork Costs Lives."[20]

These would not have seemed like unreasonable conclusions, if you'd quickly skimmed the study. It had indeed highlighted the statistic that for men, fifty grams of bacon a day – about two or three rashers – increased the risk of colon cancer by 20 per cent.[21] It was this figure that underpinned the newspaper stories.

I mean, if someone told you that your risk of getting cancer would go up by as much as 20 per cent if you ate bacon, wouldn't it sound like time to ditch the fry-up?

But before you answer that, let's look a bit closer.

When you are presented with an estimate of risk, the first thing you need to ask yourself, if you're to properly understand what it means, is this: is the risk you're being presented with an absolute risk – that is, the actual chance that something will happen to you; or a relative risk – information about a proportional increase or decrease in your risk?

Think of relative risk reduction like a discount. A 50 per cent sale can sound like a bargain, but there's a big difference between a 50 per cent reduction in the price of a £3 million yacht and a half-price £50 jacket – the starting price is the important thing when you're trying to work out if you can afford it.

The 20 per cent cancer figure is a relative risk addition – the amount by which something for which there is already a risk, getting cancer, would become more likely if, in this case, you ate 50g of bacon every day.

Eat bacon daily, and your risk of colon cancer goes up by 20 per cent.

To determine how worried you should be in this case, you would need to know your starting risk level – the baseline.

It turns out that the lifetime risk of colon cancer – the absolute risk for a man of getting cancer over his lifetime – is about 5 per cent. That's five chances in a hundred. A 20 per cent relative rise would therefore mean increasing this absolute risk by only one percentage point – from five to six chances in a hundred.

So, while an absolute risk increase of colon cancer of twenty percentage points – an increase, say, from 25 to 45 per cent –

would be really worrying, for only an additional one percentage point of risk you might just decide it's worth keeping on ordering your full English breakfast.

David Spiegelhalter, a mathematics professor at Cambridge University who enjoys the grand title of Professor for the Public Understanding of Risk, is a tireless campaigner for more sensible ways to express risks. "We are generally badly served by the way that risks are communicated to us – usually by people who want to either sell us something or change our behaviour," he says.

Spiegelhalter is particularly concerned that when doctors and pharmaceutical companies suggest a drug to us, they typically present its benefits in the form of relative risks rather than absolute risks. By doing so they are liable to skew our judgement.

He cites the example of cholesterol-busting statin drugs, which reputedly lower your risk of heart attack by approximately 30 per cent if you take them every day. Doctors often advise their patients to take statins, and sure enough, when Professor Spiegelhalter visited his GP for a check-up in his early fifties, he was encouraged to start using them. A 30 per cent risk reduction certainly looked good at first glance: but what did it really add up to? Spiegelhalter explained: "Using relative risks makes things look a lot more impressive, but it's the absolute risks that are important."[22]

Again, a 30 per cent relative risk reduction is meaningless without an absolute rate to compare it to. You need to know how likely you are to have a heart attack were you to do nothing, and compare the potential risk reduction to that.

Professor Spiegelhalter knew that a man of his age and fitness has roughly a 12 per cent chance of a heart attack in the next ten years. Taking statins would reduce this risk by 30 per cent – so in his case it would actually bring the risk down to about 8 per cent. However, there were also side-effects to consider when taking statins: an increased chance of cataracts, of liver dysfunction, and of the muscular disease myopathy. Spiegelhalter felt that compared with just a 4 per cent extra chance of beating a heart attack, he would rather pass on the pills for the time being. "The numbers mean that twenty-five people like me would have to take the tablets for ten years to prevent one heart attack or stroke – I feel that's not enough chance of benefiting," he said, though he acknowledged that "others could feel differently."[23]

What Do Your Medical Tests Really Mean?

There's another medical setting that many of us will face at some point in our lives where understanding risk and probability really matters.

You've been for a blood test or a scan, and are presented with a positive result. How do you interpret what this actually means?

Let's consider this problem by means of a more specific scenario.

Imagine you are a middle-aged woman who's just had a routine mammogram (in the UK, mammograms are routinely offered to women aged between fifty and seventy). You are given the distressing news that you have a positive test result. You know that mammograms correctly classify 90 per cent of women. What's the probability that it's wrong, and you *don't* actually have breast cancer?

Most people think the answer to this is 10 per cent.

But it isn't. The chance that you don't have cancer if your test comes back positive is actually around 91 per cent.

How can this be?

The confusion derives from the problem we have with understanding what are known as "conditional probabilities" –

the likelihood of something happening given that something else has happened. Our confusion typically stems from failing to separate two kinds of conditional probability: on the one hand, the probability that a hypothesis is true *given some evidence*, on the other hand the probability that the evidence will be true *given the hypothesis*.

Here's an everyday example. Imagine a friend hasn't been returning your emails for a few days. Surely you must have fallen out of favour, because otherwise they would be replying to your emails, right?

Not necessarily. Here, the hypothesis is that your friend is mad at you, and the evidence is the lack of reply. If you start by assuming that the hypothesis is correct and your friend is angry, it is almost certain that this is what's causing them to ignore you. But, working backwards from just the evidence – that you've not had any replies to your emails – the link to the hypothesis is much weaker. There are many other possible explanations: your friend could instead be very busy at work, or on holiday, or ill.

Back to the mammogram result – the confusion lies in mixing up the hypothesis of having breast cancer, and the evidence of the test result.

Working forward from the hypothesis: if you do have cancer, there is indeed a 90 per cent probability that the test will be correct. But we need to be working backwards from the actual evidence – the positive test result – if we are to gauge how likely we are to have the hypothetical cancer. Specifically, we need to compare two numbers: the likelihood of a correct positive, and the likelihood of a false positive.

To do so, as in the case of assessing the impact of bacon or statins on your health, you need a further bit of information – the *baseline risk*. In this case, you need to know the proportion of women over fifty who are likely to have breast cancer before you can assess how likely your test is to be wrong.

Let's say the baseline risk in this case is one in a hundred. What that means is that out of one hundred women of a similar age, one will have breast cancer. As her test will probably be accurate, we have one correct positive. But of the ninety-nine who don't have breast cancer, we'd still expect 10 per cent – another ten women – to test (falsely) positive, as the test is only 90 per cent accurate. That makes eleven positive tests, of which only one is accurate. So the probability of not having cancer if you test positive is 10/11, or about 91 per cent. As a rule of thumb, the larger the number of people being tested, and the rarer the disease, the more likely a positive result will be false.

(Note, however, that if you'd been sent for a mammogram specifically because you had symptoms, or because your family history put you in a higher-risk category, you would need to use as your baseline risk the chance that someone with similar symptoms or family history, as well as of a similar age, has cancer, rather than the considerably lower risk that a woman aged over fifty has breast cancer. In such a case, given that the baseline risk would be considerably higher, a false positive would be much less likely.

Whoever you are, if you do have a positive test, *don't ignore it*. It's important to follow it up and see where the trail leads.)

Thinking through relative risks and conditional probabilities is challenging, I acknowledge. The disturbing thing is that it's not just patients who find it hard.

In US and German studies, gynaecologists – one of the types of doctor you'd see if you had a lump in your breast – struggled to answer a question similar to the example we've just worked through. In this case they were asked to estimate the probability that a woman with a positive mammogram actually had cancer, and different values for the false positive rate and the baseline risk were used. The correct answer was 9 per cent, but 95 per cent of the American doctors wrongly estimated it to be around

75 per cent, while the average estimate of the German doctors was 70 per cent.[24]

It's frightening to think how this sort of miscalculation might lead to inappropriate treatment recommendations, and it's another useful reminder that we should ask questions and keep our brains firmly switched on when we are talking to doctors about our health.

More than that, however, it makes it all too clear that if you've got an important decision to make, it's critical that *you* understand what risk assessments really mean, especially given that the experts you meet may not.

Beyond that, assessing risk is often a series of personal decisions. It's up to you to decide whether you'd rather eat a bacon sandwich a day and increase your five out of a hundred risk of getting colon cancer to six out of a hundred, or whether you'd rather take statins and suffer potential side-effects to decrease your risk of heart attack by four percentage points. Only you can decide whether you'd rather undergo more tests than start treatment immediately on the basis of a positive test result.

These personal choices are not straightforward by any means, but unless you understand what is meant by the odds you're given, you won't have the correct information at hand with which to make them.

Context and the Coming Armageddon

"The correct information."

How elusive that can prove to be.

As we move through this chapter, we'll see that when it comes to numbers and statistics and surveys and graphs, making sense of them can be much less clear-cut than one might think.

In June 2009 the UK's low-taxation pressure group the TaxPayers' Alliance reported that civil servants were spending £8 million a year on taxis.[25] The headlines were predictable enough: "How Whitehall Takes us for a Ride," wrote the *Daily Express*.[26] And £8 million certainly sounds like an extraordinary amount to spend on taxis.

But once again, before you react, ask yourself, what does this figure actually mean?

Think about it. There are hundreds of thousands of civil servants. Of course, not all of them take taxis in connection with their job. Let's say just 20,000 are senior enough – about 4 per cent of the total. Share the £8 million between them, and it comes to about £400 a year each – or just enough for one short £8 taxi ride each a week.[27] When that enormous £8 million figure is converted to its real-life context, it doesn't seem so extravagant after all.

So, the next time you're given a number, think about who is providing it. Is it their intention to shock? If so, before you react, contextualise it. What does it actually represent? Are you still as surprised?

Focusing on a number's shock value without stopping to ask whether there is in fact anything really shocking about it is just one way of missing the bigger picture. Another is to fixate on the eye-opening extremes plucked from a spread of results.

Take some highly alarming headlines that appeared in many newspapers in January 2005. "Weather Trial Predicts 10°C Rise in British Temperatures," reported the *Daily Telegraph*. "Global Warming is Twice as Bad as Previously Thought," warned the *Independent*. Even the popular-science press was at it: "Sizzling Times Ahead for Earth," said the *New Scientist*, warning of an even greater potential temperature rise of 11.5°C.[28]

An increase of eleven degrees Centigrade. Terrifying. A rise of over three degrees is viewed by many scientists as the tipping point beyond which the earth is heading towards a no-return global-warming Armageddon.

But that figure, whether ten or eleven degrees, needed to be considered much more carefully. In this case, you'd need to go back to the original study to get an accurate understanding of what the evidence had really shown.[29]

For these alarmist headlines stemmed from the first results of a huge experiment organised by scientists at Oxford University, in which people all over the world donated their computers' down-time to produce 2,000 separate runs of a new climate-change model. The model was designed to simulate what might happen if the amount of carbon dioxide in the atmosphere doubled from its pre-Industrial Revolution level – a scenario well within the realms of possibility.[30]

So, did the experiment reveal that most of the computer runs indicated a temperature increase of ten or eleven degrees? No, it didn't. In fact, about half of the 2,000 results predicted a rise of close to three degrees – which would admittedly be bad enough. Some results actually predicted a *fall* in global temperatures.

Only one single result was in fact a rise of eleven degrees.[31]

Why had the journalists misrepresented the results so badly? The reason for this lies in part with the scientists themselves, who issued a press release alongside the study which stated that "Average temperatures could eventually rise by up to 11 deg C." The clue was of course in the words "could" and "up to," which many journalists presumably either missed or ignored.

If a number appears in a headline, the message again is to dig a bit deeper before you react. If need be, go back to the source yourself to check it. In our online age it is much easier than it used to be to locate source documents and to be sure of your own conclusions.

Families from Hell

With those newspapers for which shock and awe is their stock-in-trade, there's something else to be mindful of.

In July 2012, both the *Daily Mail* and the *Sun* devoted much newsprint to a report produced by the office of Louise Casey, a UK government official known colloquially as the "Troubled Families Tsar." The report was about the roughly 120,000 families across the nation who fell into multiple "problem" categories, such as having parents suffering from disabilities or mental-health problems, having no parent in work or with qualifications, and living in overcrowded housing and on a low income.[32]

The *Sun* claimed that the report had damned these families as "families from hell," in which "children live in fear of savage attacks and indecent assaults," and "drug use is rife." In the words of the *Daily Mail*, these families featured "a high incidence of incest and sexual abuse, physical violence and a spiral of alcohol abuse and crime."[33]

To anyone reading these articles it would have been a reasonable assumption that the government report had identified these shocking conditions in many of the 120,000 families in question.

In fact, these details were lifted from interviews that Louise Casey's researchers had conducted with just sixteen families. The newspapers had taken the data on these sixteen families – little more than one-hundredth of 1 per cent of the total – and extrapolated it to refer to every family covered in the report. It was utterly misleading, and at least one of the newspapers at fault was shamed into publishing a correction.[34]

As you can see, therefore, numbers shorn of their context are at best meaningless, and at worst thoroughly misleading.

Extreme values plucked from a spread of numbers can be alarming, until you realise they are just statistical freaks.

A figure can seem worryingly large, but after examining it closely, you may discover that it's anything but.

Risks or benefits are often presented in ways that exaggerate the difference they really make.

Probabilities can mean something very different from what you initially take them to mean.

Headlines and advertising claims involving numbers all too often provide partial truths – if they are truthful at all.

So, before you react to a figure or a statement or a claim, you need to make sure you actually understand where it's from, and have processed what it actually means.

Correlation, Causation and Top Marks at School

You also need to understand how a conclusion has been arrived at, and whether the right assumptions underpin it. A hidden set of causes, circumstances or reasons may lie beneath an easily digestible number.

Have you got a child of school age? If so, you've probably read that children who are privately educated achieve better grades. Perhaps you read the *Daily Telegraph* on 18 October 2012, which reported that private-school pupils were three times more likely to get top grades at A-level than state-school pupils?[35] Or one of the many other articles that link achievement at school and university with whether or not a child was privately educated?

No wonder 57 per cent of parents in Britain say they would send their children to private schools if they could afford to.[36]

Indeed, a 2011 survey commissioned by the Independent Schools Council found that the most common answer parents gave to the question of why they sent their children for private schooling was "better standards of education."[37]

But should parents really be saving up the £11,700 a year on average that it costs to send a child to private school?[38] Not necessarily.

The real question is, do children who go to private schools perform better than children who don't *because* of where they went to school, or for another reason?

PISA, or the Programme for International Student Assessment, is a highly respected international comparative study of different countries' education standards. Set up by the OECD in 2000, it conducts tests and publishes its reports every three years. PISA aims to assess educational systems, methods and policies that can be compared universally. One such system is private schooling.

In 2011 PISA reported the results from its most recent study. It concluded that while results from private schools tended to outstrip those from state schools, the advantage turns out to be more down to parental socio-economics than to the private school's magic touch.[39] Privately educated children are likely to do better because they have parents who can afford to send them to private schools – the kind of parents who tend to have a high level of education themselves, a good occupation, and a relatively high income. In fact, when privately educated children in Britain are compared to state-school students from similar socio-economic backgrounds, they actually perform worse at school and university than their state-educated but equally wealthy counterparts.[40]

It seems that the family, not the school, is what makes the real difference in children's educational prospects.[41]

If you are presented with a conclusion, before you unthinkingly accept its underlying logic, ask yourself whether the inferences made necessarily stack up. The numbers may actually be acting as a red herring, distracting you or drawing your mind away from the underlying cause and effect.

Don't Pick the Cherries

There's more still to remember from your schooldays – if indeed you were concentrating in class ...

When you're presented with a claim, you also need to interrogate the data upon which it is based.

In particular you want to consider whether the data has been chosen specifically to support a particular position, be it political, economic or moral. In other words, has the data been cherry-picked?

This is something politicians are prone to do with numbers in order to reinforce their argument and damn their opponents. Take just one of the claims made by Mitt Romney in the run-up to the 2012 US presidential election. Romney suggested that President Obama had allowed petrol prices to rise uncontrolled: "When the president took office, the price of gasoline here in Nassau County was about $1.86 a gallon. Now it's $4 a gallon," Romney said during one of the presidential debates.[42]

But was this implication that Obama was responsible for the gas-price hike fair? Did it provide a balanced picture of what accounted for the rise in gas prices in recent years?

Now that we're switched on to the dangers of reaching the wrong conclusions based on erroneous assumptions, it's easy to come up with alternative reasons for why the price may have shot up, regardless of who was in office. It could have been down to a number of factors including the Arab Spring, and sanctions against Iran, to name just a couple of possibilities. Arguably, putting the blame directly on Obama was unfair.

But even if these global conditions had not played a part, Romney's statement was unfair for another reason too. If you look at how consumer petrol prices have risen this century you would on the whole see an upward trend. Obama's inauguration on 20 January 2009 happened to coincide with a sudden and extreme drop in the price of oil – probably an early effect of the economic crisis, as over-leveraged investors became worried about the prospects of a worldwide slowdown and rapidly liquidated their assets.[43] A few months later the price of oil began to stabilise again as the initial panic subsided.

By picking an isolated and unusual moment in time to set as the benchmark for the price of gas, Romney was able to paint the picture that from the moment of Obama's inauguration it only went in one direction – sharply up.

The thing is that President Obama could have used the same technique as Romney to suggest that he had actually *lowered* gas prices while in office, if he too had cherry-picked his dates.

On 7 July 2008, only four months before Obama's election and just before the collapse of Lehman Brothers, the average US gasoline price was at a record high of $4.11 per gallon – around the figure Romney referred to in the debate to criticise Obama.[44] The world's demand for petroleum seemed to be increasing faster and faster, driven by oil-thirsty economic development in India and China.

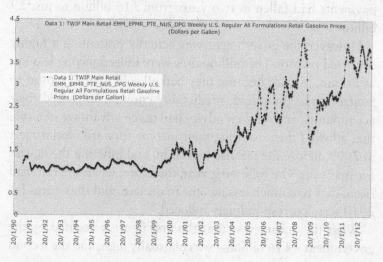

201

Compare this with four years later, on 9 July 2012, when the world was in a much less optimistic state, so gas was much cheaper at only $3.41 per gallon, and it would look as if Obama had presided over a drop in the price.

Unfortunately, Mitt Romney is not the only politician guilty of cherry-picking dates and numbers to suit his own purposes.

In March 2012 the UK's coalition government under David Cameron announced a tax cut for the rich – a hugely controversial move in the midst of a deep recession, at a time when government spending on the poor was being cut in the name of austerity.

In order to justify this tax cut, the government claimed that the tax rate in question – which had been raised just two years previously, in 2010 – had been so off-putting that many millionaires had left the country and were now paying no British tax at all. It pointed to a report that compared the tax years 2009–10 and 2010–11.[45] The implication was that the tax-rate rise had resulted in a net loss to the nation. The figures seemed to bear out this version of events: millionaires' tax payments had fallen in two years from £16 billion to just £9 billion.

However, the government was actually presenting a highly distorted picture. The millionaires were indeed paying less tax in Britain, but not because they had all sold up and moved to Switzerland. Many had, predictably enough, consulted their accountants, and on their advice had taken advantage of a rule that allowed them to bring their income forward, declaring it in 2009, before the tax rise kicked in, and inflating the figures for that year. The following year, therefore, when the rate had risen, they had much less income to declare, and the figures for 2010 were correspondingly reduced.[46]

What this meant was that the first figure presented by the government – £16 billion – was unusually high, and the second figure – £9 billion – was unusually low. HMRC, the government's own revenue department, made this clear to anyone who asked, adding that it was unlikely that any millionaires had left the country at all, and that tax receipts would soon return to normal, because this accounting tactic would only work once.[47]

Winnowing the data in this way created an unrepresentative picture that was used to support a political argument. Either the British government did not realise that its analysis of the data was deeply flawed, or it carried out an extraordinary deception to justify a tax cut for the rich when the less well-off were really struggling.

So remember, without proper context, numbers can be manipulated to mean very different things. Whether it's a politician or a marketer, a financial adviser or your sales department whose claims you are considering, make sure to *check the time span for the particular data set you have been presented with.*

Was there something untoward or unusual going on in this period – a spike, a temporary trend that may be distorting the picture? Or can you really take the numbers at face value?

Beware of Partisan Opinion Polls

It's not just dates that can be cherry-picked, of course. So too can any data that comes from a larger pool.

Take opinion polls. Partisan supporters will often seize on those which show their party or candidate ahead, and ignore those which show the opposite.

For example, look at these twelve national polls which were published on Monday, 5 November 2012, the day before the US presidential election:[48]

Monday's National Polls

Pollster	Monday Poll	Change from Prior Poll
American Research Group	tie	unchanged
Angus Reid	Obama +3.0	Obama +3.0
CVOTER / U.P.I.	Obama +1.0	unchanged
Democracy Corps	Obama +4.0	Obama +1.0
Gallup	Romney +1.0	Obama +4.0
Google Consumer Surveys	Obama +2.3	Obama +2.0
Ipsos / Reuters (online)	Obama +2.0	Obama +1.0
Monmouth U. / SurveyUSA	tie	Obama +3.0
Public Policy Polling	Obama +2.0	Obama +2.0
RAND Corporation	Obama +4.4	Obama +1.2
Rasmussen Reports	Romney +1.0	Romney +1.0
Wash. Post / ABC News	Obama +3.0	Obama +2.0
Average	Obama +1.6	Obama +1.5

On average, they showed Obama ahead by just under two points. But if an Obama supporter cherry-picked the best four polls for their candidate, they would show him nearly four points ahead on average. And if a Romney supporter chose his best four polls, they could claim that it was actually the Republican who was leading, by half a point.[49]

This is a pretty crude way of cherry-picking, although it is not beneath politicians and their teams to present data in this kind of way. But you can be more subtle. Rather than focusing on the three or four best polls for your candidate, you can instead *ignore* three or four of the worst ones.[50]

In this case, if you threw out four polls, your claim would seem more credible because it would be based on eight polls. An Obama supporter excluding the President's four worst polls could claim he was leading by about three points, making him the near-certain winner. Meanwhile, a Republican ignoring the worst four for Romney would say Obama's lead was less than one point – "a virtual tie."

Advertisers use a similar technique. We've all seen those testimonials for cosmetics that claim that "eight out of ten women prefer it" to rival products. But where did this number come from? Would it mean as much if you knew that it was taken from a pool of consumers who had *already* reported that they liked the product? And what about those before-and-after photos of women following cosmetic surgery that we've seen in magazine adverts? We might feel differently about them if we were more aware that the women had been chosen from a pool of those post-operative patients who actually did look good afterwards. Those who return to have their "work" improved never make it onto the glossy pages.

When you are given data to consider, you need to ask yourself what you are *not being shown* as well as what you are seeing. And why? If different available data was included, how would that affect your assessment?

Useless Data that Gets in the Way

At this point you may well be thinking that there is too much information out there to cope with already. It's an understandable feeling. Perhaps you feel that there is so much data that you can't see the wood for the trees.

More information isn't always useful if it's the wrong kind of data.

In the case of the US presidential election, national polls were often quoted to show how close the race was, but the only polls that really mattered were those in a few swing states, in which Obama had a fairly unassailable lead.[51] Time and again, the public was presented with information that was irrelevant when it came to predicting the likely winner.

So sometimes it is vital to remove extraneous information to help us get at the truth.

Scientists and engineers often refer to the need for a good "signal-to-noise ratio" – the useful information must be distinguishable from the useless. If someone throws too much data at you, you risk the noise drowning the signal out. Simply piling in vast quantities of irrelevant data will at best do nothing, and at worst can mask useful information.

When you are addressing a problem, you must consider what kind of information will be useful – on either side of the argument – and set out to capture as representative a picture as possible, warts and all.

Get your data set wrong – ignore key points, be overly tunnel-visioned, collect misleading data from too narrow or too wide a set, or simply look in the wrong place – eyes wide open *without* brain switched on – and you'll get a distorted result and end up making bad decisions.

Why Graphs Might Not Be Fair and Balanced

So, too much data can be a problem, too little data can be a problem, and cherry-picked data is also problematic. But these are not the only things to look out for – the way data is visually represented can lead you badly astray too.

Take a look at this graph of the FTSE 100 share index in 2012:[52]

What's the story? A big drop in spring, downward spikes again in July, August and November, and numerous peaks and valleys along the way. Seems like a really rocky year for investors. Now take a look at another graph:

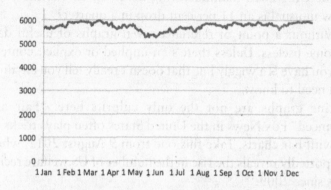

The data is exactly the same. But the story it tells is very different. Here what one sees is a slight drop in May, but not much change overall. From this graph it looks as if it was actually a pretty flat year for investors.

The trick here is one of the most common in graph-making. In the first case, the y axis (the vertical one) starts at 5,200; in the second, it starts at zero. The effect of starting the y axis at such a high number is to make small changes look big, and to make every tick up or down seem dramatic. So, how to avoid being fooled?

The most important rule is always to check the y axis. If it doesn't start at zero, try to imagine what the graph would look like if it did. Since axis-manipulation impairs your ability to judge the size of any changes just by looking at the graph itself, look at the numbers as well. In the first graph, you can see that while the drop from March to June looks huge, the numbers only change from just over 5,900 to just under 5,300: a little more than 11 per cent.

More than this, to really understand what the graph is telling you, you need to put it into some sort of context. How does this year compare to British share-price movements over a longer period? Or to stock-market movements elsewhere? Or to the UK's 2012 manufacturing data? Or to another year? How unusual is an 11 per cent drop in a quarter?

Without a point of reference, even graphs of useful data become useless. Unless there's an implied or explicit context, all you have is a wiggly line that doesn't really tell you anything you need to know.

Line graphs are not the only culprits here. "Fair and balanced" Fox News in the United States often plays tricks on us with bar charts. Take this one from 9 August 2012, which purportedly reveals the rise in the number of US welfare recipients since 2009:[53]

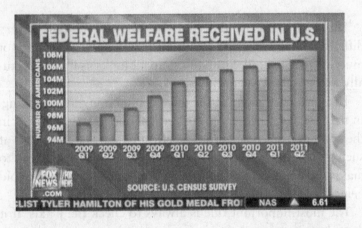

If you looked at the chart quickly – presumably it would only have been shown on screen for around five seconds – you would probably get the impression that the number of people on welfare shot up between 2009 and 2011, during Obama's first term. This is because the height of the bars – our visual cue – in this chart increases by over 300 per cent. It's that messing-with-the-y-axis ploy again. If the vertical axis had started at zero, instead of at ninety-four million, you would have a very different picture. It would then have been clear that the rise was only a little over 10 per cent, perhaps not unexpected given the dire economic conditions of this period, and the lag in impact of the financial crisis.

There's a secondary trick here too, which Fox News uses to compound the misleading effect of starting the y axis at ninety-four million, that you might not immediately have noticed: the numbers on the y axis do not match the horizontal lines. There are eight numbers on the y axis, marking every two million, but there are ten lines going across the graph, with smaller spaces between them. This makes it almost impossible to work out the actual numbers represented by the bars.

When you're looking at a chart or a graph, watch out for these kinds of y-axis deceits. If you spot this type of anomaly, there is a fair chance that the graph has been constructed with a particular bias in mind.

By now, you may not be surprised to learn that it's not just the y axis that can be manipulated to change the story a graph tells.

On 17 April 2011, the *Wall Street Journal* used a graph (see overleaf) in an editorial headlined "Where the Tax Money Is" to demonstrate that most taxable income in the United States comes from middle-earners.[54]

The story appears straightforward: the group paying the most tax is those earning between $100,000 and $200,000 per year – the well-off, but not extremely wealthy.

But look a bit closer. Why have the earners been grouped in this way? There is one group consisting of those earning $25–$30,000 (a $5,000 range), another of those earning $100–200,000 (a $100,000 range), and another of those earning $5–10 million (a $5 million range). The sample groups, being of different sizes, inevitably produce a distorted analysis.

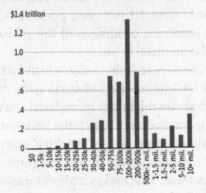

The Middle Class Tax Target

The amount of total taxable income for all filers by adjusted gross income level for 2008

To show how such decisions affect this graph's story, the news magazine *Mother Jones* created the same graph the following month, but grouped everyone earning $200,000 or more together.[55] Suddenly, with exactly the same data, you have a graph that could instead be used to support the claim that most taxable income comes from the United States' highest earners.

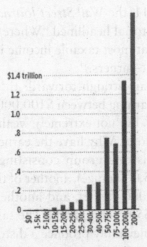

Depending on how data is sliced and diced, it can be used to tell very different stories.

These kinds of tricks are not, of course, confined to the heated worlds of partisan politics and newsrooms. Distorted graphs or charts can be presented to you in a whole host of circumstances, whether you are trying to analyse performance data in your work environment, assessing which financial products to invest your savings in, or attempting to make sense of the information you are being given in your daily newspaper.

A number of studies reveal examples of financial data being misrepresented by companies intent on promoting a very particular story in just the kind of ways we have seen – graphs' axes being used that are disproportionate to the underlying figures;[56] heights and widths of graphs being chosen with the express intention to distort;[57] bar charts being used rather than line graphs, because trends represented in that format look significantly more pronounced.[58] There are even cases of US banks having made loans on the basis of misleading graphs that provided more favourable impressions of a company's performance than was warranted.[59]

So, the next time you're presented with a graph, whether by your marketing department, chief finance officer, investment adviser or doctor, make sure to ask some basic questions.

Look carefully at the x and y axes. Ask yourself, if different choices had been made – if the y axis had started at zero, if the x-axis grouping was cut in another way – would the graph tell a different story? Is this bar chart trying to influence me in a particular way? And how would the information seem if it was presented in a different form altogether?

Yoghurt Drinks, and How Numbers Get Manufactured

We've looked at the need to contextualise figures, warned of cherry-picking and commonly used methods to distort how data is represented. We've also looked at the difficulties involved in understanding probabilities and risk.

But when you're presented with data, there is another set of factors you need to take into account if you are going to end up making a smart decision. Make sure to ask yourself how the numbers were generated. What was the methodology that underpinned them? And how does it relate to the claims being made?

Take Danone's 2009 claim that "seventeen clinical studies on over 3,000 people" had shown that the company's probiotic drink, Actimel, was "scientifically proven to help support your kids' defences."[60] A claim that it advertised across print, television and the internet. It even published links to the studies on its website.

This claim would make you think that if you want to keep your children healthy you should definitely buy Actimel, right? Indeed, since the mid-1990s, yoghurt drinks containing "beneficial" bacteria have led the so-called "functional foods" market, capitalising on our increasing demand for healthier food products. They are set to be worth £180 billion in 2013.[61]

But following a complaint, the UK's Advertising Standards Authority investigated the TV ad. It emerged that all of Danone's studies were carried out on very particular groups of children – either on babies under the age of two, whose immune systems hadn't yet fully developed, or on hospitalised children in India who were receiving treatment for diarrhoea and gastritis.[62]

This means that the company's claims were valid only for small babies and seriously sick children. From these studies we have no idea whether Actimel would help a healthy child stay well.

Nestlé and Coca-Cola used a similar statistical ploy when they jointly marketed Enviga, a green-tea-based energy drink that "burned calories" and sped up your metabolism. But again, who made up the sample they studied to support these claims? In this case only young, relatively thin people who consumed at least three cans a day – and they were only studied for three days.[63] Coke and Nestlé were ordered by a US court to stop their generalised weight-loss claims.[64]

Both of these cases are examples of what is known as "sample bias." The sample being studied is not representative of the group of people the claims are subsequently made for. Sample bias is a potential problem whenever you're considering generalisations based on partial data. Remember how representativeness was also a big problem when we were looking at the inferences we could draw from Twitter data?

When It Comes to Medicines, Women May Be from Venus

Beyond the supermarket and social media, we should be just as wary of methodological errors.

You've probably read that if you're middle-aged and want to cut your risk of heart attack, you should take an aspirin a day.[65]

You might even already be doing so.

But if you are female, did you know that the research that underpins this study was carried out on men, not women? And did you know that men and women typically metabolise many drugs differently? Women metabolise some antidepressants, for example, slower than men, and certain epilepsy, asthma and anti-inflammatory medications faster.

Indeed, when the effect on women of taking aspirin every day was actually studied, it turned out that, unlike men, before the age of sixty-five women got no benefit at all.[66] Yet female takers were bearing the downside risks of daily aspirin use, which include stomach inflammation, stomach ulcers and bowel irritation.

Such differences can even prove fatal. Seldane, an antihistamine, was withdrawn from sale after a number of young women who were taking it died unexpectedly because of a previously unknown gender difference in response to it.[67]

It's not just women who may be being prescribed drugs on the basis of research that isn't applicable to them, and whose health is thereby being jeopardised.

As drug-trial costs increase, we're seeing a dramatic increase in the "outsourcing" of clinical trials to poorer parts of the world, including countries in Africa and Asia.[68] This is despite the fact that your ethnic make-up is a factor that affects how you metabolise drugs. The way your body transports, targets and responds to drugs is determined by enzymes that may vary dramatically depending on your genetic background.[69]

So, a drug that is tested in Lagos may have a very different outcome on a patient in Las Vegas or Leeds.

If you are given the details of a study on which to base a personal decision, whether at the doctor's surgery or the supermarket, the first thing to check is whether the study was carried out on people similar enough to you.

Whom Did You Ask? The Dangers of Self-Selection Bias

Staying with research methodology a little longer, let's turn to surveys. For these can be as misleading as those dodgy bar charts with their manipulated axes.

We could all fill out hundreds of surveys a day, from online opinion polls to customer satisfaction questionnaires. But we don't. Typically, we choose to engage only on topics that we care about.

So, if it's survey data you're confronted with, the first thing to ask is, who filled it in? And why?

Take the survey results published as a headline by the *Observer* in February 2012, as debate raged around health-care reforms: "Nine out of 10 Members of Royal College of Physicians [RCP, the body that represents over 27,000 doctors and administrators] Oppose NHS Bill." The evidence of this poll seemed damning, and it undoubtedly had the potential to influence the newspapers' readers, and perhaps even government opinion. The article continued: "92.5 per cent of RCP members want the health and social care bill withdrawn" – an apparently devastating rejection of the government's reforms.

However, this particular statistic was based on an online survey organised by a group of activist doctors, formed with the express purpose of opposing the legislation.[70] The survey was only circulated among a very particular group – doctors on their contact list, and visitors to their blog: in other words, those who were already likely to object to the planned legislation.

An obvious bias. Moreover, as no proof of membership of the RCP, or indeed any identification, was required, it would have been possible for anyone to fill out the survey multiple times, and thus further distort the results.[71]

Did this survey's questionable methodology matter? It sure did. If we compare its results with those of another carried out the next month by the Royal College of Physicians itself, the impact is very clear. This later, official, survey posed an almost identical question to that posed by the activist doctors. Yet now only 49 per cent of respondents said that the RCP should "seek withdrawal of the Bill."[72] Two surveys in rapid succession, asking the same question, but with radically different outcomes.

With polls and surveys, methodology is crucial.

Even if a study is carefully and scientifically prepared, there is no guarantee that respondents will always tell the truth. One of the most famous polling effects observed in surveying is the so-called "Bradley Effect." This phenomenon was named after Tom Bradley, the black Mayor of Los Angeles and Democrat candidate for the governorship of California in 1982. He appeared to be leading the race by a considerable margin, even in exit polls on election day itself, only to find that he narrowly lost. Fewer white electors were found to have voted for him than had claimed to do so in polls.

In this case the problem wasn't one of survey design. The data was flawed because the respondents, wanting to appear in a more positive light to their questioner, did not answer truthfully. A proportion of white Californian voters did not reveal their true intentions because they didn't want to seem racist.[73] Similarly, studies reveal that men underplay their fear of crime in surveys because of social pressure to look tough.[74]

This is a reason why the listening-in opportunities we discussed in earlier chapters are so exciting: they enable us to get away from such biases, and hear what people really think, directly and in the raw – while recognising of course the potential online herding effect.

So, if poll or survey results are involved in your decision-making, the lesson to take away from this section is this – not only make sure you know how the survey was conducted and who the sample group actually were, but also reflect upon whether the questions asked are likely to prompt a particular response over another, for reasons of social or other pressure.

Takeaways

At a time when we increasingly have to behave as information-gatherers and fact-checkers ourselves, when traditional experts cannot be counted upon to translate the world for us accurately, when those trying to sell us ideas or products are ever more manipulative with the tools available – it is critical that we ditch any feelings of math anxiety and become much more number-savvy and confident.

For how can we properly respond to what a doctor advises us, unless we properly understand probability and risk?

Or to what a financial adviser recommends, unless we understand the ways in which data can be visualised?

How can we properly assess advertising, if we don't know the basics of sampling and survey design?

Or the claims of politicians, if we lack the math skills to check their stories?

We can't.

If we leave it to others to interpret the world for us, we do so at our own peril.

To be better informed for decision-making is therefore partly about getting better at analysing what it is we are being told by other people, about getting better at evaluating and interrogating research, charts and numbers.

But, as ever, there's more to do if we are to become wiser.

To make smart decisions we also need to understand something else – ourselves. Making wise choices isn't just about gathering the right information and interrogating it properly. Nor is it simply about being aware of how easily others can steer us in directions that serve their interests, and putting in place measures to avoid their manipulations. Nor is it just about freeing up sufficient time and space to think. Or about having the confidence to challenge the certainties of experts and seek out insights from unusual sources. Although these are all essential steps to take, there's still more to consider. As we'll see in the next chapter, our moods, our emotions, our physical states – whether we're tired, or hungry, or just plain horny – also have a major impact on the choices we make.

QUICK TIPS FOR OVERCOMING YOUR MATH ANXIETY

- **Don't succumb to math anxiety.** You *can* become more number literate.

- **Before you act on numbers you've been presented with, ask yourself some key questions.** Does whoever's presenting them to you have a particular agenda? If so, are the numbers being spun in a particular way? If you're unsure, go back to the original source. If it's a graph you're presented with, are any common data-visualisation distortions being used? Check to see if the y axis starts at zero. Look at how things are grouped on the x axis. Then ask yourself, how might the data come across if different visual-representation choices had been made?

- **Put the number before you into its appropriate context.** Think about what it's expressing; think about how it compares or relates to what else you know. Even a very large number that initially seems shocking can actually prove rather mundane when it's put into its proper context.

- **Check to see if the data you're being presented with has been cherry-picked – sliced and diced in a particular way so as to make a particular point.** Things to look out for include carefully selected time frames – is there something untoward or unusual going on in that period that may be distorting the picture? Also be mindful of carefully picked subsets of data – are you only being shown polls that favour a particular politician's chances, say, or the testimonies of consumers who only have something positive to report?

- **Whenever you're given data to consider, think about what you might not be being shown, and why.** What additional data might you want to seek out so you can be sure you have a fully representative picture?

- **Before you take a claim (such as the effectiveness or the side-effects of a drug) based on the results of a study as gospel, make sure that the study was conducted on the same kind of people the claims are being made for.** If not, it may not be valid. Remember how Danone made a claim about the effectiveness of probiotics on *all* children, based on research conducted partly on sick children in India. Think too about how many drugs are only tested on men, despite the fact that men and women metabolise many drugs very differently, and so may have very different reactions to the same drug.

- **Think about the explanation you're being provided with for why a particular statistic or numerical reading is relevant.** Are there alternative explanations for why it could hold?

- **Before you act on the basis of survey data, think about the following:** who is likely to have responded, and might they have a particular agenda? How likely is it that respondents are answering truthfully? How representative is the group that was polled?

- **When you are presented with an estimate of risk, before you factor it in, check whether it's an estimate of absolute risk – i.e. a 1 per cent chance that you will have a heart attack – or an estimate of relative risk – i.e. a 30 per cent decrease in your chance of experiencing a heart attack.** Remember that if it's relative risk you're presented with, you need to know your baseline risk (in this case your risk of getting a heart attack) before you can determine how significant a decrease (or increase) in risk would be.

- **Don't assume that your doctor understands what positive test results mean.** As we've seen, they often significantly overestimate the probability that a positive result means you actually have the disease in question. To understand your real odds you need to know both the accuracy of the test and the baseline risk you should be relating it to. Also remember that you need to establish the odds of whether someone who tests positive actually has the disease, not whether someone with the disease will test positive. They are not the same thing.

STEP NINE

Monitor Your Emotional Thermostat

A Hero Called Leigh Pitt

Leigh Pitt, Reprographic operator, Aged 30, Saved a drowning boy from the canal at Thamesmead, but sadly was unable to save himself. June 7 2007.

These few modest words are found upon the Memorial to Heroic Self-Sacrifice in Postman's Park, near St. Paul's Cathedral in the City of London. Built on the site of a former burial ground, the wall is covered with beautifully decorated tiles in blue, green and white – each remembering someone who sacrificed their own life to save another.

Leigh Pitt's memorial is the most recent. He jumped into the canal near his home after seeing a nine-year-old struggling in the water, and managed to keep the boy afloat while rescuers used a hosepipe to winch him to safety from above. Unfortunately, the 4.5-metre-high canal walls had no bars, or anything else to hold on to. By the time someone jumped in to save Leigh, it was too late.

This is just one of the many stories of selfless heroism immortalised in these moving ceramics.

What is it that makes people defy the human instinct for self-preservation? In non-emergency circumstances, we would not decide to run into a burning building, or throw ourselves in the path of an oncoming train. Yet add emotion, stress and the desperation of a fellow human being into the mix, and the decisions people make can be truly astonishing, belying a whole host of unconscious variables that underpin our decision-making – variables that we began to touch upon in the first three Steps.

The Thing about Fear – from Spiders to Skin Excisions

Reflect, for just a moment, on past instances of acute stress. We've all been there. For some it will be triggered by speaking in public, for others by rumours of a round of redundancies, or by a full-blown media crisis on their watch. In some cases it might simply be a spider in the bath.

I'm sure you've experienced the sensation: heart thumping loud in your ears, sweaty palms, a quickening of the breath and goosebumps prickling down your arms. Each of these is a sign that your body is on high alert, and preparing you either to fight or to run for your life.

Although the intensity of fear may vary – a spider in the bath is hardly the same as one of your ancestors coming face to face with a hungry lion – the chemical chain reaction both events set off hasn't changed a bit.

What has changed is the *kind* of frightening and stressful situations modern humans come up against. This mismatch between what our fight-or-flight system evolved for and what it now faces can lead to catastrophic decision-making.

But before we get to that, let's look a bit closer at that spider.

Having just stepped into the shower, you turn around to see a huge, hairy specimen scurrying towards your bare and unprotected toes. It makes you shriek with surprise and leap towards the shower hose, your nearest weapon. As this bathroom drama is unfolding on the outside, there's a whole lot more going on inside your body.[1] Adrenaline and cortisol, the two most important stress hormones, are released from the adrenal glands that sit on top of the kidneys. Adrenaline is the first to take effect, quickly flooding the system and triggering many of the tell-tale signs of fear, shock and stress, such as an increased heart rate and dilated pupils.[2]

The second hormone, cortisol, is released more slowly, but it has its own important role. It tells the liver to release glucose into the bloodstream, so the body has fuel if it needs to run.

And the cortisol does something else too: it sharpens our attention.[3] In video-game simulations in which US police officers were tested to see whether they were able to correctly distinguish between a suspect carrying a revolver or a mobile phone, officers who had been exposed to an acutely stressful experience just prior to playing the game made more accurate calls than when they were tested in a stress-free state. Similarly, trainee surgeons recalled the steps needed to perform tracheotomies and skin excisions better when they were taking an exam than either prior to or after it.[4]

So, while adrenaline makes your heart beat faster, cortisol helps us ignore everything that is perceived as non-critical. It enables us to become more vigilant, alert and accurate, and helps concentrate our attention on the job in hand.[5] It also acts as adrenaline's break, slowing down its production, thereby enabling us to maintain control and avoid panic.[6]

Hurrah for cortisol – nature's little helper.

Not so fast …

Although it may be useful if you're taking an exam, giving a presentation or confronting a criminal to have a jolt of cortisol-fuelled focus, acute stress can also really mess up your decision-making.

This is because when we're in an anxious or acutely stressed state we are more likely to succumb to many of the thinking errors we've considered in previous Steps. We're more likely to anchor our thinking on inappropriate numbers, fail to contemplate alternative courses of action, and more prone to default to what is familiar and habitual. That's not always a bad thing. It's why pilots, astronauts and soldiers are drilled so hard on procedure – so that in times of stress their life-saving actions come naturally, and require minimal cognitive effort.

The trouble is that for many of us the familiar patterns we default to when under severe stress can be caricatured and prejudiced.[7]

Take doctors. Studies show that in situations of acute stress, such as when responding to an emergency call from a patient with chest pain, doctors tend to evaluate Hispanic or black patients as much less likely to have coronary heart disease or angina than Caucasian ones, and are less likely to refer non-Caucasians to see a heart specialist.[8] This despite the fact that Hispanics and blacks are at *higher* risk of cardiovascular disease than Caucasians.[9] Judges, when stressed, have also been found to tend to revert to their unconscious biases. So, if you have a Hispanic-sounding name, say, beware going before a judge with an overly heavy caseload – if she's got a general predisposition to racial stereotyping, the chances are that you'll receive a harsher sentence because she's stressed.[10]

It's not just acutely stressful situations that can skew our decision-making. The day-to-day, ongoing stress that many of us increasingly feel nowadays can be just as influential. Chronic stress can lead to excessive tunnel vision, which we've already seen is bad news for decision-making. It can also generate all-consuming self-doubt, and inordinate focus on negative thoughts – both of which can also powerfully impair our decision-making performance in both our professional and personal lives.[11]

Lessons from Hollywood and the White House

This doesn't mean that you should give up your job if it is high-pressured. Many of us find that these kinds of jobs are also stimulating and rewarding, and help define our sense of identity. But it does suggest that we need to be more aware of our stress levels, and how to manage them through techniques like exercise and meditation. We also need to give time and thought to whether any of our environmental stressors can actually be removed.

A good example is the basics of the space where you work. Is it adding to your stress? We established in Step One that our working environment can ramp up stress levels. But did you know that if you work in an open-plan office the constant hum of noise and the continuous fear of interruption are likely to cause your adrenaline levels to rise?[12]

If your workplace has fluorescent lighting – bad luck. That too may well be adding to your stress.[13] And as for the constant drip, drip, drip of information – the phone calls, texts, emails, tweets that incessantly ping and ring, and the consequent out-of-control feeling you're probably all too familiar with ... the state of continuous disruption we referred to earlier in the book? You've got it – very stress-inducing, too.[14]

So, is there a door you can close if you have a significant decision to make? How about convincing your boss to pay for a set of noise-reducing headphones?

Can you unplug from the digital stream for at least a beat, so that you can think clearly about one thing at a time? Once more I'm highlighting the value of taking a pause.

Can you go for a walk, even? Preferably in a park, where you can breathe in some fresh air and feel closer to nature. Actively distancing yourself from the kind of urban environmental stressors we are surrounded by in typical work spaces will improve your decision-making and also your productivity.[15] Such simple steps can really make a difference.

You should also ask yourself whether you have taken on too much. Can you reduce the number of demands being made of you? Too many people coming to you for advice or answers at one time can be very stressful, and can thereby impact on the quality of the decisions you make.[16]

Legendary Hollywood film producer Dick Zanuck told me over lunch that one of the main things he did for both Tim Burton and Steven Spielberg was to help them "shut everything off."

I said to Steven [Spielberg] when he was twenty-three [Zanuck produced both The Sugarland Express, *Spielberg's first feature film, and* Jaws],"I want you to concentrate on how we're going to make this goddam picture; how are we going to do it? And I don't want you thinking about returning a telephone call. I will return a telephone call. I will deal with the agencies, I will deal with the whiney actors and all of the interruptions. I am your bodyguard."*

You may not have a multiple-Oscar-winning movie producer to hand to act as a gatekeeper for you, but is there someone you can deploy to take on some of your less pressing responsibilities at moments when you have a really important decision to make? Trusting other people to support you will not only lighten your workload, it will also give you the time and space to focus on the things that really make a difference.

If this is just not possible, can you remove some distractions yourself, so that you are better able to focus on what matters, and less likely to be affected by stress?

President Barack Obama takes this question to an extreme that the fashion-conscious among us may feel is just a step too far.

Obama has talked about the ways in which he tries to "pare down decisions." He explains: "You'll see I wear only grey or blue suits ... I don't want to make decisions about what I'm eating or wearing ... You can't be going through the day distracted by trivia."[17]

And he's right – if you've got big decisions to make, you can't allow your attention to be consumed by inconsequential details. Small and irrelevant things can be incredibly distracting and mentally exhausting, and can tip you over the edge of your stress limits.

So, ask yourself whether what is consuming your attention is actually necessary, or whether it falls into the category of trivia or irrelevance. What could you delegate? What could you ignore or get rid of entirely?

Feelings and Decisions – Why Being Happy May Be a Bad Thing

When it comes to distorting our decisions, stress is of course not the only culprit. Our moods and emotions more generally have this effect on us too. People leave bigger tips – regardless of the level of service – when the weather is sunny, because they're in a better mood. When a national football team loses in a country mad about the sport, its stock market typically plunges because investors are feeling gloomy.[18] Whilst the extent to which you trust a colleague, it turns out, depends less on their qualities and more on how it is you are currently feeling.[19]

In a crowded north-eastern American railway station, using the promise of candy bars to tempt in 120 volunteers, Jennifer Dunn and Maurice Schweitzer from the University of Pennsylvania set out to test how people's responses are affected by their mood. They asked forty people to list three to five things that made them angry. They were then asked to provide an in-depth account of a time in their life when they felt angrier than ever before. The other eighty volunteers were asked to write about either a happy or a sad memory instead. What Dunn and Schweitzer were angling for was to really stoke the participants' emotions. But this was just a prelude to the next task.

The volunteers had been asked to name a colleague or acquaintance at the start of the experiment. Now they were asked to rate how highly they would trust them, on a scale of 1 to 7, to pay back a $40 loan. They were also asked how they would feel if the colleague complimented them on a new haircut. Would they trust their comments to be genuine?

Ten questions later, the results were clear. People who had written about a happy memory were significantly more likely to be trusting than those who had conjured up sad thoughts, and the angry group were the least trusting of all. The volunteers' emotions, although completely unrelated to the trust task, were colouring their judgement.[20]

Our feelings, then, can distort our ability to make good decisions – if you've ever pressed "send" on an email in anger, I'm sure you've subsequently regretted it – but at the same time we actually need our emotions to help us make choices. Indeed, *without* emotions, we wouldn't be able to make any decisions at all.

The Trouble with Elliot

Dr. Antonio Damasio, a neurologist at the University of Southern California's Brain and Creativity Institute, has carried out research on patients with damage to their prefrontal cortex, a part of the brain that we use for everyday decision-making. One such patient was "Elliot."[21]

After reaching his thirties, businessman Elliot began to suffer from crippling headaches. The cause turned out to be a brain tumour just behind his eye socket, in a specific part of the prefrontal cortex known as the ventro-medial prefrontal cortex. This area is thought to be the interface between emotion and decision-making, with strong connections being made between it and one of the centres of human emotion in the brain, the amygdala.

Although the tumour was successfully removed, the surgeons were unable to prevent damage to the prefrontal cortex. It was now that Elliot's life began to unravel. Once he was back at his job, his previously excellent performance went into free-fall. He got fired. He secured a new job, but was fired again. His family life also fell apart: he and his wife divorced, and he subsequently remarried. His bride of choice was a prostitute. Suffice to say this second marriage was very short-lived.[22] By the time Elliot met Dr. Damasio he was living with his brother, unable to hold down a job or look after himself.

Despite this, Elliot's intellectual ability showed no signs of impairment at all. His IQ remained above average, and he was able to complete a battery of cognitive tests with normal or above normal scores. When asked, for example, "If you broke your wife's favourite vase, how could you prevent her from becoming angry?," he made a credible suggestion, and provided a valid justification for why he had chosen it. And when he was then asked, "What else could you do?," he was able to provide a normal number of suggestions, with valid justifications for why he had chosen them.

However, what Dr. Damasio soon realised was that Elliot was incapable of choosing between his various suggestions. At the end of the experiment he wailed, "And after all this, I still wouldn't know what to do!" Further examination revealed what Damasio had already suspected – that Elliot had been rendered unable to feel emotion. Even the most gruesome pictures of accidents and disasters failed to elicit any response. Here was a man with a perfect ability to reason, but who could not feel at all.[23]

We do need feelings, it turns out, to make decisions. For our rational, conscious decision-making is guided by our internal emotional cues.

Because Elliot's brain damage prevented him from bringing emotion into the mix when given different options to choose from, none of the solutions to the broken vase problem resonated with him. Devoid of an emotional compass or satnav, he was left unable to choose between them.

More recent studies of brain-damaged patients who are unable to experience emotions confirm that they too make very bad decision-makers, even if their other cognitive functions, such as IQ, work perfectly. Like Elliot, without any emotional cues these patients proved mentally paralysed, unable to choose one path over another.[24]

So, the journey to becoming a smarter decision-maker does not involve forcing our emotions out of the picture. But given that our emotional compass can, as we've already seen, lead us astray, is there a way to manage our emotions so they don't impair our decision-making?

How Self-Aware Are You?

Step forward US researchers Myeong-Gu Seo and Lisa Feldman Barrett. They wanted to try to answer this very question, and designed an online stock-investment simulation to do so.[25] Participants were given $10,000 to invest in any of twelve anonymous stocks selected from the US stock market, and had a daily opportunity to buy or sell their shares. Just before making their decisions, they were asked to make a detailed record of their emotions. After twenty days the aim of the game was to make the highest profit, with the added incentive of being able to take home between $100 and $1,000 in actual money, depending on their performance.

So who did best? Not the participants with the most muted emotions, but those who were most self-aware, and therefore best able to *identify* their emotions and their potential biases. These subjects made significantly better investment choices than the others.

What Seo and Barrett discovered was that one of the most important considerations when it comes to making decisions is whether you recognise and respond to whatever emotion you are feeling. It's about being able to introspect, to think, "OK, waiting for these hospital test results is making me feel pretty nervous today. This could make me unintentionally cautious. I must bear that in mind."

It seems too good to be true that merely acknowledging your emotions could make you a better decision-maker, but a number of other studies also suggest that this is indeed the case.[26]

It turns out that when someone is unaware of their underlying emotions, they tend to make decisions that support that emotion. So, for example, if someone is happy, they are more likely to be lenient, or – as we saw in the railway station experiment – trusting in their behaviour. However, when a person is aware of their emotions, through thinking or writing about them, or if someone else points them out to them, they automatically start to compensate, thereby returning to the more calibrated or balanced state that we should ideally be in when we make decisions.

Think of it as a kind of mood-management system.

Researchers have repeatedly been able to demonstrate that people who start out in a negative frame of mind, and are then asked to think about that negativity, spontaneously start behaving more positively over time. The reverse is also true. It's not the case that happy people suddenly became depressed – more that being aware of our emotions tends to move us towards the middle ground, the equilibrium of feeling at which we are more likely to make good decisions. Just as our homes have a thermostat to keep the temperature within sensible limits, it seems that we have a similar system for our emotions.

So, how can we become more self-aware about our emotions and how they might be influencing us?

Well, one option for the future could be to buy a bracelet. Seriously.

A few years ago, electrical giant Philips developed a proto-type emotional reader called the "EmoBracelet." This chunky, futuristic-looking device is one half of what Philips and its collaborators, Dutch bank ABN AMRO, are calling a "Rationalizer." Targeted at the investor working from home, but presumably suitable for anyone else too, the idea is pretty simple: you snap the bracelet onto your wrist and it silently monitors your "arousal component," which is techno-speak for keeping track of the non-perceptible amounts of moisture on your skin that stem from being emotionally aroused.[27] It then displays its findings in real time via a "dynamic light pattern" on the bracelet itself or its twin component, the "EmoBowl," which looks a bit like the interior of a flying saucer. The more emotionally "aroused" you become, the more moisture is detected on your skin, and the more jazzy and zippy the light show on the bracelet or bowl becomes, going from soft yellow to orange, and right up to red. When the lights are red and are moving quickly, that's when you're most emotional – so that's when it's time to take a breather from making any big decisions, and to note how it is you're feeling.

But until this bracelet is properly trialled and comes to market – we're told to expect a product utilising some of the technology "a few years from now"[28] – what should we do?

It's time to get all Zen ...

Omm

Imagine this scenario. A family member has won the lottery. They offer you a small portion of their winnings. Would you accept?

It turns out that how people answer this question depends on what percentage of their winnings their relative has offered. If they offered you above 30 per cent, the vast majority of us – 95 per cent – would say yes. But if only offered 5 per cent, say, most of us would refuse to take it; in fact only a little over a quarter would accept the offer.

Why the difference? Because our emotions have come forcefully into play. We feel angry that our relative is being mean, sharing so little with us. So we cut our nose off to spite our face. Of course, even if your sister won a million pounds and only offered you a hundred, you'd still be financially better off taking the cash than rejecting it.

Ulrich Kirk, a bespectacled professor from Virginia Tech who arrived at neuroscience via literature and aesthetics, was interested in finding out whether a particular group of people would respond any differently.

So he posed the hypothetical "Would you accept 5 per cent of her winnings?" question to a group of Buddhist monks, and scanned their brains as they were making their decisions. What he saw was fascinating. Unlike regular folk, when the monks were confronted with the decision, their brains went into introspection mode. He could see this on the fMRI scan, which revealed increased activity in their posterior insula, the part of our brain that, among other things, notes how our bodies feel.[29]

The monks' training in "mindfulness" – the concept that we should continuously note, but not judge, our emotions – meant that their mood-management thermostat was second nature.

It's as if, when confronted with negative emotions, they immediately noted them, and therefore calibrated for them, thereby balancing their emotions effectively in their decision-making.

This made a big difference to the monks' response to the 5 per cent offer. Almost twice as many monks accepted the offer than "regular" people.

You don't have to be a Buddhist monk, able to meditate for hours at a time, to reap the benefits of mindfulness and a well-calibrated emotional thermostat. A 2011 study in *Psychiatry Research: Neuroimaging* revealed that even novice meditaters showed an increase in grey-matter concentration in the part of our brains that regulates emotion.[30]

In an age of downloadable mobile-phone apps, we can all access "guided meditations" that allow us to escape from our immediate surroundings, and check in with how we are feeling, even if only for five minutes. However busy we think we are, we can all find a few minutes a day if we really want to.

Learning to spot, label and understand our emotions is vitally important in decision-making. It enables us to detach ourselves from our feelings, to separate those that may bias or distort a decision from those that are essential to getting it right.

Conversely, being unable to identify our emotions and calibrate them makes it much harder to make good decisions. In the Seo and Barrett stock-market experiment, people without these skills made significantly lower profits.[31]

If you're reading this and thinking that you need to improve your emotional self-awareness, but are not ready to commit to a regular meditation practice, there is something simpler and even less time-hungry that you can try.

Seo and Barrett recommend that people carry out regular self-audits at the point of making a decision. Literally ask yourself how you're feeling – and try to be specific. Don't use general terms such as "I feel down," but instead think about exactly which emotions are at play. Is it sadness, desperation, nervousness, calm, boredom? What is causing it?

Answering these questions is the first step to being able to remove the potential bias caused by how you are feeling. Just by noting your emotions, your inner emotional thermostat will do the rest.

What We Can Learn from Victoria's Secret Models and Fizzy Drinks

Of course, some emotions are easier to identify or control than others. Take our deep-rooted "animal" emotions – physical sensations such as hunger, thirst, pain, craving and sexual desire.[32] What impact do they have?

Much of the research into these kinds of visceral emotions has focused on the way they drive people to find solutions that ease their discomfort – be it food if you're hungry, or a glass of water if you're thirsty. But what is often overlooked is the way they can very substantially affect our decision-making, in a much broader way that goes beyond our immediate animal needs.

Take what happened when a group of male undergraduate students were shown either "neutral" images of rocks, trees and other objects, or "hot" images of lingerie-clad Victoria's Secret models, and were then asked to assess how happy they would feel if they were given $100 in cash immediately.

Both groups said they would be pretty happy.

They were then asked a slightly different question: how would they feel if they had to wait a month for the $100? This time there was a clear difference. The "hot" group were now far more dismissive of the gift, and far more willing to dispense with it, than the group who had been looking at pictures of rocks.

It's as if when we're a bit hot under the collar and want to feel sated in a visceral sense, these feelings spill over to our wider decisions – we want it, and we want it now.[33]

Indeed, waiting is something we become progressively worse at when our bodies are crying out for some kind of sustenance, whether to satiate our lust or, more innocently, hunger.

This was highlighted when X.T. Wang and Robert Dvorak at the University of South Dakota looked into how even very mild hunger might affect people's financial decisions.

Using a somewhat unusual research tool of choice, fizzy drinks, the researchers started by asking their volunteers to come to the experiment having not eaten for at least three hours. After their blood sugar had been tested and recorded, the volunteers were offered various sums of money. The choices, as in the Victoria's Secret study, involved either a small amount of money soon ($90 tomorrow) or a much larger amount in the future ($570 in 939 days' time). The rational choice, of course, would be to take the larger amount at the more distant date.

Halfway through the experiment, the volunteers had a break and were asked to drink a can of cola: half the group were given a full-sugar version, the other half a sugar-free diet one. Neither group was told which they were given, nor the import of the drink to the task at hand. They then had their blood sugar tested again, and continued with the "Take the money now or later?" task.

What the researchers found was that those who had had the full-sugar drink tended to choose to wait for the larger sum of money, whereas those who had had the sugar-free diet version tended to prefer the more immediate but less valuable pay-off. In other words, low blood sugar made the participants more impulsive, and more likely to make the wrong investment choice. Another case of "I want it, and I want it now!"

It's not only financial decisions that you risk distorting if you haven't recently had a snack, or kept an eye on your blood sugar. Pilots are cautioned in numerous training manuals that hunger can impair their decisions. Hunger is identified as one of the key external stressors that can harm a surgeon's performance.

As for judges – who we have already seen can be flawed decision-makers – how does hunger affect them? Not too well, it turns out.[34]

In a recent study of parole decisions in Israel, the key factor that determined whether or not a judge granted parole was not the gender of the prisoner, their ethnicity, or even the severity of their crime, but *whether or not the judge had eaten recently*.

If a prisoner came before a judge whose blood sugar was low in advance of his ten o'clock mid-morning snack of a sandwich or piece of fruit, it was terrible timing. At such times the accused had hardly any chance of getting parole – pretty much 0 per cent. Immediately after the snack, their chances shot up to 65 per cent. Just before lunch was another dire time, with only a 10 per cent chance of parole. Just after lunch, their chances soared to 65 per cent once again.[35]

It's frightening to think that a decision about something as serious as a person's liberty can be profoundly affected by whether someone has had a piece of fruit or not, but this is a powerful example of how the way we feel on a very basic, visceral level can fundamentally impact the way we think and decide.

At the other end of the justice equation, it turns out that people arrested for a range of impulsive criminal actions, from domestic violence to destruction of property, from embezzlement or arson to public masturbation, often suffer from low blood sugar, or have poor glucose tolerance.[36] This isn't to say that eating a meal would have stopped their anti-social and criminal behaviour, but a lack of sugar in the brain may have played its part, especially in preventing them from undertaking the planning necessary *not to get caught*.[37]

You know the old adage, don't act on an empty stomach?

Well, don't.

When You Need to Go

Not all physical discomforts are bad for decision-making. Some can actually be of use to us when we have choices to make.

In a recent Dutch study, participants imbibed either a small amount of water or 700ml (over a pint). Forty-five minutes later, the second group understandably felt the urge to urinate. At this point they were given a similar conundrum to the cola drinkers and the Victoria's Secret model-gazers we met earlier in this chapter. They were given a choice between receiving sixteen euros the next day, or thirty euros over a month later. Surprisingly, the people who needed the toilet chose to wait for thirty euros – the rationally superior choice – more often than those who didn't need to excuse themselves.

Why didn't drinking lots of water and then needing the toilet encourage a quick fix, as it did with hunger or sexual arousal?

One interpretation is that it all comes down to the nature of the physical discomfort. When we're hungry or thirsty or sexually aroused, we feel a very strong need to eat, consume, be sated – the "I want it and I want it now" phenomenon – so we prefer the monetary reward today (even though it's considerably less). Needing to go to the bathroom but being unable to, on the other hand, makes us conscious that we're holding back and must control our impulses. This visceral feeling spills over into our decision-making, providing us with the mettle to wait and therefore receive the more valuable prize.

We Need to Take Sleep More Seriously

This Step isn't just about gorging or peeing or being sexually aroused. There's another physical state that affects our decision-making too.

Is it just coincidence that disastrous decisions relating to Three Mile Island, Chernobyl and the *Exxon Valdez* oil spill all happened in the early hours of the morning?[38] No, it's not. Investigations into these disasters found that sleep deprivation played a critical role in each. The Presidential Commission into the *Challenger* Space Shuttle disaster highlighted lack of sleep as a significant factor – key managers had been sleeping as little as two hours a night in the run-up to the launch.[39] More recently, it was revealed that the pilot of Air France Flight 447, which crashed in June 2009 killing all 228 people on board, had managed only an hour of sleep the night before.[40]

If you've ever pulled an all-nighter you'll know the symptoms of sleep deprivation all too well: difficulty concentrating, inability to think quickly and efficiently, memory lapses – it's as if you're on autopilot.[41] But did you know that if you go twenty-four hours without sleep, or spend a week sleeping only four or five hours a night, and you'll have given yourself a mental impairment akin to a blood-alcohol level of 0.1 per cent. To put that in context, you're legally over the limit to drive if your blood-alcohol level is 0.08 per cent.[42]

This is pretty worrying for any of us who work too hard, or burn the candle at both ends. Especially as in today's go-go-go world sleep deprivation is almost a badge of honour, and tiredness is tantamount to an admission not only of physical but also of mental weakness. Especially worrying is that this strange pride in sleep deprivation crops up time and again among the very people – doctors, CEOs, bankers, politicians – whose decisions can affect each and every one of us if they get them wrong.

Take doctors. When a group of orthopaedic surgical residents were tracked over a two-week period, it was found that when fatigued, they were 22 per cent more likely to make errors than when they were well rested.[43] And a study of 2,737 medical residents revealed that after working shifts of more than twenty-four hours, which in the US and many other countries is not uncommon, they were twice as likely to suffer a needlestick or other sharp injury (although this was still an infrequent occurence).[44] These are frightening statistics, yet it's still the case that the importance of sleep is not respected or recognised in many critical work environments, in the way that being sober or well-trained would be non-negotiable.

What's more, these overworked doctors were not only a threat to patients, but also to themselves: they had more than double the rate of accidents while driving after extended work shifts compared with non-extended shifts.[45]

This is partly because if you are overtired, your motor skills and memory become increasingly debilitated. But it's also down to something else going on in our brains.

Brain scans of people who have not had enough sleep reveal that the ventromedial prefrontal cortex – the part of our brain that not only serves as the interface between emotion and decision-making, but also relates to us overestimating our chances of success – is more active after losing a night's sleep, while the left anterior insula, a part of our brain that plays a key role in assessing risk, effectively switches off when we're overtired.[46]

So if our brain is sleep-deprived, we tend not to weigh up the pros and cons of a decision sensibly. Instead we become more impulsive and less measured, more likely to take unnecessary risks, and less likely to realise our decisions could end in disaster. We become prone to dangerous overconfidence.[47]

It's as if when we're overtired our measured voice of caution falls asleep, while the gung-ho, manic part of our personality stays wide awake.

By the way, don't think that a cup of strong coffee will return you to a state of equilibrium. It won't. Although a big dose of caffeine may help you to feel more alert and able to focus, studies in which sleep-deprived subjects are given caffeine reveal that it doesn't actually help us to appraise information any better, or to make decisions with any greater accuracy.[48]

Also, don't buy into the "I function perfectly well on four hours of sleep" myth. Seventy per cent of consultant surgeons think that "Even when fatigued, I perform effectively during critical times," for example. Yet sleep deprivation disrupts the decision-making part of the brain even in people who think they feel fine.[49]

In the medical sphere, a lack of sleep can obviously have life-threatening consequences, so this is something we should watch out for if we or our loved ones are in the care of doctors. Alongside a good bedside manner, it's perfectly legitimate to expect our clinicians to have had a good night's sleep. And to ask them whether they have.

More generally, the importance of sleep when it comes to good decisions makes the host of business and political leaders who claim to function on only a few hours of sleep look less macho and more short-sighted.

Remember 2012 US presidential candidate Mitt Romney? Back in 2008 he remarked to the *Wall Street Journal* that his New Year's resolution for 2009 was to "stop wearing a suit and tie to bed."[50] A self-professed workaholic, perhaps it was Romney's lack of sleep that led him to make so many disastrous gaffes during his campaign.

If you are sleep-deprived and liable to overlook the negative consequences of this, you may be more likely to question London's preparedness for the Olympic Games, call Iran's leaders "crazy people," or claim that 47 per cent of Americans pay no tax and are dependent on the state.[51] Interestingly, a campaign spokesperson declined to discuss Romney's sleep patterns on the record.[52]

This isn't a partisan issue. Democrats go crazy if sleep-deprived too.

President Clinton, in an interview with CNN's Anjali Rao late in 2008, confessed: "In my long political career, most of the mistakes I made, I made when I was too tired ... You make better decisions when you're not too tired. So that would be my only advice."[53]

It's no wonder then that staff at MI5 are told to make sure they get enough rest, even at times of huge national emergency. (I was told this by a spook so senior that were I to reveal his name he'd have to kill me.) Given the level of mental aptitude needed to quickly determine exactly what happened and what the next steps should be in such circumstances, sleep is explicitly recognised by the British intelligence services as a key factor for success.

Takeaways

We are not robotic decision-makers, dispassionately weighing various bits of information and coming to our choices in a purely logical fashion. We saw in earlier Steps how our pasts could steer us in particular directions, as could colours, words, touch and smell. Here we have seen that how we feel and our physical state have a profound impact on our decision-making too.

This is not necessarily a bad thing. Often our emotional steers help us from making disastrous decisions – fear can, after all, be a very useful warning signal, as our hunter-gatherer ancestors knew all too well.

Yet, unchecked, unacknowledged and uncontemplated, our emotions can lead us to make pretty bad choices. Especially as, in a world as complex as ours, our adaptive evolutionary feelings will not always prove either appropriate or intelligent.

The good news, as we've seen in this Step, is that there are positive measures we can take to ensure that our emotions and animal impulses do not rule us unwittingly. We can remove ourselves from extraneous stressors, close our doors, unplug, delegate non-essential matters to someone else. We can pare down the number of decisions we have to make, so as not to take on more than we can handle. We can note our emotions, and also take that proverbial beat before we respond.

Given how our physical state can massively affect the quality of our decision-making, when the stakes are high and we've got a big decision to make we should treat ourselves like Olympic athletes: get an early night, and eat slow-release carbohydrates to keep our glucose levels constant. If you are willing to put up with some discomfort, you might also want to wait before you empty your bladder!

Don't forget, though, that decision-making is often not a solo pursuit. Much of the time we make decisions alongside others – our colleagues, friends, team, family – or with their advice and input in mind.

So, if we are to make smart decisions it's not enough that we better understand ourselves, and how our wants, desires, feelings and experiences impact our decisions. We also need to understand how group dynamics and our social spheres affect our decision-making.

QUICK TIPS FOR MONITORING
YOUR EMOTIONAL THERMOSTAT

- **Don't let your blood sugar fall.** Eat regularly, and don't make big decisions on an empty stomach.

- **Try to get enough sleep before making important decisions.** If that's not possible – say you're in the midst of a crisis – make sure that at least some of your team or support system are properly rested, and bounce your sleep-addled thoughts off their fresh-thinking minds.

- **Note how you are feeling before you make a decision.** Are you stressed, happy, angry? Get better at this through meditation practice or carrying out self-audits.

- **When you can, wait before you act. Take that beat.** This isn't always going to be possible, but if you can at least pause, it can really pay off. If you've written an angry email, wait until the morning to send it. When you return to it in a calmer frame of mind, you may well make some changes.

- **If you know you're stressed, watch out that you're not falling back on innate and probably unconscious stereotypes or prejudices.** Ask yourself if you would be treating the person before you any differently if they were of the same gender or colour as you.

- **Seek to reduce workplace stressors.** Angle for your own office. If that's not possible, invest in noise-reducing headphones and identify a place at work where you can shut the door if you've an important decision to make.

- **Unplug when possible.** Step away from your computer and emails, even if only for a short time, so you can think clearly about the one key thing at hand.

- **Pare down your decisions.** What trivial decisions can you park or get someone else to deal with on your behalf?

- **Identify who can serve as your gatekeeper.** Who can help keep the demands on you at a more manageable level?

SHAKE THINGS UP

STEP TEN

Embrace Dissent and Encourage Difference

The Building Is on Fire

It is 1968. The Vietnam War is ongoing, Stanley Kubrick's *2001: A Space Odyssey* has just premiered, and Martin Luther King has been assassinated in Memphis.

In New York, a place of *Mad Men*-style ad agencies, rising skylines and late-night discos, two psychologists, Bibb Latané of Columbia University and John M. Darley of neighbouring NYU, invite a group of male students and professionals from Columbia University (women will not be admitted to study there for another fifteen years) to discuss "some of the problems involved in life at an urban university."[1]

When they arrive, the volunteers are directed to an interview room to fill out a preliminary survey. Some are sent into the room on their own, and some go in with two others who, unbeknownst to them, are actors.

As they finish filling out the first couple of pages of the questionnaire, puffs of white smoke start appearing from a wall vent in intermittent bursts. The smoke is made of titanium dioxide – the compound found in white fireworks and military weapons used to obscure parts of a battlefield.

Latané and Darley wanted to see how people's decisions would be influenced by others. When it appeared obvious that an emergency was taking place, what would it take for people to act decisively?

The subjects who were sent into the room alone acted pretty rationally. They got up, wandered over to the vent, checked the temperature of the smoke, sniffed at it, and generally tried to suss it out. Seventy-five per cent of them then reported it to the administrators, and left the room before the test was over. Those who were in the room with two actors responded very differently. The actors had been instructed to stare briefly at the smoke, shrug their shoulders, make no comment, and return to the questionnaire. They played their part admirably, wafting away the smoke with their papers so they could see the questions, and responding with "I dunno" to queries from the real participant when he asked what was going on.

Remarkably, in this scenario only one of the ten participants reported the smoke. The other nine sat there coughing and spluttering, rubbing their eyes to try to help them read the questions. A few got up to open the window, but only one of the ten actually left the room. Although something was clearly wrong, and their lives might even have been in danger, most of the participants conformed to the collective inaction.

We don't make decisions in isolation. Decision-making is not just about gathering the right information, processing and screening it correctly, and noting our own emotional and physical states. All of these things are very important, as we've seen in previous chapters, but whether we are facing choices about what to wear, or who to hire, or decisions as big as whether or not to go to war, we are also profoundly influenced by what those around us say, think, do or don't do.

Ultraconformists

It was social psychologist Solomon Asch who pioneered much of the early academic research into how influenced we are by other people.

Asch was driven in part by his own experience, a bewitching memory from his own childhood of partaking in his first Passover Seder with his Jewish family. As his grandmother poured glasses of wine, Asch noticed she had poured an extra glass, and he asked his uncle who it was for. The uncle told him it was for the prophet Elijah. Asch was intrigued, and asked if Elijah would actually take a sip. His uncle's response was assertive: "Oh, yes. You just watch when the time comes." Asch studied the glass, and lo and behold, he was convinced that the level had indeed gone down, as if by magic.[2]

Nearly forty years later, Asch used this psychological phenomenon as the basis of an experiment to see how far a group could be swayed by what others claimed.[3] Unlike the smoke experiment, which was designed to test how people responded to a group's inaction, this experiment aimed to see how people responded to a group's active behaviour – however ludicrous.

The experiment involved assessing the length of a line. A group of eight participants were shown three lines, varying in length from half an inch to 1¾ inches, on one card, and a single line on another. The single line was the same length as one of the other three lines. The question was simple: which did it match?

As with the smoke-filled-room research, Asch did not tell his subjects that some of their fellow participants were actors. In this case a team of seven actors worked in concert to test how robust the participants' conviction in their own perceptions was when faced with a majority pulling the other way.

The results were surprising to anyone new to this area of psychology. Despite the very obvious differences in the length of the lines, when all seven actors gave identical, incorrect answers, the participants conformed with the majority choice a third of the time. As many as 70 per cent of participants went along with the misleading majority opinion at least once when they were tested multiple times.

This is an experiment that has been repeated many times since. And although there have been found to be some "cultural" differences – Asians on average tend to conform more than Americans, Americans more than Brits, Norwegians more than French, women more than men, young people more than old – and although in some countries conformity levels are less today than they were at the time these experiments were first carried out – Asch's basic conclusion remains pretty robust.[4] Most of us are "ultraconformists" at least some of the time – willing to yield to the group even when we have overwhelming evidence to the contrary.[5]

Peer Pressure and the Myspace Brain

Why are we prone to being so easily influenced?

There are many potential explanations. Clearly at the core is a desire to fit in and be liked: social or peer pressure in some shape or form. In fact, put us back in that brain scanner we've come across in previous Steps, and we can actually see this at play.

Dr. Gregory S. Berns is a neuro-economist by trade, with joint professorships in Psychiatry and Economics at Emory University. He became hot property following the financial crash in 2008, as magazines and TV stations like ABC, CNN and PBS all sought mavens to explain why traders were behaving the way they were, and causing such havoc. But before media fame found him, Berns had sought to understand the brain behaviour of a much younger group: teenage music fans.

In 2006, working from his lab in Atlanta, Berns studied the brains of twenty-seven children between the age of twelve and seventeen while they were played sixty tracks in three of their favourite genres by unsigned musical artists found on Myspace. Lying down in an fMRI scanner, the subjects were played each track for fifteen seconds, and then asked to rate it on a star system from one to five. They were then played the same fifteen-second clip again. In two-thirds of these replays, participants were flashed a "popularity" star rating for the song they were listening to. With this popularity score still in front of them, they were then asked to re-rate the song. For the other one-third of occasions, no popularity rating was shown.

The results were pretty illuminating. When no popularity rating was shown, the kids only switched their choices 11.6 per cent of the time when asked to re-rate the song. But once exposed to others' ratings, that figure almost doubled: 21.9 per cent of the original scores were now changed. And in what way? In 79.9 per cent of cases, in the direction of the popularity score.

In keeping with earlier studies such as Asch's, not all the kids proved to be "ultraconformists." Some of us, it seems, manage to resist the weight of peer pressure. Yet what was so interesting was that Berns saw something very similar going on in the brains of his young subjects who clearly wanted to fit in. Looking at his fMRI scans, he noted that a complex constellation of changes was occurring in their brains, creating a kind of cognitive/emotional dissonance.[6] The children were thinking one thing and feeling another, and this made them feel anxious.

It was as if they were distressed that their own tastes weren't in line with what they should be in order to fit in. And this anxiety was what drove them to alter their choices.[7]

We established in earlier Steps the propensity of people to herd online. Now we have some insights into the physiological factors at play. Think about this the next time you're looking at reviews on a recommender site such as Amazon. Did the reviewer share their true feelings, or were they unconsciously seeking to conform to what others had written before them, so as to fit in? If the reviews have a similar thrust or are mono-thematic, perhaps there is more going on than straightforward, independent consumer feedback.

People Like Us

It's not just that we are prone to follow the crowd.

It turns out that when it comes to who we are most likely to follow, what kind of people we're most likely to copy, who we are most likely to socialise with, or even who we are most likely to hire, we are prone to imitate, befriend or seek the advice of a particular type of person – *a person just like us*.

A person who looks like us, speaks like us, acts like us, has the same political or religious beliefs as us, is of the same ethnicity, comes from the same place or went to the same school.[8]

Many of us will have witnessed this tendency in operation at big universities, campuses with 25,000 students or more. Despite the fact that there are more people and more types of people to get to know than we may have previously ever experienced, many of us still end up in social groups full of people just like ourselves.[9]

But did you know that research has shown that we are especially likely both to mimic the behaviour and do the bidding of people with the same name as our own?[10] How revealing is that of the extent of our innate narcissism?

Similar patterns of homophily – our tendency to associate and bond with people similar to us – often play out at work.

In the absence of any clear interview guidelines (and sometimes despite them), many of us use our own identities as templates of suitability, and select people with interests and hobbies similar to our own.[11] Around 80 per cent of staff in elite US professional services companies acknowledge that they use the "airport test" when interviewing, asking themselves, "Would you mind being stuck in an airport with this person during a snowstorm?" As one investment banking director said, "The question I ask myself is, are they the kind of person I enjoy hanging with?"[12]

It's not just hiring practices that are thus distorted. We see such tendencies of homophily affecting work dynamics in other ways too. Managers who think they treat everyone equally are shown in fact to favour and gravitate towards colleagues who look and sound most like them.[13] At investment banks, executives are more likely to seek input from people of the same nationality, even when they are not best-placed to help them, and even if their performance suffers as a consequence.[14]

The Case for Dissent

So, we copy, conform with and surround ourselves with people like us – that much is clear. But how does this affect our decision-making?

Badly.

Although several heads can be better than one if we're trying to solve challenging problems, making forecasts or facing complex decisions, all those extra minds will not be of any real use if they are just replicas of our own.

If the views they espouse, the ideas they bring to the table and the approaches they suggest are simply echoes of what we already believe, know and do, then they take us no further forward. They offer us nothing new in the way of challenge. They tell us little about whether we've got our plans right or wrong. Indeed, the more "clubby" the environment, the less willing people will be to voice dissenting views – often the very views we need to hear in order to improve our decision-making.

History is littered with bad decisions and erroneous predictions made because of excessive conformity and insufficient divergence. US President Lyndon Johnson notoriously discouraged dissent, with many historians now believing that this played a significant role in the decision to escalate US military operations in Vietnam.[15] Excessive group-think is now recognised to have underpinned President Kennedy's disastrous authorisation of a CIA-backed landing at Cuba's Bay of Pigs.[16]

Think back too to the billions of pounds spent by corporations preparing for Y2K – the bug that was expected to bring down computer networks worldwide on the stroke of midnight at the beginning of the new millennium. As we now know, nothing significant happened beyond a feeling that we'd all been expensively duped and acted like a global flock of sheep that had failed to challenge what quickly became a kind of media group-think.

Staying with business a bit longer, the refusal of the Detroit car industry's leadership to challenge the received wisdom that the American public would be reluctant to buy compact and fuel-efficient cars turned out to be more than a bum steer.

Time and again we see that if everyone sings from the same hymn sheet, there is a significant risk that everyone will end up singing the wrong song.

It's not just that group-think can act as a barrier to good decision-making.[17] Countless studies and experiments have found that when group members are actively encouraged to openly express divergent opinions, they not only share more information, but consider it more systematically and in a more balanced and less biased way. That by embracing people with different opinions and views from our own we become much more able to properly interrogate critical assumptions and identify creative alternatives. And that an atmosphere that encourages dissent leads to a better chance of us having our more mediocre ideas challenged and replaced by sharper thinking, with better overall outcomes generated as a result.[18]

This means that if we are to make smarter decisions, we need to actively take steps to bring dissenters and challengers into our inner circle, our network, our management team. Abraham Lincoln was renowned for this. His "team of rivals" was comprised of people whose intellect he respected but who were confident enough to take issue with him when they disagreed with his point of view.[19]

Yet most of us rarely voluntarily surround ourselves with challengers. Instead we are prone to seek out the comfort and self-validation of people like ourselves, who confirm what we already believe. That "airport test" identified among executives in the United States may actually end up being your worst enemy, if it means the best ideas and the most stretching opinions never surface.

The Value of Difference

So, dissent is key to good decision-making.

So too is difference. For if we are to make smarter decisions, we also need to include in our decision-making people with different experiences and backgrounds from our own. People who look different to us, sound different to us, and have different skills.

A considerable number of studies point to the superior performance of groups that are characterised by difference.

These include evidence of higher returns for companies with more women at senior levels of management or on their boards, better grades for students exposed to racially diverse groups than those in a more homogeneous environment, and superior thinking skills among those who've been exposed to divergent and diverse perspectives.[20]

This suggests that hiring students with a diverse range of degrees and backgrounds may well be a more effective policy than only interviewing economics graduates, say, from the still predominately white Oxbridge.[21]

It is not as simple as surrounding ourselves with a Benetton-ad-like group of people who simply look different, and expecting this on its own to guarantee better business practices and decision-making. If we are to gain the benefits of difference, not only will those qualifying as "diverse" actually need to have different experiences, backgrounds and perspectives from the dominant white male ones and from each other (which of course will not be true of every person of colour or every woman), they will also have to be willing to express their differences.[22] And we will need to listen to them.

"Different" does not only mean different skin colour or sex, however.

It can also mean a difference in age. Indeed, some of the strongest empirical evidence for the benefits of diversity comes from research done on groups that are demographically rather than racially or gender diverse.[23]

Multi-generational management teams perform better than teams made up of people of a similar age.[24] Firms in the financial sector with a greater age distribution outperform those whose professionals cluster in the thirty to fifty age range.[25] Indeed, some Wall Street firms expressly practise what is known as "barbelling" – the pairing of young financial professionals with those over fifty, with the explicit purpose of taking advantage of both the adventurousness of youth and the caution born of experience.[26] In doing so they help to assure that different types of "eyes" are deployed. A recent study showed that in companies where creative problem-solving is at a premium, a 10 per cent increase in age diversity would increase productivity by 3.5 per cent per year.[27]

Perhaps it's not surprising that age differences produce more diverse ways of doing and seeing. As Scott Page, Professor of Complex Systems, Political Science and Economics at the University of Michigan, who has studied the benefits of difference extensively, has written, "Those who arrive at the same time think the same way."[28]

World War II Code-Breaking and the Curious Role of Seaweed

We've highlighted the ways in which diversity of gender, ethnicity and age can improve how we think and the way we arrive at decisions. But the power of difference doesn't stop there. If smarter problem-solving and decision-making is the goal, then a team of people made up of different disciplines and different skills may well be what we need to deliver on the most complex challenges.

During the horrors of World War II, one particular front in the fight against the Third Reich tells us something powerful about the value of a diverse team.

A key element of the Nazi armoury was the Enigma machine, a secret encoding device that allowed the German forces to coordinate attacks, deliver supplies and communicate with each other without giving anything away to the enemy.

The code was so complex that the chances of cracking it were estimated to be 150 million million million to one.[29]

Yet somehow, against all the odds, the British succeeded in breaking it.

What accounted for their remarkable success? A key factor was the way in which British intelligence assembled a team of code-breakers with difference at its heart.[30]

They were housed at Bletchley Park, an estate in Buckinghamshire, where around 10,000 people worked in secrecy, trying to break the cipher.

Some of those involved in this herculean task were the kind of people you might expect to be deployed – mathematicians and engineers trained to spot and process highly complex sequences of data. But also thrown into the mix were a fair few wild cards. Authors and linguists, Egyptologists and classicists, moral philosophers, bridge players and antiquarian booksellers.[31]

The American lawyer and intelligence officer Telford Taylor, who visited Bletchley Park during the war, contrasted the British and American teams. He noted that the code-breakers at the Pentagon were mostly professional lawyers, while those at Bletchley were "a very motley but exciting group" made up of writers, teachers and "guys that play chess."[32]

Many were sceptical about this unorthodox approach to recruitment. Jon Cohen, a civilian code-breaker, recalled an occasion when the military police saw personnel at Bletchley Park "walking about, officers and ratings, people in uniform and people not in uniform," and mistook the place for a services lunatic asylum.[33] Even Winston Churchill, surveying the bizarre assembly of talent, reportedly remarked: "I told you to leave no stone unturned in your recruiting. I did not expect you to take me so literally."[34]

However, it is precisely this intellectual diversity that was pivotal to their ultimate success. "New schemes for tackling a job were never snubbed," remembered Joy Ettridge, a Cambridge graduate who joined Bletchley in 1942 and worked in the Control Room.[35] Rather, they were actively encouraged. Harry Hinsley, plucked out of his second year at Cambridge to work in Bletchley's Naval Section, recalled that it *was a delightful amateur place which gradually became an enormous hive of professional activity. It never lost what I think was the key to its success – that as in University, which was very much what it was like, there was no discipline, no hierarchy, in terms of what anyone got on with. You were all left free to get on with your own work and it had that atmosphere of real academic preoccupation.*[36]

Outsiders were similarly won over by this arrangement. US Colonel Alfred McCormack, visiting Bletchley, was especially impressed by how much the British had accomplished by eschewing rigid military formalities and getting "the best man for the job."[37]

By coming together, by pooling their knowledge as well as expressing their differences, this secret British team played a vital role in defeating fascism. Indeed, without the intelligence gathered by Bletchley Park's ragbag assortment of crossword addicts and chess-champion code-breakers, it is believed that the war would have lasted for at least two more years.[38]

At the more eccentric end of the code-breakers at Bletchley Park, one key asset turned out to be a Geoffrey Tandy of Block D, a friend of T. S. Eliot and an expert in cryptogams: non-flowering plants like ferns, mosses and seaweed.[39] Tandy was posted to Bletchley by the Admiralty because his posting officer had confused "cryptogams" with "cryptograms" (the word for messages signalled in code), and had therefore thought Tandy was an expert code-breaker. Although Tandy knew nothing about code-breaking, his work on seaweed actually proved invaluable.

One of the challenges the teams at Bletchley Park faced was the fact that the Enigma machine constantly altered the system of encryption it used.

Code books pulled from the wreckage of Nazi U-boats therefore became highly prized materials for the code-breakers.[40] They provided clues and hints, the kind of specific detail that just might make the difference to cracking the Enigma code.

But, salvaged from the sea soaking wet, how useful could these code books be? This is where Tandy's contribution proved significant.

Thanks to his expertise in cryptogams, and a pre-war job specialising in algae at the Natural History Museum,[41] Tandy knew just what to do when the British navy recovered soaked code books from a German U-boat. Requesting from the museum some of the special absorbent paper he had used to dry out seaweed in his old job, Tandy put it to work to dry out those valuable documents.[42] Thus the navy was able to preserve the coded messages on the documents rescued from the sea – messages that played an integral role in cracking the Enigma.[43]

Games Consoles Could Save Your Life

More recent work points to similar ways in which diverse skills and disciplines can provide a boon to problem-solving and decision-making.

A study by Karim Lakhani and Lars Bo Jeppesen, professors at Harvard Business School and Bocconi University in Milan respectively, showed that in 30 per cent of cases the most stubborn corporate research-and-development problems could be solved by an external expert from another discipline coming at them from a different angle.[44]

Foldit, a game developed in 2008 by a team at the University of Washington to help solve complex medical biochemistry problems, has seen significant success by people who are not biochemists: in one remarkable case, gamers cracked a problem in just a few days that had been defying doctors and scientists for decades: the structure of an enzyme called "M-PMV retroviral protease," a protein which plays a key role in developing a virus very similar to AIDS.[45] This outcome has been seen as a significant breakthrough in the quest to find a cure for AIDS.

And who were these gamers? Only one-eighth of them worked in the science industry, and two-thirds had no biochemistry experience at all beyond high school.

The finance industry has made similar breakthroughs when it has embraced divergence. A study of 199 banks found that the most innovative were those led by a team made up of people with good educational backgrounds but also very different functional areas of expertise.[46] Those firms that adopted or developed the most products, programmes and services were propelled by senior leadership teams with a patchwork of different expertise: some came from an accounting background, others from operations, lending or even information systems or sales. Their divergent experience and expertise was a powerful factor driving their success.

Perhaps most surprisingly, the US Navy is currently collaborating with video gamers to try to improve its decision-making. In 2011 it introduced MMOWGLI, a computer game that asked players to contribute ideas on how to deal with piracy off the coast of Somalia. Players were given a scenario – one began: "Three pirate ships are holding the world hostage. Chinese–US relations are strained to the limit and both countries have naval ships in the area ..." They were asked to propose a solution in 140 characters – the same as a tweet.

The navy has not yet gone public on how useful this process is proving, but it seems something about it is working. After piracy it issued calls on a number of other hard-to-solve problems, including energy security.[47]

Bringing different people's skill-sets to bear in order to help you improve your decision-making is not of course as simple a matter as giving an English major a computer programming problem, or a philosopher an engineering challenge to work on. Don't forget that for some problems and some decisions there is a level of prior training or knowledge required before you can even explain what needs to be done. Nor is it to dismiss the importance of domain-specific experience – we've seen the value of this in earlier Steps. But provided you can speak enough of the same lingo to allow for real communication (and this *does* need to be carefully managed), and provided the intrinsic ability meets the requisite threshold, difference really can deliver.

So, next time you're recruiting for your company, or your team has been struggling to solve a problem, don't forget what a difference it can make to expose yourself to diverse perspectives and refreshingly left-field ways of thinking.

This seems straightforward, but it's surprising how many of us fall into the same patterns with the same groups of people, and lose out on the myriad benefits of hearing different and dissenting views.

Hear No Evil, Speak No Evil at Lehman Brothers and Beyond

At work, say, how actively does your boss encourage the airing of divergent and sometimes contrarian views? Is he comfortable with being challenged in this way? How diverse is your management team? Does it include a range of perspectives and experiences? And how creative are you when it comes to seeking input from non-traditional sources?

When it comes to diversity and difference at work, the situation in most organisations remains bleak. Even today, decades after equality legislation, the vast majority of management teams remain white, male and middle-aged. Globally, only 21 per cent of all senior manager positions are held by women. In the US the figure is as low as 17 per cent, while in the UK's FTSE 250 companies, only 9.4 per cent of directors are female.[48]

It's a similar picture in most countries when it comes to the gender of those who make political decisions. Following David Cameron's September 2012 reshuffle, the British cabinet is now over 80 per cent male, with only four of its twenty-two members being women. Every one of the twenty-two is white. The UK government is sadly not alone in this. The vast majority of senior decision-making forums globally have a similar lack of diversity. This despite the fact that the more homogeneous the group, the less likely that those different and dissenting views we know are so important will out.

Moreover, it's all too common to see CEOs receiving "too little criticism and too much confirmation" not only from their board and senior staff, but also from their advisers – their bankers, accountants and lawyers – all of whom are likely to have similar backgrounds to their own.[49]

Managers reporting to the CEO typically damp down the concerns and points of disagreement they have, especially if they are a few rungs down the hierarchy. And dissenting views are often seen as evidence that someone is not a team player, with bearers of bad news being considered pariahs.[50] Too often, employees espouse what they think their bosses want to hear, rather than what they need to hear.[51]

Indeed, former employees of the now defunct bank Lehman Brothers have told the *Harvard Business Review* that voicing dissent there was considered a career-breaker.[52] Perhaps if it hadn't been, the bank's leadership would have thought twice about taking on so much debt and using creative accounting to inflate its assets (at the time of its collapse Lehman had $1 in the bank for every $30 of its liabilities).[53]

Lack of dissent was also cited as a contributing factor in the decision of the medical company Synthes to sell surgeons a form of bone cement despite it not meeting US government regulations – a practice that resulted in patient fatalities and the conviction and imprisonment of four of the company's executives.[54] Several employees from the company have revealed that Synthes' corporate culture was one that didn't tolerate dissent.[55]

Perhaps most catastrophically of all, at the site of the Fukushima nuclear plant explosion, the author of the independent report on the disaster, Professor Kiyoshi Kurokawa, spelled out plain and clear the role that conformity played in what unfolded: the "fundamental causes are to be found in the ingrained conventions of Japanese culture: our reflexive obedience; our reluctance to question authority; our devotion to 'sticking with the programme'; our groupism."[56]

World News: Brought to You by Your Friends

Outside work it's also important to reflect upon how different the people you surround yourself with are in terms of gender, age, ethnicity, education and political affiliation. How often do you get input from people with different points of view? These lessons about the value of diversity, difference and dissent do not only hold in the workplace. If we are to make smarter decisions in our personal lives, we have to make sure that we are not unwittingly surrounding ourselves only with people like us.

Yet here too we score badly. For most of us, our track record for exposing ourselves to different, diverse and dissenting perspectives and views away from the workplace is pretty poor.

Earlier, we looked at examples that reveal our propensity for homophily. We saw the way in which we seek out people of similar nationalities, ethnicities and age as friends – people who dress like us, look like us, went to the same schools and universities as us. This is of particular concern in our digital age. For although, as we saw in earlier Steps, we have the potential today to access raw information direct from source, all too often we cope with the resultant deluge by focusing in on the information favoured by only a very narrow group – our friends.

It's as if, having jettisoned traditional gatekeepers to curate our information landscape, we increasingly turn to our social networks to do so in their stead.[57]

The Dangers of Narrowcasting

A recent study of internet news consumption found that 19 per cent of people now access their news via social media such as Facebook, Twitter, Google Plus and LinkedIn.[58] This figure rises to 33 per cent among adults under thirty.[59] So what, you might be thinking. But this does matter – because if our friends are all too similar to us we risk unwittingly locking ourselves into information bubbles containing only views and opinions similar to those we already hold. We risk shutting ourselves off not only from a host of new ideas and opinions as yet undiscovered, but also from all the benefits of diversity, difference and dissent this chapter has laid out.[60]

This isn't far-fetched. On Twitter we are more likely to follow people who tweet about similar topics to us, are of a similar age and from the same country.[61] On Facebook we are more likely to read news stories posted by people superficially similar to us – white users are more likely to click on content recommended by whites. Black users are more likely to select news from individuals they identify as black.[62] When we co-create information it's our pre-existing social networks we are most likely to turn to – remember how Nico Zeifung discovered he had Legionnaires disease. Moreover, online we also actively shut out dissenting views: one in five users of social networking sites have blocked or hidden all posts from a "friend" because they disliked their posts on political subjects.[63]

The risk of inadvertently what I call "narrowcasting," relying on a small group of people to screen the information landscape on our behalf, is only likely to get worse, given new technologies such as Facebook's Open Graph, which reveals to our friends what news stories we're reading. If you see that your friend has been reading a story on the *New York Times* website, you are more likely to click on it too, at the expense of other stories, or the same story viewed through a different lens. Or how about Facebook's recently launched Graph Search, which will try to answer your questions using information from your friends?[64] Or the *Wall Street Journal*'s proposed social network for likeminded professionals?[65] What might you never discover if your primary source of information becomes people like you?

These personal choices are reinforced by social media sites themselves. The algorithm that companies like Facebook use to determine which content to display on our newsfeeds is partly based on our past selection preferences. Given that we are most likely to have clicked on the link of someone most like us, this means that we risk discovering the world only through the eyes of people all too similar to us, not only today but in perpetuity[66] – inadvertently condemning ourselves therefore to eternal narrowcasting.

All this is very worrying. Especially given that people who look like us, are the same age as us, the same gender and race and from the same socio-economic background, are likely to hold the same views and opinions as us. By "narrowcasting" we risk only hearing echoes of our own preferences, tastes and beliefs. This is then likely to consolidate our comfortable, unchallenged sense of being "right" – if others in our social network all seem to think the same as us, we are likely to think that the opinions we hold must be true and valid. We also risk missing the opportunity to discover the contradictory information that could serve to make us wiser, better decision-makers. And never discovering a world outside our Facebook- or Twitter-perimetered ghetto – a world of different tastes, cultures, experiences and beliefs to those of our all too homogeneous friends.

Of even greater concern, perhaps, is the fact that the more we associate online with people who think like us, the more exaggerated our beliefs are likely to become. Social networks act like a stereo amplifier, whether it's rap or Rachmaninov, racist or radical views – the more corroborating views we hear, the more extreme our own positions are likely to become.[67]

Some Answers to These Problems

So, the risks of sameness and conformity are pretty clear. They lead to significant mistakes, less creative and successful decision-making, and a narrow world-view despite our globalised and virtualised societies.

How do we avoid these pitfalls? How can we ramp up our dissenter and difference quotients? How can we ensure that we expose ourselves to contrarian views, and make room at the table for a wider range of experiences, from people who will bring us new ideas and help us break with static conventions? How can we counter our natural tendency to follow the majority and copy those most like us, and instead remain open-minded and inquisitive? How do we broaden our spheres of influence?

Good Leaders Seek Out Difference and Dissent

At work, this means consciously putting together teams whose members' experience and insights can add to each other. Hiring people who don't only have the skills needed for the job at hand, but also have different and diverse backgrounds and experience.

To ensure that this happens we need to put safeguards in place so that we don't end up hiring only people like us.

Structured interviews rather than informal chats can help in this regard. By asking the same or very similar questions of every candidate, and giving interviewers a clear, defined and structured way in which to rate candidates, you are forced to focus on relevant information only. As Organisational Behaviour Professor Julie McCarthy, who has carried out research in this area, says, "The crazy questions like your favourite colour or what kind of animal you would be – that's when cultural biases slip in and the similarity attraction might be stronger."[68]

Informal chats play to the old-boy network, and risk delivering an identikit team with an identikit approach, which is why they are faulty as a screening mechanism. If it's diversity you're after, it is vital that they do not form the basis of your hiring decisions.[69]

Surrounding ourselves with different and diverse people at work is only the first step. We also have to ensure that we actively draw out their views and perspectives.

This is not straightforward. Some types – introverts, say – will always be less likely to express dissent, especially in public. More generally, if dissent is not welcomed in the workplace, employees are very likely to recognise that expressing difference may come at a significant personal cost. If they just toe the line, whether or not they agree with it, they're less likely to be singled out and to pay any subsequent price if things go wrong.

This fear that dissent may lead to being marginalised or even fired is a symptom of an unhealthy workplace. But it's one that's endemic. As renowned Yale economics professor Robert Shiller wrote of his role on the economic advisory panel to the Federal Bank of New York:

> *While I warned about the bubbles I believed were developing in the stock and housing markets, I did so very gently, and felt vulnerable expressing such quirky views. Deviating too far from consensus leaves one feeling potentially ostracised from the group, with the risk that one may be terminated.*[70]

In all too many work environments it's as Keynes famously said: "Worldly wisdom teaches that it is better for reputation to fail conventionally than to succeed unconventionally."[71] The tendency to rein in what you truly think, and to err on the side of failing conventionally, is of course exacerbated in cultures that explicitly value deference.

So, if you're intent on getting diverse and different views on the table, you have to make clear that they are actually what you want to hear from your team.

It takes courageous leadership to do this in the business environment. It requires leaders to have the confidence to allow themselves to be challenged by their teams, and for their mistakes or misperceptions to be pointed out to them, despite their seniority.

The pay-off, however, is worth it. Not only does it show your colleagues that you trust and respect their views, but the end result is very likely to be better problem-solving, and consequently improved decision-making.

We saw in Step Five how suggestion schemes and prediction markets can be used with good effect to draw out non-traditional views and to tap into disagreement. In this Step we've seen how biochemists and the US Navy have been using games as a way to get unusual individuals with different experiences to participate in problem-solving. But there are many other ways to signal that you encourage nay-sayers, dissenters and those with different perspectives to come forward.

If you're leading a meeting, you might want to ask those present to explicitly articulate what they're thinking but haven't hitherto expressed.

Eric Schmidt, Executive Chairman of Google, says, "What I try to do in meetings is to find the people who have not spoken, who often are the ones who are afraid to speak out, but have a dissenting opinion. I get them to say what they really think and that promotes discussion, and the right thing happens."[72]

You might consider circulating key agenda items and soliciting input in advance of the meeting. This can help to ensure that the introverts among you, or those less comfortable with airing differences, also get the opportunity to air their views.

To shake the group dynamic up, you might even want to get people to change seats. With regular meetings we very quickly assign ourselves the same places to sit. If you mix this up, the way your group interacts is likely to change too.[73] You might also want to bring a critical outsider in, that Challenger in Chief, to directly challenge the dominant thinking of your team or facilitate a change in style.[74]

And if you are truly championing the dissent ethic at work, it's important that you be seen to listen to and consider views that don't chime with your own, and to value those with different ideas, perspectives and opinions from yours – from wherever in the organisation they come.

In part, this is about ensuring access. Google holds a weekly meeting at which any employee can ask Larry Page, Sergey Brin or any other top executive any question they like, either in person or electronically. As Senior Google VP Laszlo Bock says of that meeting, "Everything is up for question and debate."[75]

But it's also about how you communicate that this is your intention. So, don't roll your eyes at a comment you don't agree with, or summarily cut colleagues off. Instead, ask the speaker questions, engage – listen attentively, making it clear that you haven't yet made your mind up. Make sure that you are seen to consider the opinions of the nay-sayers and contrarians as well as the yes-men.

This doesn't mean, of course, that as a leader you always have to follow your advisers' decisions, or that you should not act until consensus has been reached among your team. Sometimes the right thing to do, having considered opposing views, is to reject them. But at those times that your decision does not correspond with the views of those around you, share with your team the reasons why you are taking that decision, so they understand that their views are valued by you, and properly considered, even if they are not always acted upon.

If possible, also make clear that you continue to value their advice even if you've had to cut the discussion short. This is what Abraham Lincoln did. Having allowed his cabinet to debate whether to abolish slavery for months, he finally decided to issue his historic Emancipation Proclamation. Bringing his cabinet together, he told them that although he no longer needed their advice on the main issue, he was keen to hear their thoughts on how best to implement his decision to free the slaves. And indeed he took on board the suggestion of one of his cabinet members to wait for a victory on the field before he issued the Proclamation.[76]

To successfully manage dissent needs care. If you're going to have contrarian views circulating, they must not come across as pointless confrontation or personal attacks. You don't want your team screaming at each other. Nor do you want dissent to come at the expense of collaboration and cooperation. If it does, there will be a considerable cost.[77] So the dissent ethic must be underpinned by a clearly shared purpose and underlying respect if it's to work in practice.[78] And care must be taken over the language in which dissent is expressed. You still want cooperative discourse to be used: "That's a good idea, but what if I play devil's advocate?" rather than "You lose – I win."[79]

Dissent and Difference in Your Day-to-Day Life

What about outside work? How do you ensure that you receive enough opposing, diverse and different views so that the decisions you make in your personal life are properly informed? Especially in a world in which we are increasingly likely to edit and curate the data deluge ourselves, via our social networks, to narrowcast, and to co-create information through them too?

This will continue to be a challenge, especially given the way in which the technologies themselves serve to narrow the field of who it is we hear and learn from. But once we are aware of the challenge, there are steps we can actively take.

We can commit to getting our news and information from a broader variety of sources than we currently do. We can consciously seek out multiple views offline as well as on. We can follow people on Twitter who are very different from us, with different interests and opinions. We can seek out bloggers from other countries. On Facebook we can commit to befriending people of different ages, genders, colour and political persuasion, and to clicking on stories from friends we would normally ignore.

Takeaways

If we are to have the capacity to shift paradigms, to make breakthroughs, to destroy myths, to solve difficult problems and make wise choices, we must create environments in which ideas constantly battle it out, our own opinions are fiercely challenged, and different thoughts from different viewpoints are actively sought out and fearlessly brought to the centre of our discussions.

Progress comes about not only from the creation of ideas, of course, but also from their destruction. John Stuart Mill pointed out long ago that alternative perspectives are essential for reflection and growth.[80] The onus is on us to ensure that we surround ourselves with such alternative views.

This is truer today than ever before. If we are to make smarter decisions it is essential that we not only apply all the lessons in earlier Steps, but also break away from our mirrored echo-chambers, whether at work, at home or online.

QUICK TIPS FOR ENCOURAGING
DIFFERENCE AND EMBRACING DISSENT

- **Shake up your social network.** If everyone in it is similar to you – same age, same background, same beliefs – you risk discovering only what you already know, and amplifying the beliefs you already hold.

- **Be careful of digital narrowcasting** – filtering the information landscape only through people like you. Follow people on Twitter with different interests to you; befriend people on Facebook of different ages, gender, colour and political persuasion; seek out bloggers from different countries to yours. And don't block or hide posts from people with different views from your own. It's important to see the world through different lenses and to expose yourself to alternative perspectives.

- **Be aware of the herding tendencies of online reviewers.** Just because most people have given five stars to something, it doesn't mean that is how they would have evaluated it if they hadn't seen what came before. More generally, be on guard against *group-think* – the majority view is not necessarily the correct view.

- **Actively solicit dissent and contrarian views both at work and within your circle of informal advisers.** Encourage people to speak their minds and to challenge you, and don't roll your eyes at comments you don't agree with, or be seen to value only those with similar ideas and opinions to your own. And at those times when you do override the views of your team, explain why, and try to involve them in the implementation process.

- **At work, consciously build diverse teams,** made up of people of different ages, gender, ethnicities, background. This will ensure that different eyes are deployed, and a range of perspectives and points of view are brought to the table. Of course you need to speak a common enough lingo to be able to work together productively – without this, difference is not practical. So think about how to ensure that your team can properly communicate with each other while retaining difference and diversity.

- **When interviewing a candidate for a position, be careful not to be overly swayed by how similar they are to you.** The right candidate will not necessarily have similar hobbies and interests, or pass the "airport test."

- **In meetings, draw out the views of the person who hasn't spoken.** What do they really think? Before the meeting, circulate the agenda and solicit input so that the introverts among you, or those less comfortable about publicly airing differences, can also contribute.

- **Bring outsiders in to help you solve challenging problems.** New insights and ways of doing things will help challenge the dominant thinking and lead to smarter decision-making.

Epilogue

I wake up from surgery.

My partner is waiting. The crease between his eyes that reveals his concern is clearly discernible, yet he is smiling.

Morphine muffles the hope I feel. "How did it go?" I ask.

"Great." He squeezes my hand gently. "It all went great ..."

Time to Take Control

We won't always, of course, have such happy-ever-after endings to our decisions, however carefully and thoughtfully we approach them. The ever more complex and unpredictable nature of twenty-first-century life means that there will always be some curveballs thrown our way.

But I wanted to research and write this book so that I and my readers would have a much better chance of getting those high-stakes decisions in our personal and professional lives right. Decisions such as which job to take and which to walk away from, which investments to make and which acquisitions to champion, whose advice to take and whose to disregard, which medical treatment to agree to for ourselves or our loved ones.

Life is a series of big decisions. But if we take control of the decision-making process, eyes wide open and brains switched on, we can at least stack the odds of making the right calls firmly in our favour.

The onus is on us – *we must make this an age of self-empowerment.*

An age in which we take control, in which we get vastly better at understanding the world around us and become first-class decision-makers in our own right.

We must no longer just blindly accept the words of shamanic experts or science-wielding dissemblers, in the hope or naïve belief that they will always be correct in their analysis. As we've seen, traditional experts can often fail us – remember the professor of nutrition who advised that I ate more sugar? Or all those financial mavens who failed to anticipate the financial crisis? We must accept that this is an age in which those who filter and translate the information landscape for us can no longer be guaranteed to be either trustworthy or correct.

Yet we must also acknowledge that we are lucky to be living at a time when something truly exciting is unfolding – knowledge is being democratised in a way we've never hitherto experienced. Today we can gather with remarkable ease information and insights in a raw, unspun, unedited form, direct from the source. The old custodians of truth have lost their privileged position. We can all now take on the role of information hunter and gatherer. *We all now have this power*.

Not that this role is an easy one to successfully realise. The deluge flows fast, its volume is immense.

The democratisation of knowledge makes new demands on us. If we are to successfully navigate this new information landscape we will need to consider information from a more diverse range of sources than we might previously have relied on. We will need to improve our screening capabilities, so that we are better able to determine what information to act upon and what we can safely ignore. And we must improve our verification skills, so that we can cover new terrains with confidence and with all the facts before us.

For some of us this may mean becoming more confident about numbers. For others it may mean recognising in ourselves a predisposition to overvalue what is represented in a numerical form. For some of us this may be about focusing on the bigger picture. For others it's about properly pondering alternatives, including those that don't immediately resonate with us. In yet other cases it may mean acknowledging our limitations and building a team around us who can complement our own skills with a variety of aptitudes and experiences.

Time to Free Up Head-Space

All this takes time and effort.

I recognise that for those of us with ever-expanding to-do lists, committing to this may feel like an overwhelming and impossible ask. I acknowledge too the increasing pressure we often feel under nowadays to respond instantly, and to make our decisions on the hoof. Yet it's vital that we free up head-space and thinking time when we have important decisions to make. Remember how the best ER doctors manage to do this even in the emergency room? Or how one of the busiest men on the planet, President Obama, counselled Prime Minister David Cameron to carve out plenty of thinking time?

It's only by allowing ourselves that beat, that pause, that we can ensure that our brains are sufficiently switched on.

So, which of your pre-existing commitments might you be able to set aside at critical junctures, or actually dispense with altogether? Which of your daily distractions might it be time to give up? Who can act as your personal "gatekeeper" – at home or at work – to free up more time for you to think and plan properly? What can you let go of and delegate to others so that you have more space for the things that really matter? Can you get stronger at pushing others back when their demands for immediate reactions are unreasonable? Tell them you'll get back to them? That you want to sleep on it?

Can you practise getting quicker at determining when you actually need to hone in on details, and when a snapshot over-view will suffice? Can you get better at deciding when infor-mation or advice is untrustworthy or bad, and can be summarily junked? Can you work out which of the short cuts you use actually *do* enable you to find the information that really makes a difference quickly, and which serve instead to occlude or confuse? Can you employ a Chief Intelligence Officer to help you with such tasks?

Time to Rebel

Successfully managing the new information landscape along-side the ever more intense demands made of us is crucial if we are to become smart decision-makers.

But to become empowered thinkers, there's more still that we will need to commit to.

We will need to embrace our inner rebel – the part of us that is willing to challenge both our knee-jerk acquiescence to men in white coats and our innate desire to seek comfort in conformity. The part of us that is willing to trade off popular-ity for truth, and to become, when need be, the "difficult" patient, the "annoyingly questioning" colleague, the contrarian or the nay-sayer – the person who rocks the boat, the Challenger in Chief. The part of us that regards doubt not as an albatross weighing our decisions down, but instead as a sabre, enabling us to cut through spin, lies and inaccuracies.

Time to Know Ourselves Better

We will also need to commit to greater introspection. Acknowledge the need at times to quiet our own egos – for not only must we be more willing to challenge others, we also have to be willing to let others challenge *us*. Time and time again we've seen that many of our best ideas, solutions and choices arise not from those "Kumbaya" moments when we all clap each other on the back in self-congratulation, but instead from those moments of discord and conflict, when someone's shaken us out of our complacency or exposed our own tunnel vision to us. We need to acknowledge our own thinking traps and our own biases, however smart we may think we are.

We must also commit to interrogating our initial reactions and responses – as we've seen, the steer they provide us with will at times be misleading. To this end we must practise noting our own emotions, moods and feelings, so that these neither inadvertently become the reasons we choose one path over another, nor are summarily disregarded, with the cues and clues they may *usefully* proffer ignored.

We need too to recognise that this is a time in which the truth is increasingly determined by market forces. In which those who seek to influence us for their own gain are becoming ever more sophisticated when it comes to triggering our most primitive reactions and urges. Remember all the ways in which politicians and marketers try to manipulate our decisions via our senses and the evocation of particular emotions?

And we really must get better at monitoring our basic physical needs – for as we now know, a lack of sleep or food can seriously imperil our decision-making.

Time to Accept the Chaos

We have to get better at something else, too. At accepting the chaos around us – the complexities and uncertainties that are part and parcel of our age.

This means that we have to counter our desire to oversimplify the world and have others spoon-feed us information in comforting forms. It is also about acknowledging that for many decisions there is no one-size-fits-all solution, no answer that is right for all and sundry. Even if the decision relates solely to our own situation, we need to accept that there will be different levels of risk we're willing to take on at different times of our lives, and that we will find particular trade-offs acceptable at particular moments, but not at others.

Accepting the chaos is also about recognising that the right decision today may not be the right decision even tomorrow. Knowing this, we need to detach ourselves from past successes, but also from past failures, so that these do not become of themselves misleading lodestars, nor the reason either for overconfidence or paralysing pessimism. We must also think about how to mitigate worst-possible scenarios, or whether we can break a decision up into discrete parts so that we can change tack with more ease if need be along the way. More generally, we need to be more confident about admitting to others the necessarily contingent nature of our decisions, making explicit that if the facts change we *will* change our minds, and that that is OK.

Closing Words

Empower yourself.

Take control.

Be a rebel.

Encourage dissent.

Know yourself better.

Allow yourself time and space to think.

Understand the world around you.

Accept uncertainty.

Give yourself permission to change tack.

Keep your eyes wide open and your brain switched on.

All of these things are possible, and are within your grasp.

They will help make you a better decision-maker.

I wish you well on your journey.

Acknowledgements

Many people have helped me over the past six years to uncover the research that underpins this book and further develop my thinking. I am grateful to all of them.

In particular I would like to thank my research assistants who checked and rechecked the many sources, stories, facts and data that underpin this work.

To Charlotte Owen, Daniel Janes, Paola Grenier, Andrew Somerville, Anna Lacey and Alexa Clay – I greatly appreciate the care you took with this project and look forward to witnessing all your accomplishments in years to come.

I also want to thank Lee Mager, Rose Cook, Joanne Reinhard, Nicky Ferguson, David Lee, Sara Dosa, Ian Redpath, Bernard Keenan, J.B. Fournier, Carl Miller, Sasha Brown, Nessa Malone, Heather McRobie, Jussi Nybom, Bryanna Hahn, Dan Hillman, Simon Wibberley, Daniel Lanyon, David Barker, Joe Gladstone, Jonathan Graham, Jonathan Jones, Antonio Andreoni, Eimear Nolan, Emma Howell, Imran Jina, Natalie Leeder, Jonathan Lamptey, Amna Silim, Victoria Van Tetz, Anastasia Kichigina, Aryanna Garber, Johannes Hillje, Andrea Gobbo, Kyle Gerow, Isodora Kourti, Shannon Hale, Jesko Thron, Flora Hevesi, Kenneth Sandin and Christoph Futter – each of you contributed to this book and I appreciate your help.

I would like to thank too those colleagues and friends who so graciously and thoughtfully looked over and commented on draft chapters despite having very busy lives of their own. Professor Debora Spar, Joshua Ramo, Professor Richard Sambrook, Jamie Bartlett, Jeremy Reffin, Professor Sarah-Jayne Blakemore, Stuart Roden, Sander van der Linden, Justin Fox, Professor Doron Kliger and Professor Olivier Oullier all served to make this a better book and me a smarter thinker – any errors of course remain my own.

I also want to thank the late Philip Gould whose belief in me and this book continues to mean a great deal.

Thanks also to my editors at HarperCollins UK and US, David Roth-Ey and Hollis Heimbouch – I am very lucky to have you championing this book. Thank you for believing in this project so wholeheartedly and supporting me so thoroughly. Thanks too to Hannah MacDonald who was so pivotal to this book for much of its life.

At HarperCollins Victoria Barnsley, Jamie Joseph, Robert Lacey, Stephen Guise, Katherine Patrick, Minna Fry, Caroline Crofts, Jess Fawcett, Laura Roberts, Sharmila Woollam, Tara Al Azzawi, Leanne Williams, Catherine Friis, Stephanie Selah, Mark Ferguson and Katherine Beitner have all helped to make writing and publishing this book a great experience – I'm really fortunate to have such a stellar team behind this project.

And of course huge thanks as ever to my agent, Ed Victor – who's always there for me, and has been such a strong advocate for this book from the start. And also to his wonderful team – Rebecca Jones, Maggie Phillips, Morag O'Brien, Linda Van and Hitesh Shah – thank you for all your support over the years.

I also want to express my gratitude to Professor Dirk Schoenmaker, Bernd Jan Sikken and Jeroen van Loon at the Duisenberg School of Finance; Professor George Yip; my colleagues at CIBAM, Judge Business School and UCL; and the Holland Financial Centre. All of you helped enable me to write this book and I appreciate your support.

Thanks too to Robert Senior, Morris Pondfield, Michael Schouten, Anton Emmanuel and Alexis Johansen for their input. To Lili and Dick Zanuck, Len Blavatnik, Martha Lane Fox, Henry Porter, Dave Wirtschafter, Julia Hobsbawm, Simon Sebag Montefiore, Robert Cialdini, Ken Burns, Kyu Kim, Dominic Barton, Michael Lynton, Don Tapscott, Julia White and Trine Adler for their support. And to Abby Turk, William Orbit, Simon Franks, David Costa, Caroline Michel, Jill Daamen, Jo Summers, Kirsten Orchard, Caroline Daniel, Elisa Angel, Gary Trainer, Paola Ceccarelli, Ed Blake, Molly Nyman, Liza Marshall, Fi Glover, Hannah Robson, Diane McGrath, Richard Symons, Samara Fagoti Mohamad Jalloul and Liza Cawthorn for their care.

Special thanks also to all those who helped me come up with the title *Eyes Wide Open* – in particular Chris Malone who helped me put some of the lessons of my book into action, but also Richard Cohen and Jonny Angel. Thanks also in this regard to my friends on Facebook, my colleagues on LinkedIn and my followers on Twitter who fed back on earlier possible titles and were frank and honest about those they did not like.

I want to thank too my late mother Leah Hertz, who continues to serve as an inspiration; my sister Arabel Hertz, my aunt Shoshana Gelman, my father Jonathan Hertz, and my new family, the Cohen Family, not only for the support they gave me throughout, but also for their patience at my protracted absences while I was writing this book; and also Rachel Weisz, Tim Samuels, Estelle Rubio, Michelle Kohn, James Fletcher, Adam Nagel, Gina Bellman, Roderick Miller, Roddy Skeaping, Szilvia Keffert, and Kevin Plummer for not only encouraging me throughout the writing period but also making sure I did manage to snatch at least some moments of fun.

Finally I want to thank my husband, Danny Cohen. Your insights, intelligence, care and love made this process so much better than it would have otherwise been – without you this book would be a lesser one, and I a lesser person.

Notes

STEP ONE: Get to Grips with a World in Hyper-Drive

1. Douglas, K. (2011). Decision time: How subtle forces shape your choices. *New Scientist*, 14 Nov. 2011, 38–41. http://www.newscientist.com/article/mg21228381.800-decision-time-how-subtle-forces-shape-your-choices.html.

2. A study by Cornell University researchers Brian Wansick and Jeffrey Sobal shows that 139 people underestimated the food decisions they made: "The average participant believed they made 14.4 food-related decisions per day. On aggregating the actual number of decisions made by the participants, they made an average of 226.7 decisions per day." Wansick, B. & Sobal, J. (2007). Mindless eating: the 200 daily food decisions we overlook. *Environment and Behavior*, 39, 1, 112.

3. Robinson, L. & Bawden, D. (2009). The dark side of information: overload, anxiety and other paradoxes and pathologies. *Journal of Information Science*, 35, 5. http://jis.sagepub.com/content/35/2/180.

4. Richtel, M. (2010). Attached to Technology and Paying a Price. *New York Times*. http://www.nytimes.com/2010/06/07/technology/07brain.html; Bohn, R. & Short, J.E. (2009). How much information? 2009 report on American Consumers. Global Industry Information Centre, University of San Diego, California, p.12.

5. McKinsey Global Institute (2011). Big data: The next frontier for innovation, competition and productivity, June 2011, p.16, www.mckinsey.com/.../Big per cent20Data/MGI_big_data_full_report.ashx cites a series of white papers published by IDC and sponsored by EMC: The expanding digital universe (2007). The diverse and exploding digital universe (2008). As the economy contracts, the digital universe expands. (2009). The digital universe decade – Are you ready? (2010). www.emc.com/leadership/programs/digital-universe.htm.

6. Klingberg, T. (2008). *The Overflowing Brain: Information Overload and the Limits of Working Memory.* Trans. by Betteridge, N. Oxford University Press, Oxford, p.10. Note also that the internet is not only changing the way we find information, it might also be changing the way

we think. Kassirer, J.P. (2010). Does instant access to compiled information undermine clinical cognition? *The Lancet*, 376, 9751, 1510–1511.

7. Miller, G. (1956). The Magical Number Seven, plus or minus two: some limits on our capacity for processing information. *Psychological Review*, 63, 81–97; Klingberg, T. (2008). *The Overflowing Brain: Information Overload and the Limits of Working Memory*. Trans. by Betteridge, N. Oxford University Press, Oxford, p.10.

8. Granka, L.A., Joachims, T. & Gay, G. (2004). Eye-tracking analysis of user behavior in WWW search. Proceedings of the 27th annual international ACM SIGIR conference on research and development in information retrieval. http://www.cs.cornell.edu/People/tj/publications/granka_etal_04a.pdf Retrieved on 26.10.06.

9. Lewis, P., Newburn, T., Taylor, M., Mcgillivray, C., Greenhill, A., Frayman, H. and Proctor, R. (2011). *Reading the riots: investigating England's summer of disorder*. Reading the riots, The London School of Economics and Political Science and the *Guardian*, London.

10. Palme, J. (1984). You Have 134 Unread Mail! Do You Want to Read Them Now? *Computer-Based Message Services, proceedings of the IFIP WG 6.5 Working Conference on Computer-Based Message Services, Nottingham, England, 1–4 May, 1984*, Amsterdam; New York, 175–176.

11. Temple, K. (2011). What Happens in an Internet Minute?, *Intel.com*. 13 Mar. 2012. http://scoop.intel.com/what-happens-in-an-internet-minute/. This was also reported by Tsukayama, H. (2012). Intel offers snapshot of an "Internet minute." *Washington Post*, 15 Mar. 2013. http://articles.washingtonpost.com/2013–03–15/business/37737029_1_intel-video-views-mobile-data.

12. Bohn, R. & Short, J. (2012). Measuring consumer information. *International Journal of Communication*, 6, 980–1000, quoted in Hudson, A. (2012). The Age of Information Overload. BBC News. http://news.bbc.co.uk/1/hi/programmes/click_online/9742180.stm. Note that the study refers to waking time in the home.

13. Conversation with colleague of Kissinger.

14. Richtel, M. (2010). Attached to Technology and Paying a Price. *New York Times*. http://www.nytimes.com/2010/06/07/technology/07brain.html.

15. Cisco Connected World Technology Report (2011). p.22. http://www.cisco.com/en/US/solutions/ns341/ns525/ns537/ns705/ns1120/CCWTR-Chapter1-Report.pdf.

16. McCafferty, J. (1998). Coping with Infoglut. *CFO Magazine*, Sept. 1998.

17. Iqbal, S.T. & Horvitz, E. (2007). Disruption and recovery of computing tasks: field study, analysis and directions. *Proceedings of the ACM Conference on Human Factors in Computing Systems*, 677–686; Hemp, P. (Sept. 2009). Death by information overload. *Harvard Business Review*, 87, 9, 83–89. http://hbr.org/2009/09/death-by-information-overload/; Jackson, T., Dawson, R. & Wilson, D. (2001). Case study:

Evaluating the use of an electronic messaging system in business. Proceedings of the Conference of Empirical Assessment Software Engineering, p.55.

18. Iqbal, S.T. & Horvitz, E. (2007). Disruption and recovery of computing tasks: field study, analysis and directions. *Proceedings of the ACM Conference on Human Factors in Computing Systems*, 677–686.

19. Marulanda-Carter, L. & Jackson, T.W. (2012). Effects of e-mail addiction and interruptions on employees. *Journal of Systems and Information Technology*, 14, 1, 82–94.

20. Wilson, G. (2010). The "Infomania" Study, DrGlennWilson.com, 16 January 2010. http://www.drglennwilson.com/Infomania_experiment_for_HP.doc. Note that only a small number of people were studied in this piece of research.

21. Banbury, S. & Berry, D.C. (1998). Disruption of office-related tasks by speech and office noise. *British Journal of Psychology*, 89, 500.

22. Klingberg, T. (2008). *The Overflowing Brain: Information Overload and the Limits of Working Memory.* Oxford University Press, Oxford, pp.19–20. Smith-Jackson, T.L. & Klein, K.W. (2009). Open-plan offices: Task performance and mental workload. *Journal of Environmental Psychology*, 29, 2, 279–289. http://dx.doi.org/10.1016/j.jenvp.2008.09.002. Carr, N. (2011). *The Shallows: How the Internet is Changing the Way We Think, Read and Remember.* W.W. Norton, New York, pp.118–119.

23. Schumpeter (2011). Too much Information. *The Economist.* http://www.economist.com/node/18895468; 2008 research by the Queensland University of Technology, Oommen, V.G., Knowles, M. & Zhao, I. (2008). Should health service managers embrace open plan work environments? A review. *Asia Pacific Journal of Health Management*, 3 (2), pp.37–43, also linked distractions in open-plan offices and stress problems including flu and high blood pressure.

24. Richtel, M. (2010). Attached to Technology and Paying a Price. *New York Times.* http://www.nytimes.com/2010/06/07/technology/07brain.html.

25. Yahoo! & The Nielsen Company (2011). Mobile Shopping Framework: The role of mobile devices in the shopping process. http://advertising.yahoo.com/article/the-role-of-mobile-devices-in-shopping-process.html.

26. Richtel, M. (2010). Attached to Technology and Paying a Price. *New York Times.* http://www.nytimes.com/2010/06/07/technology/07brain.html.

27. Independent UK panel on breast cancer screening (2012). The benefits and harms of breast cancer screening: an independent review. *The Lancet*, 380, 9855, 1778–1786. http://www.thelancet.com/journals/lancet/article/PIIS0140-6736(12)61611-0/.

28. Giles, J. (2005). Internet encyclopaedias go head to head. *Nature*, 438, 7070, 900–901.

29. Tetlock, P.E. (2005). *Expert Political Judgement.* Princeton University Press, Princeton, NJ.

30. See for example Groopman, J.E. (2008). *How Doctors Think*. Houghton Mifflin, New York, NY, p.59. On p.180 of this highly recommended book, Groopman says that in a study of radiologists, those "who performed poorly were not only inaccurate; they were also very confident that they were right when they were in fact wrong." Original study cited is Potchen, E.J. (2006). Measuring observer performance in chest radiology: some experiences. *Journal of the American College of Radiology*, 3, 423–432.

31. See for example Greenberg, J. (1976). The role of seating position in group interaction: A review, with applications for group trainers. *Group & Organization Studies*, 1, 3.

32. For a discussion on the impact of visuals on decision-making see Step Three, which covers this in detail.

33. Danziger, S., Levav, J. & Avnaim-Pessoa, L. (2011). Extraneous factors in judicial decisions. *PNAS*, 108, 17, 6889–6892.

34. Tuk, M.A., Trampe, D. & Warlop, L. (2011). Inhibitory spillover: Increased urination urgency facilitates impulse control in unrelated domains. *Psychological Science*, 22, 5, 627–633.

35. As well as these books – Gladwell, M. (2007). *Blink: The Power of Thinking without Thinking*, Little, Brown, New York, NY; Thaler, R. & Sunstein, C. (2009). *Nudge: Improving Decisions about Health, Wealth and Happiness*, Penguin, New York, NY; and Suroweicki, J. (2005). *The Wisdom of Crowds*. Anchor Books, New York, NY – other interesting books in this space include Kahneman, D. (2011). *Thinking, Fast and Slow*. Farrar, Straus and Giroux, New York, NY; and Ariely, D. (2008). *Predictably Irrational: The Hidden Forces That Shape Our Decisions*. HarperCollins, New York, NY.

STEP TWO: See the Tiger and the Snake

1. I first came across this study in Ramo, J.C. (2009). *The Age of the Unthinkable: Why the New World Disorder Constantly Surprises Us and What We Can Do About It*. Little, Brown, New York, NY, p.158. The reference for the original study is Chua, H.F., Boland, J.E. & Nisbett, R.E. (2005). Cultural variation in eye movements during scene perception. *Proceedings of the National Academy of Sciences*, 102, 35, 12629–12633.

2. This as opposed to computers: Visa, the credit card company, can analyse two years of records, 73 billion transactions in just thirteen minutes, while every single hour Walmart captures 167 times the amount of information that is contained by all the books in the American Library of Congress. *The Economist* (2010). Data, data everywhere. http://www.economist.com/node/15557443.

3. Cunningham, M.R. (1986). Measuring the physical in physical attractiveness: Quasi-experiments on the sociobiology of female facial beauty. *Journal of Personality and Social Psychology*, 50, 5, 925–935.

4. Buss, D. M. (1989). Sex differences in human mate preferences: Evolutionary hypotheses tested in 37 cultures. *Behavioural and Brain Sciences*, 12, 1–49.

5. Kurzban, R. & Weeden, J. (2005). HurryDate: Mate Preferences in Action. *Evolution and Human Behavior*, 26, 227–244; Rosenbloom, S. (2011). Love, Lies and What They Learned. *New York Times*. http://www.nytimes.com/2011/11/13/fashion/online-dating-as-scientific-research.html?pagewanted=all; Hitsch, G.J. et al. (2006).What Makes You Click? Mate Preferences and Matching Outcomes in Online Dating. http://papers.ssrn.com/sol3/Papers.cfm?abstract_id=895442, 21.

6. Lauer, R., Lauer, J. & Kerr, S.T. (1990). The long-term marriage: Perceptions of stability and satisfaction. *International Journal of Aging and Human Development*, 30, 189–195; Parker, R. (2002). Why Marriages Last: A Discussion of the Literature. *Australian Institute of Family Studies*, 28, 26. http://www.aifs.gov.au/institute/pubs/parker2.html.

7. Stiglitz, J.E., Sen, A. & Fitoussi, J-P. (2009). Report by the Commission on the Measurement of Economic Performance and Social Progress. http://www.stiglitz-sen-fitoussi.fr/documents/rapport_anglais.pdf.

8. Daly, L. & Posner, S. (2011). Beyond GDP: New Measures for a New Economy. Demos.http://www.demos.org/sites/default/files/publications/BeyondGDP_0.pdf.

9. See for example Stewart, M.A. (1984). What is a successful doctor-patient interview? A study of interactions and outcomes. *Social Science & Medicine*, 19, 2, 1672; Ong, L.M.L., de Haes, J.C.J.M., Hoos, A.M. & Lammes, F.B. (1995). Doctor-patient communication: A review of the literature. *Social Science & Medicine*, 40, 7, 90.

10. Freedman, D.H. (2010). Lies, Damned Lies, and Medical Science. *The Atlantic*. http://www.theatlantic.com/magazine/archive/2010/11/lies-damned-lies-and-medical-science/308269/.

11. Hyman Jr., I.E., Boss, S.M., Breanne, M.W., McKenzie, K.E. & Caggiano, J.M. (2010). Did You See the Unicycling Clown? Inattentional Blindness while Walking and Talking on a Cell Phone. *Applied Cognitive Psychology*, 24, 597–607.

12. Mack, A. & Rock, I. (1998). *Inattentional Blindness*, MIT Press, Cambridge, MA; Simons, D.J. & Chabris, C.F. (1999). Gorillas in our Midst: Sustained Inattentional Blindness for Dynamic Events. *Perceptions*, 28, 1059–1074; Fougnie, D. & Maois, R. (2007). Executive Working Memory Load Induces Inattentional Blindness. *Psychonomic Bulletin and Review*, 14, 142–147.

13. Mack, A. (2003). Inattentional Blindness: Looking Without Seeing. *Current Directions in Psychological Science*, 12, 5, 180–184.

14. Wellcome Trust (2012). Study reveals how memory load leaves us "blind" to new visual information. http://www.wellcome.ac.uk/News/Media-office/Press-releases/2012/WTVM056461.htm. See also de Fockert, J.,

Rees, G., Frith, C. & Lavie, N. (2004). Neural Correlates of Attentional Capture in Visual Search. *Journal of Cognitive Neuroscience*, 16, 5, 751–759; Lavie, N. (2010). Attention, Distraction, and Cognitive Control Under Load. *Current Directions in Psychological Science*, 19, 3, 143–148.

15. Cohen, N. (2010). Take $787 Billion. Now Show Where it's Going. *New York Times*. http://www.nytimes.com/2010/03/22/business/media/22link. html.

16. Tufte, E.R. (2003). *The Cognitive Style of PowerPoint*. Graphics Press, Cheshire, CT. Also see Columbia Accident Investigation Board Report, Vol. 1 (2003), p.191.

17. Columbia Accident Investigation Board Report, Vol. 1 (2003). http:// anon.nasa-global.speedera.net/anon.nasa-global/CAIB/CAIB_lowres_full. pdf.

18. Naughton, J. (2003). How PowerPoint Can Fatally Weaken Your Argument. *Observer*. http://www.guardian.co.uk/technology/2003/dec/21/ comment.business.

19. Ricks, T.E. (2007). *Fiasco: The American Military Mission in Iraq*. Penguin, London. Excerpt at http://www.armedforcesjournal. com/2006/08/1936008/.

20. Bumiller, E. (2010). We Have Met the Enemy and he is PowerPoint. *New York Times*. This also cites concerns that PowerPoint "stifles discussion, critical thinking and thoughtful decision-making." See also Ricks, T.E. (2007). *Fiasco: The American Military Mission in Iraq*. Penguin, London; Hammes, T.X. (2009). Dumb-Dumb Bullets. *Armed Forces Journal*; Burke, C. (aka Starbuck) (2009). The TX Hammes PowerPoint Challenge. *Small Wars Journal*. The phrase "hypnotising chickens" has been entered into the urban dictionary as "military and government jargon" for "the process of developing PowerPoint slides and other media that will induce coma in the audience." http://www.urbandictionary.com/define. php?term=hypnotizing per cent20chickens. It is derived from Hammes, T.X. (2009). Dumb-Dumb Bullets. *Armed Forces Journal*. http://www. armedforcesjournal.com/2009/07/4061641/.

21. See Boyle, D. (2000). *The Tyranny of Numbers: Why Counting Can't Make Us Happy*. HarperCollins, London.

22. Feiring, A. (2008). *The Battle for Wine and Love or How I Saved the World from Parkerization*. Harcourt Books, Orlando, FL.

23. Robinson, J. (1997). *Tasting Pleasure: Confessions of a Wine Lover*. Penguin, New York, NY, p.319.

24. Quoted in Bowden, M. (2012). *The Finish: The Killing of Osama bin Laden*. Grove Press, New York, NY.

25. Ibid.

26. The interviewee wished to remain anonymous, so "Ms. Broun" is a pseudonym.

27. Boyle, D. (2000). *The Tyranny of Numbers: Why Counting Can't Make Us Happy*. HarperCollins, London.

28. This is commonly attributed to Einstein, yet is now thought to be a misattribution. Some suggest that it first appeared in Cameron, W.B. (1963). *Informal Sociology: A Causal Introduction to Sociological Thinking*. Random House, London.

29. Sharot, T., Wom, C.W. & Dolan, R.J. (2011). How unrealistic optimism is maintained in the face of reality. *Nature Neuroscience*, 14, 11.

30. Akerlof, G.A. & Shiller, R.J. (2009). *Animal Spirits: How Human Psychology Drives the Economy, and Why It Matters for Global Capitalism*. Princeton University Press, Princeton, NJ.

31. Sharot, T. (2011). *The Optimism Bias: A Tour of the Irrationally Positive Brain*. Pantheon, New York, NY.

32. Sharot, T. (2012). The Optimism Bias by Tali Sharot: Extract. *Observer*. http://www.guardian.co.uk/science/2012/jan/01/tali-sharot-the-optimism-bias-extract.

33. This story (including Dr. Alter's subsequent quotes) is from Groopman, J.E. (2008). *How Doctors Think*. Houghton Mifflin, New York, NY, p.59.

34. http://www.linkedin.com/pub/harrison-alter/19/b71/548.

35. http://www.hghed.com/people/faculty.

36. Haidt, J. (2012). *The Righteous Mind*. Allen Lane, London, p.79. The study cited is Westen, D., Blagov, P.S., Harenski, K., Kilts, C. & Hamann, S. (2006). Neural Bases of Motivated Reasoning: An fMRI Study of Emotional Constraints on Partisan Political Judgment in the 2004 U.S. Presidential Election. *Journal of Cognitive Neuroscience*, 18, 11, 1947–1958.

37. Fishbein, W. & Treverton, G. (2004). Making Sense of Transnational Threats. The Sherman Kent Center for Intelligence Analysis, 3, 1.

38. This is a practice medical professor Jon Kabat-Zinn of the University of Massachusetts uses as an easy introduction to mindfulness. See Kabat-Zinn (2011). *Mindfulness for Beginners: Reclaiming the Present Moment – and Your Life*. Sounds True, Louisville, CO.

39. Conversation with Stuart Roden, Lansdowne Partners.

40. Martin, D. (2012). Richard Zanuck, Producer of Blockbusters, Dies at 77. *New York Times*. http://www.nytimes.com/2012/07/14/business/media/richard-zanuck-producer-of-blockbusters-dies-at–77.html?_r=0D36BF4B49651B3576.

41. BBC News (2012). Hollywood producer Richard Zanuck dies. http://www.bbc.co.uk/news/world-us-canada–18839577.

42. See also Balio, T. (1987). *United Artists: The Company that Changed the Film Industry*. University of Wisconsin Press, Madison, WI, p.128; Martin, R. (2000). *Mean Streets and Raging Bulls: The Legacy of Film Noir in Contemporary American Cinema*. Scarecrow Press, Lanham, MD, p.19; Purdum, T.S. (2005); *The Sound of Music*: 40 Years of Unstoppable Success. *New York Times*. http://www.nytimes.com/2005/05/31/arts/31iht-music.html; http://boxofficemojo.com/alltime/adjusted.htm.

43. Vallance, T. (2012). Richard Zanuck: Film Producer Responsible for Hits Including *Jaws* and *Driving Miss Daisy*. *Independent*. http://www. independent.co.uk/news/obituaries/richard-zanuck-film-producer-responsible-for-hits-including-jaws-and-driving-miss-daisy–7956977.html.

44. Balio, T. (1987). *United Artists: The Company that Changed the Film Industry*. University of Wisconsin Press, Madison, WI, p.128.

45. Schatz, T. The New Hollywood, in Collins, T. (1992). *Film Theory Goes to the Movies: Cultural Analysis of Contemporary Film*. Routledge, London, p.14; http://www.imdb.com/title/tt0063642/business.

46. Schatz, T. The New Hollywood, in Collins, T. (1992). *Film Theory Goes to the Movies: Cultural Analysis of Contemporary Film*. Routledge, London, p.14.

47. Warfield, S. (2008). From *Hair* to *Rent*: is "rock" a four-letter word on Broadway?, in Everett, W.A. & Laird, P.R. (eds). *The Cambridge Companion to the Musical*. Cambridge University Press, Cambridge, pp.235–249.

48. Associated Press (2008). Nokia Sales Increased 4 per cent in Quarter. *New York Times*, 18 July 2008. http://www.nytimes.com/2008/07/18/technology/18nokia.html?scp=21&sq=nokia+2007&st=nyt.

49. O'Brien, K.J. (2010). Nokia's New Chief Faces Culture of Complacency. *New York Times*. http://www.nytimes.com/2010/09/27/technology/27nokia.html?pagewanted=all&_r=0.

50. Troianovski, A. & Grundberg, S. (2012). Nokia's Bad Call on Smartphones. *Wall Street Journal*. http://online.wsj.com/article/SB100014 24052702304388004577531002591315494.html.

51. Ibid.

52. Business Wire (2012). Strategy Analytics: Apple iPhone Generates US$150 Billion of Revenues since Launch. http://www.businesswire.com/portal/site/home/permalink/?ndmViewId=news_view&newsLang=en&newsId=20120627005588&div=–410588540.

53. Ewing, A. (2012). Nokia's Junk Debt Rating Dropped Lower by S&P on Losses. Bloomberg. http://www.bloomberg.com/news/2012–08–15/nokia-s-junk-debt-rating-dropped-lower-by-s-p-on-losses.html; BBC News (2012). Apple becomes the "most valuable company of all time. http://www.bbc.co.uk/news/business–19325913; *Forbes* (2013). Apple's Greatest Gift from the Holidays is its Bargain Stock Price. http://www.forbes.com/sites/greatspeculations/2013/01/10/apples-greatest-gift-from-the-holidays-is-its-bargain-stock-price/.

54. Bill Bartmann lost his debt-collection business worth up to $3.5 billion; he was declared bankrupt and indicted by US government for fraud. Later acquitted, he set up a similar business again and is now worth $100 million. http://www.forbes.com/2010/01/20/gucci-indy500-letterman-entreprenuer-management-risk-greatest_slide_14.html; http://www.inc.com/magazine/20100901/how-bill-bartmann-lost-it-all-and-got-it-back.html; George Foreman made a lot of money boxing; ten years after

retiring he was nearly bankrupt, but built it all back up again by strategic endorsements, most famously of the George Foreman Grill. http://www.success.com/articles/557-big-business-with-big-george; Jeffrey Archer was left nearly bankrupt in the 1970s by a bad investment; he resigned his seat in Parliament but made his money back by writing novels. http://www.telegraph.co.uk/culture/donotmigrate/3671588/Jeffrey-Archer-The-next-chapter.html.

55. *Scotsman* (2003). The J.K. Rowling Story. http://www.scotsman.com/lifestyle/books/features/the-jk-rowling-story-1-652114

56. Gunelius, S. (2008). *Harry Potter: The Story of a Global Business Phenomenon*. Palgrave Macmillan, Basingstoke, p. 6.

57. Kirk, C.A. (2003). *J.K. Rowling: A Biography*. Greenwood Publishing, Westport, CT, p.75.

58. Gunelius, S. (2008). *Harry Potter: The Story of a Global Business Phenomenon*. Palgrave Macmillan, Basingstoke, p. 6.

59. Groopman, J.E. (2008). *How Doctors Think*. Houghton Mifflin, New York, NY, p.74.

60. The Associated Press. (2008). Obama on Vacationing and Time to Think *New York Times*. http://www.nytimes.com/2008/07/27/us/politics/27CHAT.html?_r=1&scp=1&sq=obama per cent20vacation&st=cse&oref=slogin.

61. Gawande, A. (2011). *The Checklist Manifesto: How to Get Things Right*. Picador, London.

STEP THREE: Don't Be Scared of the Nacirema

1. Miner, H. (1956). Body Ritual Among the Nacirema. *American Anthropologist, New Series*, 58, 3, 305–7.

2. Dade, P. (2007). *All Made Up: 100 Years of Cosmetics Advertising*. Middlesex University Press, London.

3. Wansink, B. et al. (2005). How Descriptive Food Names Bias Sensory Perception in Restaurants. Food Quality and Preference. *Science Direct*, 16, 5, 393–400.

4. Kliger, D., Kudryavtsev, A., Puhan, T., Vogel, R. & Tal Or, N. (2012). The HeUristic: First-Body vs Third-Body Presentation Impression Effect on Employment Decisions. Unpublished manuscript.

5. Thibodeau, P.H. & Boroditsky, L. (2011). Metaphors we think with: The role of metaphor in reasoning. *PLoS ONE*, 6, 20, 1–11. http://www.plosone.org/article/info per cent3Adoi per cent2F10.1371 per cent2Fjournal.pone.0016782.

6. Cited in Fine, C. (2010). *Delusions of Gender: How Our Minds, Society, and Neurosexism Create Difference*. W.W. Norton & Co., New York, NY, p.55. The original study is Steinpreis, R.E., Anders, K.A. & Ritzke, D. (1999). The impact of gender on the review of curricula vitae of job applicants and tenure candidates: a national empirical study. *Sex Roles*, 41, 7/8, 509–528.

7. See Ghosh, P.R. (2008). Taking stock: Call it whatever but an apple's an apple. A Dow Jones Newswires Column. Dow Jones & Co. Inc. http://www.raghurau.com/Media/DJN_20080109_NameChange.htm; Bonner, B. (2000). Freak show. The Daily Reckoning. http://dailyreckoning.com/freak-show/.

8. Cooper, M., Dimitrov, O. & Rau, R. (2001). A rose.com by any other name. *Journal of Finance*, 56, 6.

9. Djordjevic, J., Lundstrom, J.N., Clément, F., Boyle, J.A., Pouliot, S. & Jones-Gotman, M. (2008). A rose by any other name: Would it smell as sweet? *Journal of Neurophysiology*, 99, 1, 386–393. http://jn.physiology.org/content/99/1/386.long#xref-fn-1-1.

10. Luke Birmingham of University of Southampton's research as discussed in Annual Meeting of Royal College of Psychiatrists 2000. Cited in Adler, R. (2000). Pigeonholed. *New Scientist*, 38.

11. Englich, B. (2005). "Geben Sie ihm doch einfach fünf Jahre!": Einflüsse parteiischer Zwischenrufer auf richterliche Urteile. ["Give him five years!" – Influences of partisan hecklers on judges' sentencing decisions]. *Zeitschrift für Sozialpsychologie*, 36, 215–225. http://psycontent.metapress.com/content/m66894t63660t381/?genre=article&id=doi per cent3a10.1024 per cent2f0044–3514.36.4.215. For more on anchoring see original study: Tversky, A. & Kahneman, D. (1974). Judgment under uncertainty: Heuristics and biases. *Science*, 185, 1124–1130. Also Jacowitz, K.E. & Kahneman, D. (1995). Measures of anchoring in estimation tasks. *Personality and Social Psychology Bulletin*, 21, 11, 1161–1166. Also Kahneman, D. (2011). *Thinking, Fast and Slow*. Farrar, Straus and Giroux, New York, NY.

12. Scott, P.J. & Lizieri, C. (2012). Consumer house price judgements: new evidence of anchoring and arbitrary coherence. *Journal of Property Research*, 37–41. Beggs, B. & Graddy, K. (2009). Anchoring Effects: Evidence from Art Auctions. *American Economic Revue*, 99, 3, 1027–1039. Bornstein, B. & Chapman, G.B. (1996). The more you ask for, the more you get: Anchoring in personal injury verdicts. *Applied Cognitive Psychology*, 10, 519–540.

13. Ariely, D. (2009). *Predictably Irrational: The Hidden Forces That Shape Our Decisions*. HarperCollins, London.

14. Chapman, G.B. & Johnson, E.J. (1999). Anchoring, activation, and the construction of values. *Organizational Behavior and Human Decision Processes*. *ScienceDirect*, 79, 2, 115–153.

15. Mussweiler, T., Strack, F. & Pfeiffer, J. (2000). Overcoming the Inevitable Anchoring Effect: Considering the Opposite Compensates for Selective Accessibility. *Personality and Social Psychology Bulletin*, November 2000, 26, 9, 1142–1150.

16. Slovic, P., Monahan, J. & MacGregor, D.G. (2000). Violence risk assessment and risk communication: The effects of using actual cases, providing instructions, and employing probability vs. frequency formats.

Law and Human Behavior, 24, 271–296. See also on physicians' ability to process probabilistic information and make related decisions Tversky, A. & Kahneman, D. (1981). The Framing of Decisions and the Psychology of Choice. *Science*, 211, 4481, 453–458.

17. See Slovic, Monahan & MacGregor (2000). Violence risk assessment and risk communication. See also on physicians' ability to process probabilistic information and make related decisions Tversky, A. & Kahneman, D. (1981). The Framing of Decisions and the Psychology of Choice. *Science*, 211, 4481, 453–458.

18. Gerend, M.A. & Sias, T. (2009). Message framing and color priming: How subtle threat cues affect persuasion. *Journal of Experimental Social Psychology*, 45, 999–1002.

19. Elliot, A.J. & Niesta, D. (2008). Romantic red: Red enhances men's attraction to women. *Journal of Personality and Social Psychology*, 5, 1150–1164; Schwarz, S. & Singer, M. (2012). Romantic red revisited: Red enhances men's attraction to young, but not menopausal women. *Journal of Experimental Social Psychology*. In press, corrected proof. Interestingly, these researchers found this to hold true in pre-menopausal women, but not older women.

20. Cited in Frank, M.G. & Gilovich, T. (1988). The dark side of self- and social perception: Black uniforms and aggression in professional sports. *Journal of Personality and Social Psychology*, 54, 1, 74–85.

21. Guéguen, N. & Jacob, C. (2012). Clothing color and tipping: Gentlemen patrons give more tips to waitresses with red clothes. *Journal of Hospitality & Tourism Research*. In an earlier 2008 study the authors found that only red differed from the other colours. As a consequence, in their 2012 study they assumed that blue, grey or green would not change the results as found in 2008.

22. Kliger, D. & Gilad, D. (2012). Red light, green light: Color priming in financial decisions. *Journal of Socio-Economics*, 41, 5, 738–745.

23. North, A.C., Hargreaves, D.J. & McKendrick, J. (1997). In-store music affects product choice. *Nature*, 390, 6656, 132.

24. Caldwell, C. & Hibbert, S.A. (1999). Play that one again: The effect of music tempo on consumer behaviour in a restaurant, in Dubois, B., Lowrey, T.M., Shrum, L.J. & Vanhuele, M. (eds) (1999). *European Advances in Consumer Research*, Vol. 4: *Association for Consumer Research*, 58–62; North, A.C., Shilcock, A. & Hargreaves, D.J. (2003). The effect of musical style on restaurant customers' spending. *Environment and Behavior*, 35, 712–718.

25. Crusco, A.H. & Wetzel, C.G. (1984). The Midas touch: The effects of interpersonal touch on restaurant tipping. *Personality & Social Psychology Bulletin*, 10, 4, 512–517.

26. Willis, F.N. & Hamm, H.K. (1980). The use of interpersonal touch in securing compliance. *Journal of Nonverbal Behavior*, 6, 49–55.

27. Guégen, N. & Meineri, S. (2010). Improving medication adherence by using practitioner nonverbal techniques: a field experiment on the effect of touch. *Journal of Behavioral Medicine*, 33, 466–473.

28. Lindstrom, M. (2005). *Brand Sense: How to Build Powerful Brands Through Touch, Taste, Smell, Sight & Sound*. Kogan Page Ltd, London.

29. Ackerman, J.M., Nocera, C.C. & Bargh, J.A. (2010). Incidental haptic sensations influence social judgments and decisions. *Science*, 328, 5986, 1712–1715.

30. Ibid.

31. Kay, A.C., Wheeler, S.C., Bargh, J.A. & Ross, L. (2004). Material priming: The influence of mundane physical objects on situational construal and competitive behavioral choice. *Organisational Behavior and Human Decision Processes*, 95, 1, 83–96.

32. Cunningham, B.J. (2004). *Tricks of the Trade: A Real Estate Broker's Inside Advice on Buying or Selling a Home*. Adams Media, Avon, MA, p. 8.

33. Kille, D.R., Forest, A.L. & Wood, J.V. (2012). Tall, Dark and Stable: Embodiment Motivates Male Selection Preferences. *Psychological Science*, 0956797612457392. *The Economist* (2012). Psychology: Tall, dark and stable, 14 July 2012.

34. See for example Lawrence, C.P., Finkel, S.E. & Andrus, D.C. (1981). Explorations in anchoring: The effects of prior range, anchor extremity, and suggestive hints. Manuscript, Stanford University.

35. Chapman, G.B. & Johnson, E.J. (1999). Anchoring, activation, and the construction of values. *Organizational Behavior and Human Decision Processes*, 79, 2, 115–153.

36. Wansink, B., Kent, R.J. & Hoch, S.J. (1998). An anchoring and adjustment model of purchase quantity decisions. *Journal of Marketing Research*, 35, 71–81.

37. Mussweiler, T., Strack, F. & Pfeiffer, T. (2000). Overcoming the inevitable anchoring effect: Considering the opposite compensates for selective accessibility. *Personality and Social Psychology Bulletin*, 26, 9, 1142–1150.

38. The logic here is basically as follows: removing yourself from the situation should solve the so-called "associationistic" influences on our decision-making – when we hear/smell/see a certain colour/word/number we automatically make associations, but these effects diminish when we distance ourselves from them.

39. A lecturer at University College Cardiff found that, between 1977 and 1981, 42 per cent of male students in the arts faculty received Firsts or 2.1s compared to 34 per cent for their female counterparts. The contrast was most shocking in the English department: 80 per cent of English students were female, but only 27 per cent of them got Firsts or 2.1s, compared to 45 per cent for men. In 1985, however, the university decided to introduce anonymous marking – and everything changed. Women now outperformed men: 47 per cent of women received Firsts or

2.1s compared to 42 per cent of men. This research was first published in
Belsey, C. (1988). Marking by numbers. *AUT Women*, 15 (pp.1–2).
London: Association of University Teachers. It is cited by Brennan, D.J.
(2008). University student anonymity in the summative assessment of
written work. *Higher Education Research & Development*, 27, 1, 43–54.

40. Some studies show that thinking specifically about the magnitude of the
bias the anchor has induced into the thought process – that is, the size of
your likely error – can actually eliminate the effect of the anchor. See for
example LeBoeuf, R.A. & Shafir, E. (2009). Anchoring on the "Here" and
"Now" in time and distance judgments. *Journal of Experimental
Psychology*, 35, 81–93.

STEP FOUR: Ditch Deference and Challenge Experts

1. Engelmann, J.B., Capra, C.M., Noussair, C. & Berns, G.S. (2009). Expert
Financial Advice Neurobiologically "Offloads" Financial Decision-
Making under Risk. http://www.plosone.org/article/info:doi per
cent2F10.1371 per cent2Fjournal.pone.0004957.

2. The trend of the Edelman Trust reports over the year points to a rising
trust in experts: approximately 59 per cent of those surveyed trusted
them in 2008; 64 per cent in 2010; 70 per cent in 2011. Indeed, the 2011
report describes how there has been an eight-point rise since 2009: "Trust
in all credentialed spokespeople is higher this year, signaling a desire for
authority and accountability – a likely result of the skepticism wrought
by last year's string of corporate crises." See Edelman Trust Barometer
2008, 22 Jan. 2008. http://edelmaneditions.com/wp-content/
uploads/2010/12/edelman-trust-barometer–2008-richard-edelman-
presentation_0.pdf; Edelman Trust Barometer 2010, 26 Jan. 2010. http://
edelmaneditions.com/wp-content/uploads/2010/11/edelman-trust-
barometer–2010.pdf; Edelman Trust Barometer 2011: Annual Global
Opinion Leaders Study, Jan. 2011. http://edelmaneditions.com/
wp-content/uploads/2011/02/trust-executive-summary-final.pdf. Note
that the Edelman Trust Barometer 2011 puts academic and "technical
experts from a company" top of who is trusted – above, for example,
chief executive officers. In a blog post about the results Richard Edelman
said: "Given the uncertainty in the economy and plethora of sources of
information, respondents said that they believe spokespeople with proven
expertise, in order Academics, Technical Experts from a Company (for
first time), Financial Analysts and Chief Executive Officers." See Edelman
R. (2011). Trust Transformed: Results of the 2011 Edelman Trust
Barometer, 25 Jan. 2011. http://www.edelman.com/p/6-a-m/
trust-transformed-results-of-the–2011-edelman-trust-barometer.

3. Naftulin, D.H., Ware, Jr., J. E. & Donnelly, F.A. (1973). The Doctor Fox
Lecture: A Paradigm of Educational Seduction. *Journal of Medical
Education*, vol. 48, July 1973, 630–635. http://www.er.uqam.ca/nobel/
r30034/PSY4180/Pages/Naftulin.html.

4. In 1980 Professor Scott Armstrong asked twenty management professors to rank ten management journals in terms of academic stature. The journals varied in degrees of readability according to the Flesch Reading Ease Test. The professors rated the journals that were hardest to read as the most prestigious, and the easiest to read as the least. When Armstrong rewrote passages from the difficult journals to make them easier to read, the professors ranked them lower than previously. See Armstrong, J.S. (1980). Bafflegab Pays. *Psychology Today*, May 1980, 12.

5. Fanelli, D. (2009). How many scientists fabricate and falsify research? A systematic review and meta-analysis of survey data. *PLoS One*, 4, 5. "A pooled weighted average of 1.97 per cent (N = 7, 95 per cent CI: 0.86–4.45) of scientists admitted to have fabricated, falsified or modified data or results at least once."

6. Elstein, A.S. "Clinical Reasoning in Medicine," in Higgs, J. & Jones, M.A. (eds) (1995). *Clinical Reasoning in the Health Professions*, Butterworth-Heinemann, Woburn, MA, pp.49–59. Referenced in Groopman, J.E. (2008). *How Doctors Think*, Houghton Mifflin, New York, NY, p. 288.

7. Shojania, K.G. et al. (2003). Changes in rates of autopsy-detected diagnostic errors over time. *Journal of the American Medical Association*, 289, 21, 2849–2956.

8. Groopman, J.E. (2008). *How Doctors Think*, Houghton Mifflin, New York, NY, p. 288.

9. Freeman, D.H. (2010). *Wrong*. Little, Brown, New York, NY, p. 35; original reference: Paskin, J. (2008). Ten Things Your Tax Preparer Won't Tell You. *SmartMoney*, 21 Feb. 2008.

10. Ellis, C.D. (2011). The Winners' Game. *Financial Analysts Journal*, 67, 4, 11–17.

11. German Consumer Affairs Ministry (2008). Study of Evers and Jung. *Anforderungen an Finanzvermittler*, Sept. 2008; referenced in European Commission (2011). Consumer Market Study on Advice within the Area of Retail Investment Services. http://ec.europa.eu/consumers/rights/docs/investment_advice_study_en.pdf.

12. Cranfield Study cited in Craig, D. (2005). *Rip Off!: The Scandalous Inside Story of the Management Consulting Money Machine*. The Original Book Co., London.

13. *The Economist* (1995). Garbage in, garbage out. 3 June 1995.

14. Senate Select Committee on Intelligence (1977). *Staff Report: U.S. Intelligence and the Oil Issue, 1973–1974, 95th Cong., 1st sess.* http://www.intelligence.senate.gov/pdfs/77oil.pdf. The sentence "The CIA and Intelligence Community also failed to warn of the ensuing oil crisis brought on by OPEC" appears in Central Intelligence Agency (2007). Fifteen DCIs' First 100 Days.https://www.cia.gov/library/center-for-the-study-of-intelligence/kent-csi/vol38no1/html/v38i5a07p.html. See also Szulc, T. (1978). Goodbye James Bond: In From the Cold War. *New York Magazine*, 13 Feb. 1978.

15. Tetlock, P.E. (2005). *Expert Political Judgement*. Princeton University Press, Princeton, NJ, p.68.

16. King, M. (2013). Orlando, the cat's whiskers of stock picking. *Observer*, 13 Jan. 2013.

17. Greenspan said of derivatives that they had "permitted the unbundling of financial risks." Remarks by Chairman Alan Greenspan Risk Transfer and Financial Stability to the Federal Reserve Bank of Chicago's Forty-first Annual Conference on Bank Structure, Chicago, Illinois, 5 May 2005. http://www.federalreserve.gov/boarddocs/speeches/2005/20050505/. Larry Summers also failed to recognise the need for regulation in the derivatives market, stating that "To date there has been no clear evidence of a need for additional regulation of the institutional OTC derivatives market." Treasury Deputy Secretary Lawrence H. Summers Testimony Before the Senate Committee on Agriculture, Nutrition, and Forestry on the CFTC Concept Release, 30 Sept. 1998. http://www.treasury.gov/press-center/press-releases/Pages/rr2616.aspx. Summers also said: "Mr Chairman, the American OTC derivatives market is second to none. In a few short years it has assumed a major role in our own economy and become a magnet for derivative business from around the world." See also Hansell, S. (2004). Derivatives Get a Key Supporter. *New York Times*, 26 May 2004. http://www.nytimes.com/1994/05/26/business/company-news-derivatives-get-a-key-supporter.html.

18. Kaletsky, A. (2009). Economists are the Forgotten Guilty Men. *The Times*, 5 Feb. 2009. http://www.thetimes.co.uk/tto/opinion/columnists/anatolekaletsky/article2043541.ece.

19. Martinson, B.C., Anderson, M.S. & de Vries, R. (2005). Scientists Behaving Badly. *Nature*, 435, 737–738.

20. Fanelli, D. (2009). How Many Scientists Fabricate and Falsify Research? A Systematic Review and Meta-Analysis of Survey Data. *PLoS ONE*, 4 (5): e5738. doi:10.1371/journal.pone.0005738. http://www.plosone.org/article/info per cent3Adoi per cent2F10.1371 per cent2Fjournal.pone.0005738.

21. Boutron, I. et al. (2010). Reporting and Interpretation of Randomised Controlled Trials with Statistically Nonsignificant Results for Primary Outcomes. *Journal of the American Medical Association*, 303, 20, 2058–2064.

22. Stern, S. & Lemmens, T. (2011). Legal Remedies for Medical Ghostwriting: Imposing Fraud Liability on Guest Authors of Ghostwritten Articles. *PLoS Med.*, 8 (8): e1001070. doi:10.1371/journal.pmed.1001070. To support this claim the authors cite Jureidini, J.N., McHenry, L.B.& Mansfield, P.R. (2008). Clinical trials and drug promotion: Selective reporting of Study 329. *International Journal of Risk and Safety in Medicine*, 20, 183; Lexchin, J. (2003). Pharmaceutical industry sponsorship and research outcome and quality: systematic review. *British Medical Journal*, 326: 1167–1170; Bekelman, J.E. & Li, Y.,

Gross, C.P. (2003). Scope and impact of financial conflicts of interest in biomedical research: a systematic review. *Journal of the American Medical Association*, 289: 454–465; and Schott, G., Pachl, H., Limbach, U., Gundert-Remy, U., Ludwig, W.-D., et al. (2010). See also The financing of drug trials by pharmaceutical companies and its consequences. Part 1: a qualitative, systematic review of the literature on possible influences on the findings, protocols, and quality of drug trials. *Deutsches Ärzteblatt International*, 107, 279–285; and Schott, G., Pachl, H., Limbach, U., Gundert-Remy, U., Lieb, K., et al. (2010). The financing of drug trials by pharmaceutical companies and its consequences. Part 2: a qualitative, systematic review of the literature on possible influences on authorship, access to trial data, and trial registration and publication. *Deutsches Ärzteblatt International*, 107, 295–301.

23. *Huffington Post* (2012). Benefits of Chocolate: Study Finds Eating Cocoa Daily May Improve Cognitive Impairment. 13 Aug. 2012. http://www. huffingtonpost.com/2012/08/13/benefits-of-chocolate-study_n_1773893. html.

24. Cohen, D. (2012). The truth about sports drinks. *British Journal of Medicine*, 345.

25. Bhattacharya, S. (2005). Up to 140,000 heart attacks linked to Vioxx. *New Scientist*, 25 Jan. 2005. http://www.newscientist.com/article/dn6918-up-to-140000-heart-attacks-linked-to-vioxx.html. The figure referred to there stems from Graham, D.J., Campen, D., Hui, R., Spence, M., Cheetham, C., Levy, G., Shoor, S. & Ray, W.A. (2005). Risk of acute myocardial infarction and sudden cardiac death in patients treated with cyclo-oxygenase 2 selective and non-selective non-steroidal anti-inflammatory drugs: nested case-control study. *The Lancet*, 365, 9458, 5–11, 475–481.

26. Revealed by Harris, G. & Berenson, A. (2005). 10 Voters on Panel Backing Pain Pills Had Industry Ties. *New York Times*, 25 Feb. 2005. http://www.nytimes.com/2005/02/25/politics/25fda.html?pagewanted=print&position=&_r=0.

27. Shackle, S. (2011). Who are Standard and Poor's and why should we care?. *The New Statesman*. http://www.newstatesman.com/blogs/the-staggers/2011/12/credit-ratings-agencies-france.

28. Hau, H., Langfield S. & Marques-Ibanez, D. (2012). Bank Ratings: What Determines Their Quality? Working Paper Series No. 1484, Oct. 2012. http://www.ecb.europa.eu/pub/pdf/scpwps/ecbwp1484.pdf.

29. FSA Discussion Paper 07/1 (2007). A review of retail distribution. June 2007, cited in http://blogs.telegraph.co.uk/finance/ianmcowie/100008791/10-tips-to-spot-rip-off-financial-advice/. Note that in the UK the rules imposed by the Retail Distribution Review, which came into effect in 2013, may have a positive effect on this practice.

30. This story first came to my attention in a comment piece by Aaronovitch, D. (2009). The strange case of the surveillance cameras. *The Times*, 3 Mar. 2009, p. 26. Britons "could be microchipped like a dogs in a decade."

Evening Standard, 30 Oct. 2006. http://www.standard.co.uk/news/britons-could-be-microchipped-like-dogs-in-a-decade–7207412.html. See also Kelly, T. (2009). Revealed: Big Brother Britain has more CCTV cameras than China. *Daily Mail*, 11 Aug. 2009. http://www.dailymail.co.uk/news/article–1205607/Shock-figures-reveal-Britain-CCTV-camera–14-people-China.html; and Smith, E. (2007). Friend or foe? The roadside spies cluttering up Britain. *Sunday Times*, 18 Mar. 2007, Features, p.4.

31. Armstrong, G. & Norris, C. (1999). *The Maximum Surveillance Society: The Rise of CCTV*. Berg Publishers, Oxford.

32. Ibid., p.42.

33. Aaronovitch, D. (2009). The strange case of the surveillance cameras. *The Times*, 3 Mar. 2009, p.26.

34. Tetlock talks about this in context of fame/hedgehogs: Tetlock, P. E. (2005). *Expert Political Judgement*. Princeton University Press, Princeton, NJ, p.63.

35. Friedman, J. (2007). The Prophylactic Extraction of Third Molars: A Public Health Hazard. *American Journal of Public Health*, 97, 9.

36. Rabin, R.C. (2011). Wisdom of having tooth removed questioned. *Seattle Times*, 10 Sept. 2011. http://seattletimes.com/html/health/2016162884_wisdomteeth10.html.

37. American Association of Oral and Maxillofacial Surgeons (2010). Conventional Wisdom about Wisdom Teeth Confirmed. Press release, 19 Oct. 2010. http://www.aaoms.org/docs/media/third_molars/press_release.pdf.

38. Ibid.

39. That study is: Stanley, H.R., Alattar, M., Collett, W.K., Stringfellow Jr., H.R., Spiegel, E.H. (1988). The pathological sequelae of "neglected" impacted third molars. *Journal of Oral Pathology*, 17 (3), 113–117.

40. Daley, T.D. (1996). Third molar prophylactic extraction: a review and analysis of the literature. *Gen Dent*, 44, 310–320.

41. Friedman, J. (2007). The Prophylactic Extraction of Third Molars: A Public Health Hazard. *American Journal of Public Health*, 97, 9.

42. American Public Health Association (2008). Opposition to Prophylactic Removal of Third Molars (Wisdom Teeth). Policy Date: 10/28/2008. Policy Number: 20085.

43. Insights from email correspondence with Jay W. Friedman.

44. The difference in expert agreement in financial and non-financial domains is pointed out by, among others, Shanteau, J. (2001). What does it mean when experts disagree?, in Salas, E. & Klein, G. (eds) (2001). *Linking Expertise and Naturalistic Decision Making*. Lawrence Erlbaum Associates, Mahwah, NJ. http://pilotwebmail.k-state.edu/psych/cws/pdf/ndm_chapter01.PDF.

45. Epstein, S. (1995). The Construction of Lay Expertise: AIDS Activism and the Forging of Credibility in the Reform of Clinical Trials. *Science, Technology & Human Values*, 20, 4, 408–437.

46. See for example Brooke, J. (1998). Science and Religion: Lessons from History? *Science*, 11 December 1998, 282, 5396, 1985–1986. DOI: 10.1126/science.282.5396.1985.

47. Partnoy, F (2009). Derivative Dangers. NPR, 25 Mar. 2009. http://www.npr.org/templates/story/story.php?storyId=102325715; Partnoy, F. (1997, 2009). *F.I.A.S.C.O.: Blood in the Water on Wall Street*. W.W. Norton, New York, NY; Karz, G. (2009). Who Predicted the Global Financial Crisis. Investor Home. http://investorhome.com/predicted.htm; Dealbook (2009). S.E.C. Appoints Hedge Fund Veteran as Adviser. *New York Times*, 6 Nov. 2009. http://dealbook.nytimes.com/2009/11/06/sec-appoints-hedge-fund-veteran-as-adviser/.

48. Dotinga, R. (2011). Surgeon Experience Matters in Neck Artery Procedure: Study; Patient death rate within 30 days higher if doctor has less experience with carotid stenting; *Consumer Health News* (2007). Report, 27 Sept. 2011. http://news.yahoo.com/surgeon-experience-matters-neck-artery-procedure-study–201347853.html.

49. Tetlock, P. E. (2005). *Expert Political Judgement*. Princeton University Press, Princeton, NJ. Philip Tetlock suggests that were forecasters to have to publicly keep track of their batting averages, forecasts would probably improve. He advocates applying performance metrics to prediction, arguing that if experts and groups felt their reputations were at stake, it would motivate them to try harder to distinguish "what they really know about the future from what they suspect" (p. 218).

50. Tetlock, ibid., finds for example that the accuracy of an expert's predictions actually has an inverse relationship to his or her self-confidence.

51. Ibid., p. 21.

52. Groopman, J.E. (2008). *How Doctors Think*. Houghton Mifflin, New York, NY, p. 59. Original study cited is Potchen, E.J. (2006). Measuring observer performance in chest radiology: some experiences. *Journal of the American College of Radiology*, 3, 423–432.

53. Berner, E.S. & Graber, M.L. (2008). Overconfidence as a Cause of Diagnostic Error in Medicine. *American Journal of Medicine*, 121 (5A); their reference: Podbregar, M., Voga, G., Krivec, B., Skale, R., Pareznik, R. & Gabrscek L. (2001). Should we confirm our clinical diagnostic certainty by autopsies? *Intensive Care Medicine*, 27, 1750–1755.

54. Von Hayek, F.A. (1989). The Pretence of Knowledge. *American Economic Review*, 79, 6.

55. Tetlock, P. E. (2005). *Expert Political Judgement*. Princeton University Press, Princeton, NJ.

STEP FIVE: Learn from Shepherds and Shop Assistants

1. International Atomic Energy Agency (2009). Frequently Asked Chernobyl Questions. http://www.iaea.org/newscenter/features/chernobyl–15/cherno-faq.shtml.

2. BBC News (2012). Chernobyl sheep controls lifted in Wales and Cumbria. http://www.bbc.co.uk/news/uk-wales–17472698.

3. Wright, S.M., Smith, J.T., Beresford, N.A. & Scott, W.A. (2003). Monte-Carlo prediction of changes in areas of west Cumbria requiring restrictions on sheep following the Chernobyl accident. *Radiation and Environmental Biophysics*, 42, 1, 41–47; Wynne, B. (1996). May the sheep safely graze? A Reflexive View on the Expert–Lay Knowledge Divide, in Lash, S., Szerszynski, B.& Wynne, B. (eds) (1996). *Risk, Environment, and Modernity: Towards a New Ecology*. Sage, London, pp.44–83.

4. Aspirin derives from willow bark, which was mentioned by Hippocrates in 400 BC as an effective treatment to ease labour pain. Roberts, L. (2010). History of Aspirin. *Telegraph*. http://www.telegraph.co.uk/health/healthnews/8184625/History-of-aspirin.html; *Frontline* (1998). Opium Throughout History. http://www.pbs.org/wgbh/pages/frontline/shows/heroin/etc/history.html. The Quechua people of Peru used the bark of the cinchona tree as a muscle relaxant and to treat fevers over five hundred years ago; one of its products is the alkaloid quinine, now used in anti-malaria drugs.

5. Pascale, R., Sternin, J. & Sternin, M. (2010). *The Power of Positive Deviance: How Unlikely Innovators Solve the World's Toughest Problems*. Harvard Business Press, Boston, MA.

6. Ferguson, T. (1999). E-Patients Prefer eGroups to Doctors for 10 of 12 Aspects of Health Care. *The Ferguson Report*, 1.

7. Robson, M. (2009). How Teenagers Consume Media: the report that shook the city. *Guardian*. http://www.guardian.co.uk/business/2009/jul/13/teenage-media-habits-morgan-stanley.

8. Kollewe, J. (2009). Twitter is not for teens, Morgan Stanley told by 15-year-old expert. 13 July 2009. http://www.guardian.co.uk/business/2009/jul/13/twitter-teenage-media-habits.

9. *Telegraph* (2009). Morgan Stanley's teenage star: I understood banking in a week. http://www.telegraph.co.uk/finance/newsbysector/banksandfinance/5822253/Morgan-Stanley-teenage-star-I-understood-banking-within-a-week.html.

10. Johnson, A.E. (2009). Intern in the news: Matthew Robson. *Financial Times*. http://www.ft.com/cms/s/0/22666a46–72fb–11de-ad98–00144feabdc0.html#axzz27brbdQQy.

11. I was made very aware of this when working in Russia in 1992–93, a time when expert economists were claiming, for example, that "barter is dead." I remember Anders Åslund, for example, later claiming this in his book Åslund, A. (1995). *How Russia Became a Market Economy*. The Brookings Institution, Washington, DC. But I was on the ground studying the impact of transition on firms from the bottom up and saw that bartering remained a key way of doing business.

12. Hayek, F.A. (1945). The Use of Knowledge in Society. *American Economic Review*, 35, 4, 519–530.

13. Robinson, A.G. & Stern, S. (1998). *Corporate Creativity: How Innovation and Improvement Actually Happen*. Berrett-Koehler, San Francisco, CA, p.9. Thanks to Rory Sutherland for first alerting me to this case when we both spoke at the Wired 2011 Conference.

14. Thomas, M. & Brain, D. (2009). *Crowd Surfing: Surviving and Thriving in the Age of Consumer Empowerment*. Bloomsbury, London.

15. Robinson, A.G. & Stern, S. (1998). *Corporate Creativity*. Berrett-Koehler, San Francisco, CA.

16. Hukutani, Y. (ed.) (2003). *Theodore Dreiser's Uncollected Magazine Articles, 1897–1902*. University of Delaware Press, Newark, DE; The "Golden Rule" in Business (1899). *Success* magazine. http://www.daytonhistorybooks.com/page/page/4846280.htm.

17. Pasiuk, P. (2005). *Vault Guide to the Top Tech Employers*. Vault Inc., New York, NY, p.166; Corniou, J-P. (2010). *Looking Back and Going Forward in IT*. Wiley, Hoboken, NJ, p.28.

18. LaBonte, D.A. (2008). *Shiny Objects Marketing: Using Simple Human Instincts to Make Your Brand Irresistible*. Wiley, Hoboken, NJ, p.172.

19. British Airways (2012). Fuel Efficiency Drive Saves a Packet. Press Release. http://press.ba.com/?p=2189. British Airways has generated savings of up to £20 million through fuel-efficiency savings. Staff suggestions also include replacing glass with plastic wine bottles and reducing the amount of water carried in aircraft water tanks.

20. Robinson, A.G. & Stern, S. (1998). *Corporate Creativity*. Berrett-Koehler, San Francisco, CA, pp.108–110.

21. Matthews, V. (2006). Open to Suggestions. *Guardian*. http://www.guardian.co.uk/money/2006/mar/20/careers.theguardian4.

22. *The Times 100 Business Case Studies* (2013). Building a better workplace through motivation: A Kellogg's Case Study. http://businesscasestudies.co.uk/kelloggs/building-a-better-workplace-through-motivation/mayo.html#axzz2DuPDDzVH.

23. Robinson, A.G. & Schroeder, D.M. (2004). *Ideas Are Free*. Berrett-Koehler, San Francisco, CA, pp.173–175. Yasuda, Y. (1991). *40 Years, 20 million Ideas: The Toyota Suggestion System*. Productivity Press, New York, NY.

24. Campbell-Allen, N. & Welch, S. (2004). BPIR Management Brief : Issue 10 – Employee Suggestion Schemes. *Business Performance Improvement Resource*. http://www.bpir.com/employee-suggestion-schemes-bpir.com/menu-id–71/expert-opinion.html.

25. On prediction markets, see Suroweicki, J. (2005). *The Wisdom of Crowds*. Anchor Books, New York, NY; and Sunstein, C. (2006). *Infotopia*. Oxford University Press, New York, NY.

26. Berg, J.E., Nelson, F.D. & Rietz, T.A. (2008). Prediction market accuracy in the long run. *International Journal of Forecasting*, 24, 2, 285–300.

27. They All Got it Right: Polls, Markets, and Models (2012). PBS NewsHour. http://www.pbs.org/newshour/businessdesk/2012/11/they-all-got-it-right-polls-ma.html. Whether these markets will continue to deliver such results in the wake of the closing of some US markets as of December 2012 is, however, unclear at this point. Note too that non-internal prediction markets typically need a significant volume of trades to be accurate: *The Economist* (2012). Don't bet on it: Intrade retreats from American regulators.http://www.economist.com/news/finance-and-economics/21567382-intrade-retreats-american-regulators-dont-bet-it.

28. Suroweicki, J. (2005). *The Wisdom of Crowds*. Anchor Books, New York, NY.

29. See Coles, P.A., Lakhani, K.R. & McAfee, A.P. (2007). Prediction Markets at Google. *Harvard Business School Case 607–088*; O'Leary, D.E. (2012). Internal corporate prediction markets: "From each according to his bet." *International Journal of Accounting Information Systems*.

30. O'Leary, D.E. (2012). Internal corporate prediction markets: "From each according to his bet." *International Journal of Accounting Information Systems*. Prediction Markets as a Forecasting Tool, in Lawrence, K.D. & Klimberg, R.K. (eds) (2008). *Advances in Business and Management Forecasting*, Vol. 8, Emerald Group Publishing Ltd, Bingley, Yorkshire, pp.169–184.

31. Graefe, A., Luckner, S. & Weinhardt, C. (2010). Prediction markets for foresight. *Futures*, 42, 394–404.

32. DeFond, M. L., Konchitchki, Y., McMullin, J.L. & O'Leary, D.E (2010). *Does Superior Knowledge Management Increase Shareholder Value?* Paper presented at the American Accounting Association Annual Meeting, San Francisco, Aug. 2010.

33. Wolfers, J. & Zitzewitz, E. (2004). Prediction Markets. *Journal of Economic Perspectives*, 18, 2, 107–126.

34. Schrieber, J. (2004).The application of prediction markets to business. Unpublished master's thesis. Massachusetts Institute of Technology, Cambridge, MA.

35. Wolfers, J. & Zitzewitz, E. (2004). Prediction Markets. *Journal of Economic Perspectives*, 18, 2, 107–126; Schrieber, J. (2004).The application of prediction markets to business. Unpublished master's thesis. Massachusetts Institute of Technology, Cambridge, MA.

36. Lohr, S. (2008). Betting to Improve the Odds. *New York Times*. http://www.nytimes.com/2008/04/09/technology/techspecial/09predict.html?pagewanted=print. Thompson, D.N. (2012). *Oracles: How Prediction Markets Turn Employees Into Visionaries*. Harvard Business Press, Boston, MA, p.104.

37. Sunstein, C.R. (2006). When Crowds Aren't Wise. *Harvard Business Review*, 84, 9, 20–21; Stix, G. (2008). Super Tuesday: Markets Predict Outcome Better than Polls. *Scientific American*; Cohen, N. (2008). Google's lunchtime betting game. *New York Times*; Coles, P.A., Lakhani,

K.R. & McAfee, A.P. (2007). Prediction Markets at Google. Case Study. Harvard Business Publishing, Boston, MA; and Campbell-Allen, N. & Welch, S. (2004). Employee Suggestion Schemes. *Benchmarking and Performance Improvement Resource Management Brief*, 10. http://www. bpclub.com/_Attachments/Resources/413_S4.pdf.

38. Dye, R. (2008). The promise of prediction markets: A round table. *McKinsey Quarterly*, 2, 82–93.

39. Singel, R. (2008). ETech: Google Prediction Market Datamining Shows Meatspace Matters. *Wired*. http://www.wired.com/business/2008/03/ etech-google-pr/.

40. They tend to be of particular use in big organisations, where they can mitigate the tendency for information to be stuck or hidden within the business. Although you don't need many individuals to be participating for their forecasts to be accurate: at HP and Siemens at times fewer than sixty people were trading, yet in these thin markets they still delivered valuable information.

41. Dye, R. (2008). The promise of prediction markets: A round table. *McKinsey Quarterly*, 2, 82–93, p.88.

42. Cass Sunstein makes a similar point: "When there isn't a lot of dispersed information within an organization, it's ill-advised to rely on what its members think." Sunstein, C.R. (2006). When Crowds Aren't Wise. *Harvard Business Review*, 84, 9, 20–21.

43. Wylie, I. (2002). Who Runs This Team, Anyway? *Fast Company*. http:// www.fastcompany.com/44614/who-runs-team-anyway.

44. Bonebeau, E. (2009). Decision 2.0: The Power of Collective Intelligence. *MIT Sloan Management Review*, 50, 2. http://www.worldwideopen.org/ uploads/groups_bull/files/30/decision per cent202.0.pdf#.

45. Robinson, A.G. & Stern, S. (1998). *Corporate Creativity: How Innovation and Improvement Actually Happen*. Berrett-Koehler, San Francisco, CA, p.70.

46. *Success* (1899). The "Golden Rule" in Business. http://www. daytonhistorybooks.com/page/page/4846280.htm.

STEP SIX: Co-Create and Listen In

1. BBC News. (2011).Timeline: Japan Power Plant Crisis. http://www.bbc. co.uk/news/science-environment–12722719.

2. Tabucki, H. (2011). Japanese Workers Braved Radiation for a Temp Job. *New York Times*. http://www.nytimes.com/2011/04/10/world/ asia/10workers.html?pagewanted=all&_r=0.

3. Fecht, S. (2012). 1 Year Later: A Fukushima Nuclear Disaster Timeline. *Scientific American*. http://www.scientificamerican.com/article. cfm?id=one-year-later-fukushima-nuclear-disaster.

4. Mack, E. (2011). Japan radiation monitoring goes crowd, open source. CNET. http://news.cnet.com/japan-radiation-monitoring-goes-crowd- open-source/8301–17938_105–20060639–1.html.

5. Kawasa, C. (2011). Demand for personal Geiger counters soars in Japan. Reuters. http://www.reuters.com/article/2011/05/25/us-japan-geigercounter-idUSTRE74O0WE20110525.

6. Mack, E. (2011). Japan radiation monitoring goes crowd, open source. http://news.cnet.com/japan-radiation-monitoring-goes-crowd-open-source/8301-17938_105-20060639-1.html; MacManus, R. (2011). Pachube Acquired: Why Did it Sell so Early? *New York Times*. http://www.nytimes.com/external/readwriteweb/2011/07/20/20readwriteweb-pachube-acquired-why-did-it-sell-so-early-61512.html.

7. *COSM* (2011). Crowd-sourced realtime radiation monitoring in Japan. http://community.cosm.com/node/611.

8. Wind from Fukushima I. https://play.google.com/store/apps/details?id=jp.gr.java_conf.seigo.stop_ra&hl=en.

9. Bunz, M. (2010). Anonymous Video of Neda Aghan-Soltan's Death wins Polk Award. *Guardian*. http://www.guardian.co.uk/media/pda/2010/feb/16/george-polk-awards.

10. Preston, J. (2012). Chinese Social Media Accounts Clash with Official Reports on Riot at Foxconn Factory. *New York Times*. http://thelede.blogs.nytimes.com/2012/09/24/chinese-social-media-accounts-clash-with-official-reports-on-riot-at-foxconn-factory/.

11. *Telegraph* (2012). Girl's School Dinner Blog becomes Internet Hit. http://www.telegraph.co.uk/education/educationnews/9256454/Girls-school-dinner-blog-becomes-internet-hit.html.

12. World Bank (2012). Mobile Phone Access Reaches Three Quarters of Planet's Population. http://www.worldbank.org/en/news/2012/07/17/mobile-phone-access-reaches-three-quarters-planets-population.

13. Rosen, J. (2006). The People Formerly Known as the Audience. Press think: Ghost of Democracy in the Media Machine. http://archive.pressthink.org/2006/06/27/ppl_frmr.html.

14. Diep, F. (2012). High-tech maps keep track of Colorado wildfires. CBS News. http://www.cbsnews.com/8301-205_162-57463012/high-tech-maps-keep-track-of-colorado-wildfires/.

15. Thailand Flood Crisis Information Map (2011). http://de21.digitalasia.chubu.ac.jp/floodmap/reports#.

16. Bartlett, J., Crump, J., Miller, C. & Middleton, L. (2013). *Policing in an information age*. Demos.

17. Taylor, P. (2012). Crunch time for big data. *Financial Times*. http://www.ft.com/cms/s/0/bd5a5ce2-aa57-11e1-899d-00144feabdc0.html#axzz2I4F2Recf.

18. Duhigg, C. (2012). How Companies Learn Your Secrets. *New York Times*. http://www.nytimes.com/2012/02/19/magazine/shopping-habits.html?pagewanted=all&_r=0; Hill, K. (2012). How Target Figured Out a Teen Girl Was Pregnant before her Father Did. *Forbes*. http://www.forbes.com/sites/kashmirhill/2012/02/16/how-target-figured-out-a-teen-girl-was-pregnant-before-her-father-did/.

19. Hertz, N. (2011). Women and Banks: Are Female Customers Facing Discrimination? *IPPR*. http://www.ippr.org/publications/55/8186/women-and-banks-are-female-customers-facing-discrimination.

20. Remarks by Director David H. Petraeus at In-Q-Tel CEO Summit (2012). Central Intelligence Agency. https://www.cia.gov/news-information/speeches-testimony/2012-speeches-testimony/in-q-tel-summit-remarks.html.

21. The model we settled on performed as follows: in the first seven weeks the model called both the bottom two correctly five times, and one of the bottom two the other two times. In the last three weeks it called the bottom act correctly each time. On one of the two occasions the model was wrong: the missed act was predicted third from bottom. For more on the *X Factor* project see Smith, D. (2011). Video: Noreena Hertz's Talk at WIRED 2011. Wired.co.uk. http://www.wired.co.uk/news/archive/2011-10/14/noreena-hertz-wired-2011.

22. Bollen, J., Mao, H. & Zeng, X.J. (2011). Twitter mood predicts the stock market. *Journal of Computational Science*, 2, 1, 1–8. http://arxiv.org/pdf/1010.3003v1.pdf.

23. Asur, S. & Huberman, B.A. (2010). Predicting the Future with Social Media. HP Labs. http://www.hpl.hp.com/research/scl/papers/socialmedia/socialmedia.pdf.

24. Omand, D., Bartlett, J. & Miller, C. (2012). #Intelligence. DEMOS Report. http://www.demos.co.uk/files/_Intelligence_-_web.pdf?1335197327; *Hull Daily Mail* (2011). Facebook crimes probed by Humberside Police. http://www.thisishullandeastriding.co.uk/Facebook-crimes-probed-Humberside-Police/story-13191231-detail/story.html#axzz2UnmHFVYY; *City of Westminster* (2011). Choose life, not gangs: problem kids told to clean up or face the consequences. http://www.westminster.gov.uk/press-releases/2011-09/choose-life-not-gangs-problem-kids-told-to/.

25. BBC News (2012). FBI plans social network map alert mash-up application. http://www.bbc.co.uk/news/technology-16738209.

26. Kelly, K. & Bergman, J. (2011). Why One BP Subcontractor Tweeted the Top Kill. *CNBC*. http://www.cnbc.com/id/41973297/Why_One_BP_Subcontractor_Tweeted_the_Top_Kill.

27. Krauss, C. & Broder, J. (2010). Results of "Top Kill" Effort Remain Uncertain. *New York Times*. http://www.nytimes.com/2010/05/27/us/27spill.html.

28. Kelly, K. & Bergman, J. (2011). Why One BP Subcontractor Tweeted the Top Kill. *CNBC*. http://www.cnbc.com/id/41973297/Why_One_BP_Subcontractor_Tweeted_the_Top_Kill.

29. CBS *This Morning* (2012). Whitney Houston's Death: New Details Emerge. http://www.cbsnews.com/8301-505266_162-57377195/whitney-houstons-death-new-details-emerge/.

30. Ford, R. (2011). Earthquake: Twitter Users Learned of Tremors Seconds Before Feeling Them. *Hollywood Reporter*. http://www.hollywood reporter.com/news/earthquake-twitter-users-learned-tremors–226481.

31. Chittley, J. (2011). News of earthquake travels faster on Twitter than shockwaves travel through rock. Yahoo News, 25 Aug. 2011.

32. If you're thinking of listening in on social media for trading purposes, do check the state of the law on this issue where you are. It's still a somewhat grey area.

33. Sonderman, J. (2012). News Orgs Circulate Facebook Profile, Photos of Man who Wasn't the Shooter. Poynter. http://www.poynter.org/latest-news/media-lab/social-media/198262/news-orgs-circulate-facebook-profile-of-the-wrong-ryan-lanza/.

34. Choi, H. & Varian, H. (2012). Predicting the Present with Google Trends. *Economic Record*. http://onlinelibrary.wiley.com/doi/10.1111/j.1475–4932.2012.00809.x/full).

35. Carniero, H.A. & Mylonakis, E. (2009). Google Trends: A Web-based Tool for Real-Time Surveillance of Disease Outbreaks. *Clinical Infectious Diseases*, 49, 10, 1557–1564. http://cid.oxfordjournals.org/content/49/10/1557.short. Note however that Google Trends need to be used with some caution. In December 2012 they overestimated the Christmas peak of flu season, estimating that over 10 percent of the U.S. population had flu, versus the CDC's data, which showed only around 6 percent had it. See Butler, D. (2013). When Google got flu wrong. *Nature*, 13 February 2013, 494, 7436, pp.155–156. In this case the error was probably due to media scare stories about the flu leading to searches for flu by people who were not sick. Data always needs to be contextualised and interrogated.

36. McLaren, N. & Shanbhogue, R. (2011). Using internet search data as economic Indicators. *Quarterly Bulletin*. http://www.bankofengland.co.uk/publications/Documents/quarterlybulletin/qb110206. pdf. Wearden, G. (2011). Bank of England Turns to Google to Shed Light on Economic Trends. *Guardian*. http://www.guardian.co.uk/business/2011/jun/13/bank-of-england-google-searches.

37. Webb, G.K. (2009). Internet Search Statistics as a Source of Business Intelligence: Searches on Foreclosure as an Estimate of Actual Home Foreclosures. *Issues in Information Systems*, 10, 2. http://iacis.org/iis/2009/P2009_1169.pdf.

38. Batelle, J. (2005). *The Search: How Google and its Rivals Rewrote the Rules of Business and Transformed our Culture*. Penguin, New York, NY.

39. Wu, L. & Brynjolfsson, E. (2009). The Future of Prediction: How Google Searches Foreshadow Housing Prices and Sales. Social Science Research Network. http://papers.ssrn.com/sol3/papers.cfm?abstract_id=2022293.

40. See for example http://www.google.com/trends/explore#geo=GB-ENG&q=norovirus&date=today+3-m&cmpt=q.

41. *The Independent* (2012). Seven Fake Hurricane Sandy Pictures You're Sharing. http://www.independent.co.uk/voices/iv-drip/seven-fake-hurricane-sandy-pictures-youre-sharing-8252950.html.

42. Although, encouragingly, in times of crisis altruism does seem to be the dominant mode. See Solnit, R. (2010). *A Paradise Built in Hell: The Extraordinary Communities that Arise in Disaster*. Penguin, London.

43. For a comprehensive discussion of such issues see Omand, D., Bartlett, J. & Miller, C. (2012). #Intelligence. DEMOS Report. http://www.demos.co.uk/files/_Intelligence_-_web.pdf?1335197327.

44. Duggan, M. & Brenner, J. (2013). The Demographics of Social Media Users – 2012. Pew Internet & American Life Project. http://pewinternet.org/Reports/2013/Social-media-users.aspx.

45. Online MBA. (2012). A Case Study in Social Media Demographics. http://www.onlinemba.com/blog/social-media-demographics/.

46. *Semiocast* (2012). Twitter reaches half a billion accounts: more than 140 million in the US. http://semiocast.com/publications/2012_07_30_Twitter_reaches_half_a_billion_accounts_140m_in_the_US.

47. Protalinski, E. (2012). Facebook: Over 955 million users, 543 million mobile users. CNET. http://news.cnet.com/8301-1023_3-57480950-93/facebook-over-955-million-users-543-million-mobile-users/.

48. Although according to Jamie Bartlett of Demos, this seems to be broadening out.

49. ehealthforum (2008). http://ehealthforum.com/press/site-statistics/.

50. Twitter (2012). Twitter turns 6. http://blog.twitter.com/2012/03/twitter-turns-six.html.

51. Butler, D. (2013). When Google got flu wrong. *Nature*, 14 February 2013, 494, 7346, pp.155–156.

STEP SEVEN: Scrutinise Sock Puppets and Screen Your Sources

1. BBC News (2011). Syria Gay Girl in Damascus Blog a Hoax by a US Man. http://www.bbc.co.uk/news/world-middle-east-13744980.

2. Addley, E. (2011). Gay Girl in Damascus hoaxer acted out of "vanity." *Guardian*. http://www.guardian.co.uk/world/2011/jun/13/gay-girl-damascus-tom-macmaster; Elliot, C. (2011). Open Door: the authentication of anonymous bloggers. *Guardian*, 13 June 2011.

3. BBC News (2011). Syria town of Jisr al-Shughour braces for army assault. http://www.bbc.co.uk/news/world-middle-east-13678105.

4. Lenhart, A., Simon, M. & Graziano, M. (2001). The Internet and Education. Pew Internet & American Life Project. http://www.pewinternet.org/~/media//Files/Reports/2001/PIP_Schools_Report.pdf.pdf.

5. Sambrook, R. (2012). Delivering Trust: Objectivity and Impartiality in the Digital Age, Reuters Institute for the Study of Journalism Report, July 2012.

6. Flock, E. & Bell, M. (2011) ."Paul Brooks" editor of "Lez Get Real" also a man. *Washington Post*. http://www.washingtonpost.com/blogs/blogpost/post/paula-brooks-editor-of-lez-get-real-also-a-man/2011/06/13/AGld2ZTH_blog.html.

7. WebMD forum (2010). Warning: Fake Experts. http://bit.ly/VLPdHv.

8. Bennett-Smith, M. (2012). Dave on Wheels Hoax: David Rose, Deaf Paraplegic Twitter Sensation Exposed as Elaborate Fraud. *Huffington Post*. http://www.huffingtonpost.com/2012/10/15/dave-on-wheels-hoax-parapalegic-blogger-david-rose-elaborate-fraud_n_1968454.html.

9. Chen, A. (2012). The Long, Fake Life of J.S. Dirr: A Decade-Long Internet Hoax Unravels. *Gawker*. http://gawker.com/5914621/the-long-fake-life-of-js-dirr-a-decade+long-internet-cancer-hoax-unravels.

10. Kington, T. (2012). Twitter Hoaxer Comes Clean and Says: I did it to Expose Weak Media. *Guardian*. http://www.guardian.co.uk/technology/2012/mar/30/twitter-hoaxer-tommaso-de-benedetti.

11. Thier, D. (2012). How this Guy Lied His Way into MSNBC, ABC News, the *New York Times* and More. *Forbes*. http://www.forbes.com/sites/davidthier/2012/07/18/how-this-guy-lied-his-way-into-msnbc-abc-news-the-new-york-times-and-more/.

12. The studies cited within this site are typically misrepresented, cherry-picked, or have methodological flaws. See Step Eight, for tips on how to assess research and data.

13. Thirty-one per cent of twelve-to-fifteen-year-olds think, for example, that if a search engine lists something, it must be truthful. Bartlett, J. & Miller, C. (2011). Truth, lies and the internet: a report into young people's digital fluency. Demos. http://www.demos.co.uk/files/Truth_-_web.pdf.

14. Shakespeare, W. (1599). *Julius Caesar*, I, ii, lines 315–316. First Folio.

15. US Congressional Senate Committee on Finance (1986). *Tax Reform Proposals: People Below the Poverty Line*, p.85; Barrett, G. (ed.) (2004). *Hatchet Jobs and Hardball: The Oxford Dictionary of American Political Slang*. Oxford University Press, New York, NY, p.34; *Washington Post* (1985). That Import Surcharge.

16. Nielsen Report (2012). Global Trust in Advertising and Brand Messages 2012; Flood, A. (2012). Sock puppetry and fake reviews: publish and be damned. *Guardian*. http://www.guardian.co.uk/books/2012/sep/04/sock-puppetry-publish-be-damned.

17. Streitfeld, D. (2012). The Best Book Reviews Money Can Buy. *New York Times*. http://www.nytimes.com/2012/08/26/business/book-reviewers-for-hire-meet-a-demand-for-online-raves.html.

18. See for example Huffington Post (2013). Craigslist Yelp Ad Offers Money In Exchange For Good New York Restaurant Reviews. http://www.huffingtonpost.com/2013/05/14/craigslist-yelp-money-restaurant-reviews_n_3271982.html.

19. Kenber, B. (2011). Yours for a price – a better reputation online. *The Times*, 2 June 2011.

20. See for example Starmer-Smith, C. (2010). TripAdvisor Reviews: Can we trust them. http://www.telegraph.co.uk/travel/hotels/8050127/Tripadvisor-reviews-can-we-trust-them.html; http://postingpositivereviews.blogspot. co.uk; http://www.ripoffreport.com/Search/748386.aspx.

21. Liu, B., Mukherjee, A. & Glance, N. (2012). Spotting Fake Reviewer Groups in Consumer Reviews. International World Wide Web Conference Committee. http://www.cs.uic.edu/~liub/publications/WWW–2012-group-spam-camera-final.pdf.

22. Ott, M., Cardie, C., Choi, Y. & Hancock, J.T. (2011). Finding deceptive opinion spam by any stretch of the imagination. *Proceedings of the 49th Annual Meeting of the Association for Computational Linguistics*, 309–319. http://projects.iq.harvard.edu/files/ptr/files/cardie_deception. pdf; Ott, M., Cardie, C. & Hancock, J.T. (2012). Estimating the prevalence of deception in online review communities. International World Wide Web Conference Committee. http://www.cs.cornell.edu/home/cardie/papers/www–2012.pdf.

23. See for example Richards, K. (2009). Yelp and the business of extortion 2.0. *East Bay Express*. http://www.eastbayexpress.com/oakland/yelp-and-the-business-of-extortion–20/Content?oid=1176635&showFullText=true. You can view the complaint against Yelp to the US District Court here: http://www.wired.com/images_blogs/threatlevel/2010/02/yelp-cpt-filed. pdf. NOTE: the lawsuit that followed this exposé was thrown out of court in 2011 because it did not "raise more than a mere possibility that Yelp had authored or manipulated content." Fowler, G. (2011). Judge Dismisses Suit Against Yelp. *Wall Street Journal*. http://online.wsj.com/article/SB10001424052970204505304577002170423750412.html. See also on Amazon: Flood, A. (2012). Sock puppetry and fake reviews: publish and be damned. *Guardian*. http://www.guardian.co.uk/books/2012/sep/04/sock-puppetry-publish-be-damned. And on TripAdvisor: Starmer-Smith, C. (2010). Fake TripAdvisor reviewers face legal action. *Telegraph*. http://www.telegraph.co.uk/travel/travelnews/8079786/Fake-Tripadvisor-reviewers-face-legal-action.html.

24. Federal Trade Commission (2010). In the Matter of Reverb Communications Inc. et al.http://www.ftc.gov/os/caselist/0923199/index. shtm.

25. MacKinnon, R. (2010). Testimony at the hearing "China, the Internet, and Google." http://rconversation.blogs.com/MacKinnonCECC_Mar1. pdf; Bandurski, D. (2008). China's Guerrilla War for the Web. *Far Eastern Economic Review*, July 2008. www.upf.edu/materials/fhuma/xiin/mat/guerrilla_war1.pdf.

26. Jakobsson, M. (2012). *The Death of the Internet*. John Wiley, Hoboken, NJ, p. 234.

27. Doctorow, C. (2011). HBGary's High Volume Astroturfing Technology and the Feds Who Requested It. *Boing Boing*. http://boingboing. net/2011/02/18/hbgarys-high-volume.html.

28. Hwang, T., Pearce, I. & Nanis, M. (2012). Socialbots: Voices from the Front. Interactions. http://www.gm.fh-koeln.de/~hk/lehre/sgmci/ss2012/material/Socialbots_VoicesFromTheFront.pdf; Ehrenberg, R. (2012). Social Media Sway. *Science News*. http://www.sciencenews.org/index.php/issue/view/feature/id/345532/title/Social_Media_Sway.

29. Eaton, E. (2012). There are more "Fake" People on Facebook than Real Ones on Instagram. *Fast Company*.

30. *Telegraph* (2011). A Gay Girl in Damascus: how the hoax unfolded. http://www.telegraph.co.uk/news/worldnews/middleeast/syria/8572884/A-Gay-Girl-in-Damascus-how-the-hoax-unfolded.html.

31. Addley, E. (2011). Gay Girl in Damascus hoaxer acted out of "vanity." *Guardian*.

32. See for example BBC News (2011). Internet Explorer Story was Bogus. http://www.bbc.co.uk/news/technology–14370878; Sherman, A. (2011). GE Tax Hoax Claimed by Activists Seeking $3.2 Billion Refund "Re-gifting." Bloomberg. http://www.bloomberg.com/news/2011–04–13/ge-tax-hoax-responsibility-claimed-by-activist-group-us-uncut.html.

33. Addley, E. (2011). A Gay Girl in Damascus – or a Cynical Hoax? *Guardian*. http://www.guardian.co.uk/world/2011/jun/09/gay-girl-in-damascus-truth-or-hoax.

34. Streitfeld, D. (2011). In a Race to Out-Rave, 5-Star Web Reviews go for $5. *New York Times*. http://www.nytimes.com/2011/08/20/technology/finding-fake-reviews-online.html?_r=1&hp.

35. MacDonald, G.J. (2012). Is That Online Review a Fake? *Christian Science Monitor*. http://www.csmonitor.com/Business/2012/1018/Is-that-online-review-a-fake.

36. Marks, P. (2011). Gender spotting tool could have rumbled fake blogger. *New Scientist*. http://www.newscientist.com/article/dn20581-genderspotting-tool-could-have-rumbled-fake-blogger.html.

37. Armstrong, C.L. & McAdams, M.J. (2009). Blogs of information: How gender cues and individual motivations influence Perceptions of Credibility. *Journal of Computer-Mediated Communication*, 14, 3, 435–456.

38. Fogg, B.J., Soohoo, C. & Danielson, D. (2002). How do People Evaluate a Web Site's Credibility? Results from a Large Study. http://www.consumerwebwatch.org/pdfs/stanfordPTL.pdf.

39. However, if you buy in bulk you can do better. When journalist Seth Stevenson set out to buy Twitter followers for an article he was writing for *Slate* magazine, he was offered a million followers for $1,300. Stevenson, S. (2012). I Bought 27,000 Twitter Followers. *Slate*. http://www.slate.com/articles/technology/technology/2012/10/buying_twitter_followers_is_it_worth_it_.html. Considine, A. (2012). Buying their Way to Twitter Fame. *New York Times* reports that some vendors were selling 1,000 followers for $5.

40. Goodwin, D. (2011). Top Google search gets 36.4% of clicks. http://searchenginewatch.com/article/2049695/Top-Google-Result-Gets-36.4-of-Clicks-Study

41. Bartlett, J. & Miller, C. (2011). Truth, lies and the internet: a report into young people's digital fluency. *Demos*. http://www.demos.co.uk/files/Truth_-_web.pdf.

42. Lee, Y.J., Tan, Y. & Hosanagar, K. (2009). Do I Follow my Friends or the Crowd? Information Cascades in Online Movie Rating. *Proceedings of the 19th Workshop on Information Technology and Systems* (WITS) 2009. http://www.misrc.umn.edu/workshops/2010/fall/OnlineUserRating.pdf.

43. Email exchange with Richard Sambrook, Professor of Journalism, Cardiff School of Journalism, Media and Cultural Studies at Cardiff University and former Director of BBC News and BBC World Service and Global News.

44. Turner, D. (2012). Inside the BBC's Verification Hub. Nieman Reports. http://www.nieman.harvard.edu/reports/article/102764/Inside-the-BBCs-Verification-Hub.aspx.

45. Blogmouth (2011). The Disinformation War in the Media. http://blogmouth.net/2011/04/03/the-disinformation-war-in-the-media/.

46. Carvin, A. (2011). Israeli weapons In Libya? How @acarvin and his Twitter followers debunked sloppy journalism. Storify. http://storify.com/acarvin/how-to-debunk-a-geopolitical-rumor-with-your-twitt2.

47. Meier, P.P. (2011). Verifying Crowdsourced Social Media Reports for Live Crisis Mapping: An Introduction to Information Forensics. iRevolution. net. http://irevolution.files.wordpress.com/2011/11/meier-verifying-crowdsourced-data-case-studies.pdf.

STEP EIGHT: Overcome Your Math Anxiety

1. Lyons, I.M. & Beilock, S.L. (2012). When Math Hurts: Math Anxiety Predicts Pain Network Activation in Anticipation of Doing Math. *PLoS ONE*, 7, 10.

2. Kross, E., Berman, M.G., Mischel, W., Smith, E.E. & Wager, T.D. (2011). Social rejection shares somatosensory representations with physical pain. *Proceedings of the National Academy of Sciences*, 108, 15, 6270–6275.

3. Brian, K. (2012). Math anxiety: the numbers are mounting. *Guardian*. http://www.guardian.co.uk/education/2012/apr/30/math-anxiety-school-support.

4. Harms, W. (2012). Math anxiety causes trouble for students as early as first grade. UChicagoNews. http://news.uchicago.edu/article/2012/09/12/math-anxiety-causes-trouble-students-early-first-grade.

5. *Globe and Mail* (2012). Adult math anxiety adds up to trouble with basic counting. http://m.theglobeandmail.com/life/health-and-fitness/adult-math-anxiety-adds-up-to-trouble-with-basic-counting/article4306727/?service=mobile.

6. Khatoon, T. & Mahmood, S. (2010). Mathematics Anxiety Among Secondary School Students in India and its Relationship to Achievement in Mathematics. *European Journal of Social Sciences*, 16, 1, 75–86.

7. Hawking, S. (1988). *A Brief History of Time: From Big Bang to Black Holes*. Random House, London; Chivers, T. (2010). Popular Science books take off: a big bang in physics publishing. *Telegraph*. http://www.telegraph.co.uk/culture/books/7985508/Popular-science-books-take-off-a-big-bang-in-physics-publishing.html.

8. *Ipsos Mori* (2010). Ipsos Mori Statistics Research for GetStats Programme of the Royal Statistical Society. http://www.ipsos-mori.com/Assets/Docs/Polls/Oct10Statscharts.PDF.

9. National Center for Education Statistics (2010). *The Nation's Report Card: Grade 12 Reading and Mathematics 2009 National and Pilot State Results (NCES 2011–455)*. National Center for Education Statistics, Institute of Education Sciences, US Department of Education, Washington, DC, p.34. http://nces.ed.gov/nationsreportcard/pdf/main2009/2011455.pdf.

10. Gigerenzer, G., Hertwig, R., van den Broek, E., Fasolo, B. & Katsikopoulos, K.V. (2005). "A 30 per cent chance of rain tomorrow": how does the public understand probabilistic weather forecasts? *Risk Analysis*, 25(3), 623–9. http://library.mpib-berlin.mpg.de/ft/gg/GG_30_Chance_2005.pdf.

11. Ranney, M.A., Rinner, L., Yarnall, L., Munnich, E. Miratix, L. Schank, P. (2008). Designingand Assessing Numeracy Training for Journalists: Toward Improving Quantitative Reasoning Among Media Consumers. *Proceedings of the Eighth International Conference of the Learning Sciences* (2008). http://www.soe.berkeley.edu/~schank/convinceme/papers/RanneyEtAlICLS08Preprint.pdf.

12. Wulff, H.R, Anderson, B., Brandenhoff, P. & Guttler, F. (2006). What do doctors know about statistics? *Statistics in Medicine*, 6, 1. http://onlinelibrary.wiley.com/doi/10.1002/sim.4780060103/abstract.

13. Easton, M. (2012). What happened when MPs took a math exam. BBC News. http://www.bbc.co.uk/news/uk-19801666.

14. NASA (1999). Mars Climate Orbiter Failure Board Releases Report, Numerous NASA Actions Underway in Response. http://mars.jpl.nasa.gov/msp98/news/mco991110.html; Mars Climate Orbiter Mishap Investigation Board; NASA (1999). Phase I Report November 10, 1999. ftp://ftp.hq.nasa.gov/pub/pao/reports/1999/MCO_report.pdf; Page, S.E. (2007). *The Difference: How the Power of Diversity Creates Better Groups, Firms, Schools, and Societies*. Princeton University Press, Princeton, NJ.

15. Hotz, R.L. (1999). Mars Probe Lost Due to Simple Math Error. *Los Angeles Times*. http://articles.latimes.com/1999/oct/01/news/mn-17288; Page, S.E. (2007). *The Difference*, pp.171–2.

16. See for example, Joyce, Helen (2002). Beyond Reasonable Doubt. *Plus Magazine*. http://plus.math.org/content/beyond-reasonable-doubt.

17. *Telegraph* (2001). Against the Odds. http://www.telegraph.co.uk/culture/4723455/Against-the-odds.html.

18. In Easton, M. (2012). What happened when MPs took a math exam. BBC News. 76 per cent of Tories and 72 per cent of Labour MPs claimed to feel confident when dealing with numbers.

19. World Cancer Research Fund/American Institute for Cancer Research (2007). *Food, Nutrition, Physical Activity, and the Prevention of Cancer: a Global Perspective*. Washington, DC: AICR. http://eprints.ucl.ac.uk/4841/1/4841.pdf.

20. Hanlon, M. (2007). Ignore these scaremongers – I'm not giving up my bacon butties! *Daily Mail*. http://www.dailymail.co.uk/news/article-491218/Ignore-scaremongers-Im-giving-bacon-butties.html#ixzz2L4Cz8cgL; *Mirror* (2007). Have a Long, Healthy...and Miserable Life: Experts: Avoid cancer, cut out everything you enjoy. http://www.mirror.co.uk/news/uk-news/have-a-long-healthy-and-miserable-life-517722; Morton, E. (2007). Save Our Bacon: Butty Battle. *Sun*. http://www.thesun.co.uk/sol/homepage/news/413632/Row-over-bacon-scare-Scientists-say-processed-meats-carry-higher-cancer-risk-Anthony-Worrell-Thompson-leads-revolt.html.

21. World Cancer Research Fund/American Institute for Cancer Research (2007). *Food, Nutrition, Physical Activity, and the Prevention of Cancer: A Global Perspective*. Washington, DC: AICR.

22. Spiegelhalter, D. (2009). Communicating Risk. *Risk & Regulation*. Winter, 2009. http://understandinguncertainty.org/files/090409-CARR-communication.pdf.

23. Ibid.

24. Gigerenzer, G. (2002). *Calculated Risks: How to Know When Numbers Deceive You*, Simon & Schuster, New York, NY. Note that when Professor Gigerenzer asked similar questions of radiologists they did similarly poorly.

25. The TaxPayers' Alliance (2009). Research Note No. 47: Departmental use of Taxis and Chauffeured Cars. http://www.taxpayersalliance.com/Taxis.pdf.

26. Hall, M. (2009). How Whitehall Takes Us for a Ride. *Daily Express*. http://www.express.co.uk/posts/view/113550/How-Whitehall-takes-us-for-a-ride-.

27. Sense About Science (2010). Sense about science and straight statistics. www.senseaboutscience.org/data/files/resources/1/MSofStatistics.pdf.

28. Highfield, R. (2005). Screen saver weather trial predicts 10°C rise in British temperatures. *Telegraph*. http://www.telegraph.co.uk/science/science-news/3338704/Screen-saver-weather-trial-predicts-10C-rise-in-British-temperatures.html; Connor, S. (2005). Global Warming is "Twice as Bad as Previously Thought." *Independent*, 27 January 2005. http://

www.independent.co.uk/environment/global-warming-is-twice-as-bad-as-previously-thought-488375.html; *New Scientist* (2005). Sizzling Times Ahead for Earth. *New Scientist*, 29 January 2005, 185, 2484, p.16.

29. Stainforth, D.A., Aina, T., Christensen, C., Collins, M., Faull, N., Frame, D.J., Kettleborough, J.A., Knight, S., Martin, A., Murphy, J.M., Piani, C., Sexton, D., Smith, L.A., Spicer, R.A., Thorpe, A.J. & Allen, M. R. (2005). Uncertainty in predictions of the climate response to rising levels of greenhouse gases. *Nature*, 433, 403–406.

30. See the CO2 projections issued by the Intergovernmental Panel on Climate Change (2011). www.ipcc-data.org/ddc_co2.html.

31. Blastland, M. & Dilnot, A. (2008). *The Tiger That Isn't*. Profile Books, London, pp.165–166.

32. Casey, L. (2012). *Listening to Troubled Families: A Report by Louise Casey CB, Department for Communities and Local Government*. Department for Communities and Local Government. https://www.gov.uk/government/uploads/system/uploads/attachment_data/file/6151/2183663.pdf.

33. Wilson, G. (2012). Child abuse rife in hell families. *Sun*. http://www.thesun.co.uk/sol/homepage/news/politics/4435244/Child-abuse-rife-in-hell-families.html. Shipman, T. (2012). Criminal culture at the heart of feckless families: Shocking report lifts lid on incest, abuse and spiral of alcohol abuse. *Daily Mail*. http://www.dailymail.co.uk/news/article–2175094/Troubled-Families-report-lifts-lid–120–000-problem-households.html.

34. O'Leary, J. (2012). *Sun* and *Daily Mail* Back Down over 120,000 "Problem" Families. Fullfact.org. http://fullfact.org/articles/sun_daily_mail_pcc_120000_problem_families_correction–28602.

35. Paton, G. (2012). A-level results 2012: private schools "dominate top grades." *Telegraph*. http://www.telegraph.co.uk/education/educationnews/9617603/A-level-results–2012-private-schools-dominate-top-grades.html.

36. Learner, S. (2012). Why Send Your Child to Independent School? *Telegraph*. http://www.telegraph.co.uk/education/9565079/Why-send-your-child-to-independent-school.html.

37. Independent Schools Council (2012). More Parents than Ever Favour Independent Education. http://www.isc.co.uk/press/press-releases/2012/more-parents-than-ever-favour-independent-education–2012–11–12.

38. Independent Schools Council (2012). ISC Census 2012. http://www.isc.co.uk/research/Publications/annual-census/isc-annual-census-2012.

39. OECD (2011). Private Schools: Who Benefits? PISA in Focus. http://www.oecd.org/pisa/pisainfocus/48482894.pdf.

40. Ibid.

41. See also on this point Naylor, R. & Smith, J. (2002). Schooling Effects on Subsequent University Performance: Evidence for the UK University Population. *Warwick Economic Research Papers*. http://wrap.warwick.ac.uk/88/1/WRAP_Smith_Jeremy_twerp657.pdf.

42. Full Transcript of the Second Presidential Debate (2012). *New York Times*. http://www.nytimes.com/2012/10/16/us/politics/transcript-of-the-second-presidential-debate-in-hempstead-ny.html?pagewanted=all&_r=0.

43. Officer, A.J. (2008). What Caused the Big Slide in Oil Prices? *Time*. http://www.time.com/time/business/article/0,8599,1859380-1,00.html.

44. Gas prices still on record run (2008). CNN Money. http://money.cnn.com/2008/07/07/news/economy/gas/.

45. HM Revenue & Customs (2012). The Exchequer Effect of the 50 per cent Additional Rate of Income Tax. http://hmrc.gov.uk/budget2012/excheq-income-tax–2042.pdf.

46. Tax revenues could also have been down among this group because the prevailing economic recession meant that incomes for some (especially those in finance) could have been considerably lower than usual.

47. O'Leary, J. (2012). Did Labour's 50p Tax Rate Drive 10,000 Millionaires Out of the Country? Fullfact.org. http://fullfact.org/factchecks/labour_50p_tax_rate_millionaires_leave_country–28645.

48. Silver, N. (2012). Late Poll Gains for Obama Leave Romney with Longer Odds. *New York Times*, 5 Nov. 2012. http://fivethirtyeight.blogs.nytimes.com/2012/11/06/nov-5-late-poll-gains-for-obama-leave-romney-with-longer-odds/.

49. Silver, N. (2012). Falling Prey to the Dangerous Temptation to Cherry Pick Polls. *New York Times*. http://fivethirtyeight.blogs.nytimes.com/2012/10/16/falling-prey-to-the-dangerous-temptation-to-cherry-pick-polls/.

50. Ibid.

51. Silver, N. (2012). In Swing States, a Predictable Election? *New York Times*, 28 Oct. 2012. http://fivethirtyeight.blogs.nytimes.com/2012/10/29/oct-28-in-swing-states-a-predictable-election/.

52. For more distorting graphs see Bolton, P. (2012). Statistical Literacy Guide – Commons Library Standard Note. House of Commons Library. http://www.parliament.uk/briefing-papers/SN04944.

53. Pleat, Z. (2012). Today in Dishonest Fox Charts: Government Aid Edition. Media Matters for America. http://mediamatters.org/blog/2012/08/09/today-in-dishonest-fox-charts-government-aid-ed/189223.

54. *Wall Street Journal* (2011). Where the Tax Money Is. http://online.wsj.com/article/SB10001424052748704621304576267113524583554.html.

55. Drum, K. (2011). Fun With Charts: Making the Rich Look Poor. *Mother Jones*. http://www.motherjones.com/kevin-drum/2011/05/fun-charts-making-rich-look-poor.

56. Beattie, V. & Jones, M.J. (1992). The use and abuse of graphs in annual reports: theoretical framework and empirical study. *Accounting and Business Research*, 22, 88, 291–303.

57. Beattie, V. & Jones, M.J. (1997). A Comparative Study of the Use of Financial Graphs in the Corporate Annual Reports of Major US and UK

Companies. *Journal of International Financial Management &*
Accounting, 8, 1, 33–68.

58. Beattie, V. & Jones, M.J. (2002). The Impact of Graph Slope on Rate of
Change Judgments in Corporate Reports. *Abacus*, 38, 2, 177–199.

59. Taylor, B.G. & Anderson, L.K. (1986). Misleading Graphs: Guidelines for
the Accountant. *Journal of Accounting*, 162, 4, 126–135.

60. ASA (2009). ASA Adjudication on Danone UK Ltd. http://www.asa.org.
uk/Rulings/Adjudications/2009/10/Danone-UK-Ltd/TF_ADJ_47060.
aspx

61. Biswas, S. (2010). Yoghurt and the Functional Food Revolution. BBC
News. http://www.bbc.co.uk/news/business–11926609.

62. BBC News (2009). "Healthy" Yoghurt Banned. http://news.bbc.co.uk/1/
hi/8305918.stm.

63. Center for Science in the Public Interest (2007). Watchdog Group Sues
Coke, Nestlé For Bogus "Enviga" Claims. http://www.cspinet.org/
new/200702011.html.

64. *Wall Street Journal* (2009). Coke, Nestlé Settle Enviga Dispute. http://
online.wsj.com/article/SB123571111325991605.html.

65. Derbyshire, D. (2008). How an Aspirin a Day can keep Heart Attacks
Away for the Middle-Aged. *Mail Online*. http://www.dailymail.co.uk/
health/article–1048749/How-aspirin-day-heart-attacks-away-middle-
aged.html.

66. Naish, J. (2010). Why Don't We Test Our Drugs on Women? *The Times*.
http://www.thetimes.co.uk/tto/science/medicine/article2720452.ece.

67. Young Kreeger, K. (2002). The Inequality of Drug Metabolism. *The
Scientist*. http://www.the-scientist.com/?articles.view/articleNo/13912/
title/The-Inequality-of-Drug-Metabolism/.

68. BBC News (2006). Drug Trials Outsourced to India. http://news.bbc.
co.uk/1/hi/world/south_asia/4932188.stm; Jayaraman, K.S. (2004).
Outsourcing Clinical Trials to India Rash and Risky, Critics Warn.
Nature.com. http://www.nature.com/nm/journal/v10/n5/full/nm0504–
440a.html.

69. Yasuda, S.U., Zhang, L. & Huang, S.-M. (2008). The Role of Ethnicity in
Variability in Response to Drugs: Focus on Clinical Pharmacology
Studies. *Clinical Pharmacology & Therapeutics*, 84, 3. http://www.fda.
gov/downloads/Drugs/ScienceResearch/ResearchAreas/Pharmacognetics/
UCM085502.pdf.

70. Campbell, D. & Heim, T. (2012). Nine out of 10 Members of Royal
College of Physicians Oppose NHS Bill. *Observer*. http://www.guardian.
co.uk/politics/2012/feb/26/hospital-doctors-oppose-nhs-bill.

71. http://surveymonkey.com/s/Survey_For_RCP_Doctors. If you fill the form
out claiming to be a member, but leave the email and membership
number blank, it still submits properly. I'm making an assumption here
that forms from people who don't supply these details aren't discarded –
but it is stated that this information is optional.

72. Royal College of Physicians (2012). Results of RCP Health and Social Care Hill Survey. http://www.rcplondon.ac.uk/press-releases/results-rcp-health-and-social-care-bill-survey.

73. Hopkins, D.J. (2009). No More Wilder Effect, Never a Whitman Effect: When and Why Polls Mislead About Black and Female Candidates. *Journal of Politics*, 71, 3, 769–781.

74. Sutton, R.M. & Farrall, S. (2005). Gender, Socially Desirable Responding and the Fear of Crime: Are Women Really more Anxious about Crime? *British Journal of Criminology*, 45, 2, 212–224.

STEP NINE: Monitor Your Emotional Thermostat

1. Shwartz, M. (2007). Robert Sapolsky discusses physiological effects of stress. Stanford Report. http://news.stanford.edu/news/2007/march7/sapolskysr-030707.html.

2. Habib, K.E., Gold, P.W. & Chrousos, G.P. (2001). Neuroendocrinology of stress. *Endocrinology and Metabolism Clinics of North America*, 30, 3, 695–728.

3. Erickson, K., Drevets, W. & Schulkin, J. (2003). Glucocorticoid regulation of diverse cognitive functions in normal and pathological emotional states. *Neuroscience and Biobehavioral Reviews*, 27, 233–246. http://notes.utk.edu/bio/unistudy.nsf/0/661393971aba187085256bce006f8b84/$FILE/STRESS per cent20-per cent20CS per cent20affects per cent20cognition per cent20-per cent20Erickson per cent20et per cent20al per cent202003.pdf.

4. LeBlanc, V., Woodrow, S.I., Sidhu, R. & Dubrowskia, A. (2008). Examination stress leads to improvements on fundamental technical skills for surgery. *American Journal of Surgery*, 196, 1, 114–119.

5. Erickson, K., Drevets, W. & Schulkin, J. (2003). Glucocorticoid regulation of diverse cognitive functions in normal and pathological emotional states. *Neuroscience and Biobehavioral Reviews*, 27, 233–246.

6. Wolf, O.T. (2008). The influence of stress hormones on emotional memory: Relevance for psychopathology. *Acta Psychologica*, 127, 3, 513–531.

7. This is because switching off implicit biases requires active, conscious control. When stressed we do not actively engage in such efforts. Carpenter, S. (2008). Buried prejudice: The bigot in your brain. *Scientific American: Mind & Brain*, April 2008.

8. Stepanikova, I. (2012). Racial-ethnic biases, time pressure, and medical decisions. *Journal of Health and Social Behavior*, 329–343.

9. Winkleby, M.A., Kraemer, H.C., Ahn, D.K. & Varady, A.N. (1998). Ethnic and socioeconomic differences in cardiovascular disease risk factors. *Journal of the American Medical Association*, 280, 4, 356–362.

10. Flores, D.M., Miller, M.K., Chamberlain, J., Richardson, J.T. & Bornstein, B.H. (2008). Judges' perspectives on stress and safety in the courtroom: An exploratory study. *Court Review*, 45, 76–89. Casey, P.M., Warren,

R.K., Cheesman, F.L. & Elek, J.K. (2012). Helping courts address implicit bias: Resources for education. National Center for State Courts. Part of the report: http://www.ncsc.org/~/media/Files/PDF/Topics/Gender per cent20and per cent20Racial per cent20Fairness/IB_Strategies_033012. ashx. Full report: www.ncsc.org/ibreport; Guthrie, C., Rachlinski, J. & Wistrich, A.J. (2007). Blinking on the bench: How judges decide cases. *Cornell Law Review*, 93, 1; Rachlinski, J.J., Johnson, S.L., Wistrich, A.J. & Guthrie, C. (2009). Does unconscious racial bias affect trial judges? *Notre Dame Law Review*, 84, 3: Vanderbilt Public Law Research Paper No. 09–11.

11. Gasper, K. & Clore, G.L. (2002). Attending to the big picture: Mood and global versus local processing of visual information. *Psychological Science*, 13, 33–39. See also Gasper, K. (2004). Do you see what I see? Affect and visual information processing. *Cognition and Emotion*, 18, 405–421.

12. Brennan, A., Chugh, J.S. & Kline, T. (2002). Traditional versus open office design: A longitudinal field study. *Environment and Behavior*, 34, 3, 279–299; Evans, G.W. & Johnson, D. (2000). Stress and open-office noise. *Journal of Applied Psychology*, 85, 5, 779–783; Käser, P.A.W., Fischbacher, U. & König, C.J. (2012). Helping and quiet hours: Interruption-free time spans can harm performance. *Applied Psychology: An International Review*. Epublication ahead of print.

13. Ayers, S. (2007). *Cambridge Handbook of Psychology, Heath and Medicine*. Cambridge University Press, Cambridge, p. 25.

14. See for example Hair, M., Renaud, K.V. & Ramsay, J. (2007). The influence of self-esteem and locus of control on perceived email-related stress. *Computers in Human Behavior*, 23, 6, 2791–2803. Jackson, T., Dawson, R. & Wilson, D. (2001). The cost of email interruption. *Journal of Systems and Information Technology*, 5, 1, 81–92.

15. Tenngart Ivarsson, C. & Hagerhall, C.M. (2008). The perceived restorativeness of gardens: Assessing the restorativeness of a mixed built and natural scene type. *Urban Forestry & Urban Greening*, 7, 2, 107–118. Atchley, R.A., Strayer, D.L. & Atchley, P. (2012). Creativity in the wild: Improving creative reasoning through immersion in natural settings. *PLoS ONE*, 7, 12.

16. Starcke, K. & Brand, M. (2012). Decision making under stress: A selective review. *Neuroscience and Biobehavioural Reviews*, 36, 4, 1228–1248. See also Charron, S. & Koechlin, E. (2010). Divided Representation of Concurrent Goals in the Human Frontal Lobes. Science, 16 April 2010, 328, 5976, pp.360-363. DOI: 10.1126/science.1183614.

17. Lewis, M. (2012). Obama's Way. *Vanity Fair*, 5 October 2012.

18. Edmans, A., Garcia, D. & Norli, Ø. (2007). Sports sentiment and stock returns. *Journal of Finance*, 62, 4, 1967–1998.

19. Dunn, J.R. & Schweitzer, M.E. (2005). Feeling and believing: The influence of emotion on trust. *Journal of Personality and Social Psychology*, 88, 5, 736–748.

20. There are a number of other studies that support the claim that the valence of priming affects subsequent behaviours. See for example Brinol, P., Petty, R., & Barden, J. (2007). Happiness Versus Sadness as a Determinant of Thought Confidence in Persuasion: A Self Validation Analysis. *Journal of Personality and Social Psychology*, 93, 5, 711–727.

21. Damasio, A.R. (1994). *Descartes' Error: Emotion, Reason and the Human Brain*. Grosset/Putnam, New York, NY.

22. Arnhart, L. (1998). *Darwinian Natural Right: The Biological Ethics of Human Nature*. State University of New York Press, Albany, NY, p. 225.

23. Arnhart, L. (1998). *Darwinian Natural Right: The Biological Ethics of Human Nature*. State University of New York Press, Albany, NY, p. 225.

24. Bechara, A. (2004). The role of emotion in decision-making: Evidence from neurological patients with orbitofrontal damage. *Brain and Cognition*, 55, 30–40. http://www.hss.caltech.edu/~steve/bechara.pdf.

25. Seo, M. & Barrett, L.F. (2007). Being emotional during decision making – good or bad? An empirical investigation. *Academy of Management Journal*, 50, 4, 923–940.

26. Forgas, J.P. & Ciarrochi, J.V. (2002). On managing moods: Evidence for the role of homeostatic cognitive strategies in affect regulation. *Personality and Social Psychology Bulletin*, 28, 336–345 (used p.336).

27. The Rationalizer uses galvanic skin response (GSR) sensing technology which is a method of measuring the electrical resistance of the skin by measuring moisture on skin levels. http://www.design.philips.com/philips/shared/assets/design_assets/pdf/rationalizer/Leaflet.pdf; ABN AMRO Bank N.V. & Koninklijke Philips Electronics N.V. (2009). Mirror of Emotions: Rationalizer emotion awareness for online investors. http://www.mirrorofemotions.com/.

28. ABN AMRO Bank N.V. & Koninklijke Philips Electronics N.V. (2009). Mirror of Emotions: Rationalizer emotion awareness for online investors. http://www.mirrorofemotions.com/.

29. Kirk, U., Downar, J. & Montague, P. R. (2011). Interoception drives increased rational decision-making in meditators playing the ultimatum game. *Frontiers in Neuroscience*, 5, 49.

30. Hölzel, B.K., Carmody, J., Vangel, M., Congleton, C., Yerramsetti, S.M., Gard, T. & Lazar, S.W. (2011). Mindfulness practice leads to increases in regional brain gray matter density. *Psychiatry Research: Neuroimaging*, 191, 1, 36–43.

31. Seo, M. & Barrett, L.F. (2007). Being emotional during decision making – good or bad? An empirical investigation. *Academy of Management Journal*, 50, 4, 923–940.

32. See Ariely, D. & Loewenstein, G. (2006). The heat of the moment: the effect of sexual arousal on sexual decision making. *Journal of Behavioral Decision Making*, 19, 2, 87–98. Loewenstein, G. (1996). Out of control: Visceral influences on behavior. *Organizational Behavior and Human Decision Processes*, 65, 3, 272–292. http://pisis.unalmed.edu.co/vieja/

cursos/analisis_decisiones/ComportamientodelUsuario/
racionalidadLimitada/Loewenstein1996Viceraldecisions.pdf.

33. Kim, B.K. & Zauberman, G. (2012). Can Victoria's Secret change the future? A subjective time perception account of sexual cue effects on impatience. *Journal of Experimental Psychology, General*. Epublication ahead of print. Loewenstein, G. (2000). Emotions in economic theory and economic behavior. *American Economic Review*, 90, 2, Papers and Proceedings of the 112th Annual Meeting of the American Economic Association, 426–432. http://sds.hss.cmu.edu/media/pdfs/loewenstein/EmotionsEconTheoryBehavior.pdf.

34. Loewenstein, G. (2000). Emotions in economic theory and economic behavior. *American Economic Review*, 90, 2, Papers and Proceedings of the 112th Annual Meeting of the American Economic Association, 426–432; Wang, X.T. & Dvorak, R.D. (2010). Sweet future: Fluctuating blood glucose levels affect future discounting. *Psychological Science*, 20, 10, 1–6. http://people.usd.edu/~xtwang/Papers/Wang_Dvorak per cent20(psychological per cent20science per cent2009).pdf.

35. Danziger, S., Levav, J. & Avnaim-Pessoa, L. (2011). Extraneous factors in judicial decisions. *PNAS*, 108, 17, 6889–6892.

36. Virkkunen, M. (1984). Reactive hypoglycemic tendency among arsonists. *Acta Psychiatrica Scandinavica*, 69, 5, 445–452; Gailliot, M.T. & Baumeister, R.F. (2007). The physiology of willpower: Linking blood glucose to self-control. *Personality and Social Psychology Review*, 11, 4, 303–327.

37. It is possible of course that this kind of person lives a more chaotic life, and that irregular eating is a consequence, and not a cause, of that.

38. See for example National Transportation Safety Board (1990). Marine accident report: The grounding of the Exxon Valdez on Bligh Reef, Prince William Sound, AK. Springfield, VA; Nasa (1986). Report of the Presidential Commission on the Space Shuttle *Challenger* Accident, Vol. 2, Appendix G, Washington, DC: US Government Printing Office; Division of Sleep Medicine at Harvard Medical School (2007). Sleep, Performance, and Public Safety. Produced in partnership with WGBH Educational Foundation. Last reviewed on 18 December 2007. http://healthysleep.med.harvard.edu/healthy/matters/consequences/sleep-performance-and-public-safety; Folkard, S., Lombardi, D.A. & Tucker, P.T. (2005). Safety, sleepiness and sleep. *Industrial Health*, 43, 20–23. http://www.jicosh.gr.jp/en/indu_hel/pdf/43-1-3.pdf; Alaska Oil Spill Commission (1990). SPILL: The wreck of the Exxon Valdez. Details about the Accident. Final Report published by the State of Alaska. http://www.evostc.state.ak.us/facts/details.cfm; Rogers, A.E. (2008). The effects of fatigue and sleepiness on nurse performance and patient safety, in Hughes, R.G. (ed.). *Patient Safety and Quality: An Evidence-Based Handbook for Nurses*. Rockville, MD: Agency for Healthcare Research and Quality (US).

39. NASA (1986). Report of the Presidential Commission on the Space Shuttle *Challenger* Accident, Vol. 2, Appendix G, Washington, DC: US Government Printing Office, 1986; Harrison, Y. & Horne, J.A. (2000). The impact of sleep deprivation on decision making: A review. *Journal of Experimental Psychology: Applied*, 6, 3, 236–249. http://postcog.ucd.ie/files/Hrrison%20and%20horne.pdf.

40. Samuel, H. (2013). Air France Brazil plane crash pilot "had only had one hour's sleep." *Telegraph*, 21 March 2013. http://www.telegraph.co.uk/news/worldnews/europe/france/9947133/Air-France-Brazil-plane-crash-pilot-had-only-had-one-hours-sleep.html.

41. Alhola, P. & Polo-Kantola, P. (2007). Sleep deprivation: Impact on cognitive performance. *Neuropsychiatric Disease and Treatment*, 3, 5, 553–567.

42. Bronwyn Fryer (2006). A Conversation with Charles A. Czeisler, Sleep Deficit: The Performance Killer. *Harvard Business Review, The Magazine*, Oct. 2006. http://hbr.org/2006/10/sleep-deficit-the-performance-killer/.

43. McCormick, F., Kadzielski, J., Landrigan, C. Evans,B. Herndon, J. & Rubash, H. (2012). Surgeon Fatigue: A Prospective Analysis of the Incidence, Risk, and Intervals of Predicted Fatigue-Related Impairment in Residents. *Arch Surg.*, 147(5), 430–435. doi:10.1001/archsurg.2012.84.

44. Ayas, N.T., Barger, L.K., Cade, B.E., Hashimoto, D.M., Rosner, B., Cronin, J.W., Speizer, F.E. & Czeisler, C.A. (2006). Extended work duration and the risk of self-reported percutaneous injuries in interns. *Journal of the American Medical Association*, 296, 9, 1055–1062. Normally such "sharps injuries" occur 0.076 per cent of the time. For fatigued interns this percentage increased to 0.131 per cent. Although the risk remains small, given that needlestick injuries can lead to infection by such diseases as HIV, this research should be taken seriously.

45. Barger, L.K., Cade, B.E., Ayas, N.T., Cronin, J.W., Rosner, B., Speizer, F.E. & Czeisler, C.A. (2005). Extended work shifts and the risk of motor vehicle crashes among interns. *New England Journal of Medicine*, 352, 2, 125–134.

46. Libedinsky, C., Smith, D.V., Teng, C.S., Namburi, P., Chen, V.W., Huettel, S.A. & Chee, M. W. (2011). Sleep deprivation alters valuation signals in the ventromedial prefrontal cortex. *Frontiers in Behavioral Neuroscience*, 5, 70, 1–10. Note that the left anterior insula is involved in a lot more than merely assessing risk.

47. Venkatraman, V., Huettel, S.A., Chuah, L.Y.M., Payne, J.W. & Chee, M.W.L. (2011). Sleep deprivation biases the neural mechanisms underlying economic preferences. *Journal of Neuroscience*, 31, 10, 3712–3718. This study showed that risk-taking is higher for sleep-deprived people while controlling for differences in attention; Libedinsky, C., Smith, D.V., Teng, C.S., Namburi, P., Chen, V.W., Huettel, S.A. & Chee, M.W. (2011). Sleep deprivation alters valuation signals in the ventromedial prefrontal cortex. *Frontiers in Behavioral Neuroscience*, 5,

70, 1–10. This study also proves that we "weigh" risk differently when sleep-deprived; Killgore, W.D., Balkin, T.J., Wesensten, N.J. (2006). Impaired decision making following 49 hours of sleep deprivation. *J Sleep Res*, 15, 7–13. The study shows that sleep-deprived people perform worse on the Iowa gambling tasks, i.e. sleep-deprived people are less good at anticipating loss and avoiding risky card decks.

48. Van Dongen, H.P., Price, N.J., Mullington, J.M., Szuba, M.P., Kapoor, S.C. & Dinges, D.F. (2001). Caffeine eliminates psychomotor vigilance deficits from sleep inertia. *Sleep*, 24, 7, 813–819; Killgore, W.D., Lipizzi, E.L., Kamimori, G.H. & Balkin, T.J. (2007). Caffeine effects on risky decision making after 75 hours of sleep deprivation. *Aviation, Space and Environmental Medicine*, 78, 10, 957–962; Libedinsky, C., Smith, D.V., Teng, C.S., Namburi, P., Chen, V.W., Huettel, S.A. & Chee, M.W. (2011). Sleep deprivation alters valuation signals in the ventromedial prefrontal cortex. *Frontiers in Behavioral Neuroscience*, 5, 70, 1–10.

49. Venkatraman, V., Huettel, S.A., Chuah, L.Y.M., Payne, J.W. & Chee, M.W.L. (2011). Sleep deprivation biases the neural mechanisms underlying economic preferences. *Journal of Neuroscience*, 31, 10, 3712–3718; Libedinsky, C., Smith, D.V., Teng, C.S., Namburi, P., Chen, V.W., Huettel, S.A. & Chee, M.W. (2011). Sleep deprivation alters valuation signals in the ventromedial prefrontal cortex. *Frontiers in Behavioral Neuroscience*, 5, 70, 1–10.

50. *New York* (2011). Sleep Habits. 22 Dec. 2011. http://nymag.com/news/politics/encyclopedia/sleep-2012/.

51. Crumley, B. (2012). After gaffe-filled foreign tour, Europe asks: "Is Mitt Romney a loser?" *Time World*, 31 July 2012. http://world.time.com/2012/07/31/after-gaffe-filled-foreign-tour-europe-asks-is-mitt-romney-a-loser/); Foster, P., Swaine, J. & Spillius, A. (2012). Mitt Romney struggles to keep on track as further video revelations emerge. *Telegraph*, 18 Sept. 2012. http://www.telegraph.co.uk/news/worldnews/us-election/9551740/Mitt-Romney-struggles-to-keep-on-track-as-further-video-revelations-emerge.html#; Hargro, T. (2012). Romney on "47%": I was "completely wrong." *USA Today*, 5 Oct. 2012. http://www.usatoday.com/story/news/politics/2012/10/05/romney-47-percent-i-was-wrong/1614703/.

52. Coppins, M. (2012). Restless Romney braces for high-stake debate: A sleepless night in Denver. BuzzFaux Politics, 3 Oct. 2012. http://www.buzzfeed.com/mckaycoppins/restless-romney-braces-for-high-stakes-debate.

53. Sleep Education (2010). Bill Clinton: The Importance of Sleep. Sleep Education Blog, 20 Feb. 2010. http://sleepeducation.blogspot.co.uk/2010/02/bill-clinton-importance-of-sleep.html; Bulkeley, K. (2009). Bush, Clinton, and the Politics of Sleep Deprivation. *Dream Research & Education*, 2 Oct. 2009. http://kellybulkeley.com/bush-clinton-and-the-politics-of-sleep-deprivation/; Sex, sleep, and power: A conversation with

Chelsea Handler and Arianna Huffington. CNN Money, 4 Oct. 2011. http://management.fortune.cnn.com/2011/10/04/chelsea-handler-arianna-huffington/.

STEP TEN: Embrace Dissent and Encourage Difference

1. Latané, B. & Darley, J.M. (1968). Group Inhibition of Bystander Intervention in Emergencies. *Journal of Personality and Social Psychology*, 10, 3, 215–221.
2. Stout, D. (1996). Solomon Asch is Dead at 88; A Leading Social Psychologist. *New York Times*. http://www.nytimes.com/1996/02/29/us/solomon-asch-is-dead-at–88-a-leading-social-psychologist.html.
3. Asch, S. (1955). Opinions and Social Pressure. *Scientific American*, 193, 5, pp.31–35.
4. Bond, R. & Smith, P.B. (1996). Culture and conformity: A meta-analysis of studies using Asch's (1952b, 1956) line judgment task. *Psychological Bulletin*, 119, 111–137; Nicholson, N., Cole, S. & Rocklin, T. (1985). Conformity in the Asch situation: a comparison between contemporary British and US Students. *British Journal of Social Psychology*, 24, 59–63; Milgram, S. (1961). Nationality and conformity. *Scientific American*, 205, 6, 45–52. Bond & Smith's 1996 meta-analysis shows that women conform more than men; Walker, M.D. & Andrade, M.G. (1996). Conformity in the Asch task as a function of age. *Journal of Social Psychology*, 136 (3), 367–72. This study was done on children aged three to seventeen; Pasupathi, M. (1999). Age differences in response to conformity pressure for emotional and non-emotional material. *Psychology and Aging*, 14, 1, 170–174. This study was done on people aged eighteen to ninety-one, but with a geometric-shape judgment task rather than a line judgment task; Sunstein, C. (2002). Conformity and Dissent. *Public Law and Legal Theory Working Paper No. 34*, 1–87. University of Chicago.
5. Sunstein, C. (2002). Conformity and Dissent. *Public Law and Legal Theory Working Paper No. 34*, 1–87. University of Chicago.
6. To provide some more detail: the children's brain scans revealed that knowing others' song ratings didn't change someone's emotional preference for a song, but did make them anxious because their tastes didn't match the consensus. It was this that caused them to change their scores.
7. Berns, G., Capra, C.N., Moore, S. & Noussair, C. (2010). Neural mechanisms of the influence of popularity on adolescent ratings of music. *NeuroImage*, 49, 2687–2696.
8. Yabar, Y., Johnston, L., Miles, L. & Peace, V. (2006). Implicit behavioral mimicry: Investigating the impact of group membership. *Journal of Nonverbal Behavior*, 30, 97–113; Wimmer, A. & Lewis, K. (2010). Beyond and Below Racial Homophily: ERG Models of a Friendship Network Documented on Facebook. *American Journal of Sociology*, 116,

2, 583–642. http://www.sscnet.ucla.edu/soc/faculty/wimmer/
WimmerLewis.pdf.

9. Bahns, A.J., Pickett, K.M. & Crandall, C.S. (2012). Social ecology of similarity: Big schools, small schools and social relationships. *Group Processes & Intergroup Relations*, 15, 1, 119–131.

10. Guéguen, N. & Martin, A. (2009). Incidental similarity facilitates behavioral mimicry. *Social Psychology*, 40, 2, 88–92; Pronin, E., Berger, J. & Malouki, S. (2007). Alone in a Crowd of Sheep: Asymmetric Perceptions of Conformity and Their Roots in an Introspection Illusion. *Journal of Personality and Social Psychology*, 92, 4, 585–595. A previous study by Guéguen, referred to in this article, found that we're also more likely to fill in an online survey if it's sent by someone with the same surname as ours. http://psych.princeton.edu/psychology/research/pronin/pubs/2007Conformity.pdf.

11. Rivera, L.A. (2012). Hiring as Cultural Matching: The Case of Elite Professional Service Firms. *American Sociological Review*, 77, 6, 999–1022. http://www.asanet.org/journals/ASR/Dec12ASRFeature.pdf.

12. Ibid.

13. Employers Network for Equality and Inclusion. (2012). Unconscious Bias Inhibits Employee Productivity. News, 28 September 2012. http://www.enei.org.uk/news.php/341/unconscious-bias-inhibits-employee-productivity.

14. Ertug, G. & Gargiulo, M. (2012). Does Homophily Affect Performance? INSEAD Working Paper No. 2012/121/OB.

15. Pfiffner, J. (2011). Decision Making in the Obama White House. *Presidential Studies Quarterly*, 41, 2, 247.

16. Janus, I.J. (1982). *Groupthink*. Wadsworth, Boston, MA. Although there were a few dissenters, they were marginal figures.

17. Ibid; Peterson, R.S., Owens, P.D., Tetlock, P.E., Fan, E.T. & Martorana, P. (1998). Group dynamics in top management teams: Groupthink, vigilance, and alternative models of organizational failure and success. *Organizational Behavior & Human Decision Processes*, 73, 272–305; Tetlock, P.E., Peterson, R.S., McGuire, C. & Chang, S.-J. (1992). Assessing political group dynamics: A test of the groupthink model. *Journal of Personality and Social Psychology*, 63, 403–425, cited in Klocke, U. (2007). How to Improve Decision Making in Small Groups: Effects of Dissent and Training Interventions. *Small Group Research*, 38, 437–468.

18. See on this point for example: Parks, C.D. & Nelson, N. L. (1999). Discussion and decision: The interrelationship between initial preference distribution and group discussion content. *Organizational Behavior & Human Decision Processes*, 80, 87–101; Klocke, U. (2007). How to Improve Decision Making in Small Groups: Effects of Dissent and Training Interventions. *Small Group Research*, 38, 437–468; Schulz-Hardt, S., Brodbeck, F.C., Mojzisch, A., Kerschreiter, R. & Frey, D.

(2006). Group decision making in hidden profile situations: Dissent as a facilitator for decision quality. *Journal of Personality and Social Psychology*, 91, 1080–1093, cited in ibid; Brodbeck, F.C., Kerschreiter, R., Mojzisch, A., Frey, D. & Schulz-Hardt, S. (2002). The dissemination of critical, unshared information in decision-making groups: The effects of pre-discussion dissent. *European Journal of Social Psychology*, 32, 35–56, cited in Klocke, U. (2007). How to Improve Decision Making in Small Groups: Effects of Dissent and Training Interventions. *Small Group Research*, 38, 437–468; and Johnson, D.W. & Johnson, R.T. (1989). *Cooperation and Competition: Theory and Research*. Interaction, Edina, MN, cited in ibid.

19. Goodwin, D.K. (2005). *Team of Rivals: The Political Genius of Abraham Lincoln*. Simon & Schuster. New York, NY.

20. Carter, D.A., Simkins, B.J. & Simpson, W.G. (2003). Corporate Governance, Board Diversity, and Firm Value. *Financial Review*, 38, 1, 33–53. Campbell, K. & Minguez-Vera, A. (2008). Gender Diversity in the Boardroom and Firm Financial Performance. *Journal of Business Ethics*, 83, 435–451.Sei-Fan, P. (2012). Is board diversity important for firm performance and board independence? An exploratory study of Singapore Listed Companies. MAS Staff Paper No. 52. Gender Diversity associated with better financial performance; Eisenhardt, K. & Bourgeois, L.J. (1988). Politics of Strategic Decision Making in High-Velocity Environments: Toward a Midrange Theory. *Academy of Management Journal*, 31, 4, 737–770; Erhardt, N.L., Werbel, J.D. & Shrader, C.B. (2003). Board of Director Diversity and Firm Financial Performance. *Corporate Governance: An International Review*, 11, 102–111; Phillips, K.W., Northcraft, G.B. & Neale, M.A. (2006). Surface-Level Diversity and Decision-Making in Groups: When Does Deep-Level Similarity Help? *Group Processes & Intergroup Relations*, 9, 4, 467–482; Antonio, A.L., Chang M.J., Hakuta, K., Kenny, D.A., Levin, S. & Milem, J.F. (2004). Effects of racial diversity on complex thinking in college students. *Psychological Science*, 15, 8, 507–10. Studies of prediction show that racially diverse groups predict better than all white groups; Sommers, S.R. (2006). On Racial Diversity and Group Decision-Making: Identifying Multiple Effects of Racial Composition on Jury Deliberations. *Journal of Personality and Social Psychology*, 90, 597–612, cited in Page, S.E. (2007). *The Difference: How the Power of Diversity Creates Better Groups, Firms, Schools and Societies*. Princeton University Press, Princeton, NJ, p.327.

21. Page, S.E. (2007). *The Difference: How the Power of Diversity Creates Better Groups, Firms, Schools and Societies*. Princeton University Press, Princeton, NJ.

22. Phillips, K.W., Northcraft, G.B. & Neale, M.A. (2006). Surface-Level Diversity and Decision-Making in Groups: When Does Deep-Level Similarity Help? *Group Processes & Intergroup Relations*, 9, 4, 467–482.

Part of the reason why student groups or boards that are diverse do better may also, of course, be because the women or people of colour within them are exceptional.

23. Page, S.E. (2007). *The Difference: How the Power of Diversity Creates Better Groups, Firms, Schools and Societies.* Princeton University Press, Princeton, NJ, p.358.

24. Kilduff, M., Angelmar, R. & Mehra, A. (2000). Top Management-Team Diversity and Firm Performance: Examining the Role of Cognitions. *Organisation Science*, 11, 1, 21–34.

25. Fishbein, W. & Treverton, G. (2004). Rethinking "Alternative Analysis" to Address Transnational Threats. The Sherman Kent Center for Intelligence Analysis. Occasional Papers, Vol. 3, No. 2. https://www.cia.gov/library/kent-center-occasional-papers/vol3no2.htm. (Note that the report attributes this fact to "a noted professor from the financial community.")

26. Ibid.

27. Backes-Gellner, U. & Veen, S. (2012). Positive effects of ageing and age diversity in innovative companies – large-scale empirical evidence on company productivity. *Human Resource Management Journal*, early view.

28. Page, S.E. (2007). *The Difference: How the Power of Diversity Creates Better Groups, Firms, Schools and Societies.* Princeton University Press, Princeton, NJ.

29. Enigma – breaking the unbreakable code. Bletchley Park Tour. Bletchleypark.org.uk. Accessed 15 Jan. 2012. http://www.bletchleypark.org.uk/content/museum/tour9.rhtm. Trillion in UK terminology, quintillion in US/Canadian.

30. This example is discussed in Page, S.E. (2007). *The Difference: How the Power of Diversity Creates Better Groups, Firms, Schools and Societies.* Princeton University Press, Princeton, NJ.

31. Ettridge, J. (2005). HUT 6, Bletchley Park. WW2 People's War. WW2 People's War is an online archive of wartime memories contributed by members of the public and gathered by the BBC. The archive can be found at bbc.co.uk/ww2peopleswar. http://www.bbc.co.uk/history/ww2peopleswar/stories/42/a4163942.shtml. See also Ratcliff, R.A. (2006). *Delusions of Intelligence: Enigma, Ultra and the End of Secure Ciphers.* Cambridge University Press, Cambridge, p.80.

32. Podgers, J. (1993). Remembering Nuremberg. *ABA Journal*, Oct., p.90.

33. Smith, M. (2001). *The Emperor's Codes: The Breaking of Japan's Secret Ciphers.* Arcade Publishing, New York, NY, p.147.

34. Jablonsky, D. (1991). *Churchill, the Great Game and Total War.* Routledge, London, p.148.

35. Ettridge, J. (2005). HUT 6, Bletchley Park. WW2 People's War. http://www.bbc.co.uk/history/ww2peopleswar/stories/42/a4163942.shtml.

36. Andrew, C. (2004). F.H. Hinsley and the Cambridge Moles, in Langhome, R. (ed.). *Diplomacy and Intelligence During the Second World War.* Cambridge University Press, Cambridge, p.39.

37. Ratcliff, R.A. (2006). *Delusions of Intelligence: Enigma, Ultra and the End of Secure Ciphers*. Cambridge University Press, Cambridge, p.83.

38. Hinsley, F.H. (2001). *Codebreakers: The Inside Story of Bletchley Park*. Oxford University Press, Oxford, p.5.

39. Radford, T. (2008). Dry Store Room No 1: The Secret Life of the Natural History Museum. *Guardian*. http://www.guardian.co.uk/books/2008/jan/26/history.

40. Lycett, A. (2011). Breaking Germany's Enigma Code. BBC History. http://www.bbc.co.uk/history/worldwars/wwtwo/enigma_01.shtml.

41. Algae Section Correspondence and Papers. 1920–2008. Ref: DF BOT/421. Natural History Museum Archive Catalogue. http://www.nhm.ac.uk/research-curation/library/archives/catalogue/DServe.exe?dsqServer=placid&dsqIni=Dserve.ini&dsqApp=Archive&dsqDb=Catalog&dsqCmd=show.tcl&dsqSearch=(RefNo=="DF per cent20BOT per cent2F421').

42. Fortey, R. (2008). *Dry Store Room No. 1: The Secret Life of the Natural History Museum*. HarperPress, London, p.168.

43. Lobban, I. (2012). "GCHQ and Turing's Legacy." Address delivered at the University of Leeds, 4 Oct. 2012. http://www.gchq.gov.uk/Press/Pages/Director-GCHQ-makes-speech-leeds.aspx.

44. Lakhani, K.R., Jeppeson, L.B., Lohse, P.A. & Panetta, J.A. (2007). The Value of Openness in Scientific Problem Solving. http://www.hbs.edu/faculty/Publication per cent20Files/07–050.pdf.

45. Moskvitch, K. (2011). Online game Foldit helps anti-Aids drug quest. BBC News. http://www.bbc.co.uk/news/technology–14986013.

46. Bantel, K. & Jackson, S. (1989). Top management and innovations in banking: Does the composition of the top team make a difference? *Strategic Management Journal Special Issue: Strategic Leaders and Leadership*, 10, S1, 107–124.

47. For the Mmowgli players' portal see https://portal.mmowgli.nps.edu/.

48. Grant Thornton International Business Report 2012. (2012). Women in Senior Management: still not enough. Grant Thornton International. http://www.gti.org/files/ibr2012 per cent20-per cent20women per cent20in per cent20senior per cent20management per cent20master.pdf.

49. Paredes, T. (2004). Too Much Pay, Too Much Deference: Is CEO Overconfidence the Product of Corporate Governance? *Washington U. School of Law Working Paper No. 04–08–02.* http://law-wss–01.law.fsu.edu/journals/lawreview/downloads/322/Paredes.pdf.

50. Lovallo, D. & Kahneman, D. (1993). Timid Choices and Bold Forecasts: A Cognitive Perspective on Risk Taking. *Management Science*, 39, 1, 17–31.

51. Boot, A.W.A., Milbourn, T. & Thakor, A.V. (2005). Sunflower Management and Capital Budgeting. *Journal of Business*, 78, 2, 501–527.

52. Joni, S.-A. & Beyer, D. (2009). How to Pick a Good Fight. *Harvard Business Review*, 87, 12, 48–57. http://hbr.org/2009/12/how-to-pick-a-good-fight/ar/1.

53. Foley, S. (2009). Clash of a Titan. *Independent*. http://www.independent. co.uk/news/business/analysis-and-features/crash-of-a-titan-the-inside- story-of-the-fall-of-lehman-brothers–1782714.html.

54. Loftus, P. (2011). Ex-Synthes Exec Bohner Sentenced to 8 Months in Prison in Bone-Cement Case. *Wall Street Journal*. http://online.wsj.com/ article/BT-CO–20111213–712732.html.

55. Kimes, M. (2012). Bad to the Bone: A Medical Horror Story. *Fortune Magazine*. http://features.blogs.fortune.cnn.com/2012/09/18/ synthes-norian-criminal/.

56. World Health Organisation (2013). Profile: Dr. Kiyoshi Kurokawa. Commission on Social Determinants of Health, 2005–2008. World Health Organisation. http://www.who.int/social_determinants/ thecommission/kurokawa/en/index.html.

57. Foster, R. (2012). News Plurality in a Digital World. Reuters Institute for the Study of Journalism. https://reutersinstitute.politics.ox.ac.uk/ fileadmin/documents/Publications/Working_Papers/News_Plurality_in_a_ Digital_World.pdf.

58. Newman, N. (ed.) (2012). Reuters Institute Digital News Report 2012. Reuters Institute for the Study of Journalism.

59. PEW Research Center (2012). http://www.people-press.org/2012/09/27/ in-changing-news-landscape-even-television-is-vulnerable/.

60. Sunstein, C. (2009). *Republic.com 2.0*. Princeton University Press, Princeton, NJ; Iyengar, S. & Hahn, K. (2009). Red media, blue media: Evidence of ideological selectivity in media use. *Journal of Communication*, 59, 19–39; Berners-Lee, T. (2010). Long Live the Web: A Call for Continued Open Standards and Neutrality. *Scientific American*. See also on the value of broadening the range of voices Sambrook, R. (2012). Delivering Trust: Objectivity and Impartiality in the Digital Age, Reuters Institute for the Study of Journalism, July 2012. http:// thinklikeaneditor.net/wp-content/uploads/2012/07/ Delivering_Trust_Impartiality_and_Objectivity_in_a_Digital_Age.

61. Weng, J., Lim, E,-P., Jiang, J. & He, Q. (2010). Twitterrank: finding topic- sensitive influential Twitterers. *Proceedings of the third ACM international conference on Web search and data mining*, 261–270; Aiello, L.M., Barrat, A., Cattuto, C., Ruffo, G. & Schifanella, R. (2010). Link creation and profile alignment in the anobii social network, 249–256; De Choudhury, M., Mason, W.A., Hofman, J.M. & Watts, D.J. (2010). Inferring relevant social networks from interpersonal communication. Nineteenth International Conference on World Wide Web, 301–310; Kwak, H., Lee, C., Park, H. & Moon, S. (2010). What is Twitter, a Social Network or a News Media? Proceedings of World Wide Web Conference, 10, 591–600.

62. Messing, S. & Westwood, S.J. (2012). How Social Media Introduces Biases in Selecting and Processing News Content. Preliminary Draft. Prepared for presentation at the Annual Meeting of the Midwestern

Political Science Association, Chicago, Illinois. 1–31. http://www.stanford.edu/~seanjw/papers/SMH.pdf.

63. Rainie, L. & Smith, A. (2012). Social networking sites and politics. Pew Research Center's Internet & American Life Project, 2. http://pewinternet.org/Reports/2012/Social-networking-and-politics/Main-findings/Social-networking-sites-and-politics.aspx.

64. Launch announced on 15 January 2013. See for example Ahmed, M. (2013). Facebook will use your data to challenge Google. *The Times*, 16 Jan. 2013.

65. Hullinger, J. (2013). Newscorp Reportedly Creating Social Network to Compete with LinkedIn. *Fast Company*, 29 May 2013.

66. Mutz, D. & Martin, P. (2001). Facilitating Communication across Lines of Political Difference: The Role of Mass Media. *American Political Science Review*, 95, 1, 97–114.

67. Sunstein, C. (2009). *Republic.com 2.0.* Princeton University Press, Princeton, NJ; Pariser, E. (2011). *The Filter Bubble: How the New Personalized Web is Changing What We Read and How We Think.* Penguin, New York, NY.

68. McCarthy, J.M., Van Iddekinge, C.H. & Campion, M.A. (2010). Are highly structured job interviews resistant to demographic similarity effects? *Personnel Psychology*, 63, 325–359. http://www–2.rotman.utoronto.ca/facbios/file/McCarthy_VanIddekinge_Campion_2010.pdf.

69. White, S. (2012). The downside of hiring people just like you. *Globe and Mail.* http://m.theglobeandmail.com/report-on-business/small-business/sb-managing/human-resources/the-downside-of-hiring-people-just-like-you/article555612/?service=mobile.

70. Shiller, R.J. (2008). Challenging the Crowd in Whispers, Not Shouts. *New York Times.* http://www.nytimes.com/2008/11/02/business/02view.html?pagewanted=all.

71. Keynes, J. Maynard (1935). *The General Theory of Employment, Interest and Money.* Atlantic Publishers, 2006, p.141.

72. Manyika, J. (2008). Google's view on the future of business: An interview with CEO Eric Schmidt. *McKinsey Quarterly*, 1, 136–138. http://www.mckinseyquarterly.com/Googles_view_on_the_future_of_business_An_interview_with_CEO_Eric_Schmidt_2229.

73. See for example Greenberg, J. (1976). The role of seating position in group interaction: A review, with applications for group trainers. *Group & Organization Studies*, 1, 3.

74. Campbell, S. & Sinclair, S. (2009). The crisis: Mobilizing boards for change. *McKinsey Quarterly*, 2, 20–21.

75. Bock, L. (2011). Passion, not Perks. *Think Quarterly.* http://www.thinkwithgoogle.com/quarterly/people/laszlo-bock-people-ops.html.

76. Coutu, D. (2009). Leadership Lessons from Abraham Lincoln: A Conversation with Historian Doris Kearns Goodwin. *Harvard Business Review*, 89, 4, 43–7. http://hbr.org/2009/04/leadership-lessons-from-

abraham-lincoln/ar/1. See also Rodriquez, J.P. (2007). *Slavery in the United States: A Social, Political, and Historical Encyclopedia*, Vol. 2. ABC-CLIO, p.66.

77. Ellison, S.F., Greenbaum, J. & Mullin, W.P. (2010). Diversity, Social Goods Provision, and Performance in the Firm. MIT Department of Economics Working Paper No. 10–11. This study, which analysed a firm with many small offices in the US and across the world, found that gender diversity correlated with higher revenues, although it also correlated with reduced cooperation and lower employee satisfaction.

78. Kleindorfer, P., Kunreuther, H. & Schoemaker, P. (1993). *Decision Sciences: An Integrative Perspective*. Cambridge University Press, Cambridge. Raiffa, H., Richardson, J. & Metcalfe, D. (2002). *Negotiation Analysis: The Science and Art of Collaborative Decision Making*. Harvard University Press, Boston, MA. Raiffa, H. (2002). Contributions of Applied Systems Analysis to International Negotiation, in Kremenyuk, V. (ed.) (2002). *International Negotiation: Analysis, Approaches, Issues*. 2nd edn, Jossey-Bass, San Francisco, CA.

79. Garvin, D. & Roberto, M. (2001). What You Don't Know About Making Decisions. *Harvard Business Review*, 79, 8, 108–116.

80. Mill, J.S. (1859). *On Liberty*. J.W. Parker & Son, London.

Index

INDEX